Practical Digital Evidence

Law and Technology

Part I

Dr. Ehud Roffeh, Adv

ABRIDGED CONTENTS

CONTENTS – EXPANDED

INTRODUCTION

"We cannot solve our problems with the same thinking we used when we created them"

(Albert Einstein)

The past decade was fast and rhythmical. A decade of tremendous breakthroughs within the communication and computer domains. Facebook, WhatsApp, Twitter, high speed surfing, the transformation of the mobile phone into a computer with all it implies – all these have totally changed the technical map and influenced inter-personal, global communications.

"Traditional" everyday actions have almost disappeared and been substituted by online applications, digital documents and virtual servers. Geographic boundaries have become blurred and today methods and technologies used to facilitate communications are not necessarily located within the user's country of residence.

The communications revolution has our personal information into common knowledge known to all (or at least the common knowledge of those who know how to access it) and every problem. This same exposure also opens the door to harm caused by a variety of sources, a technical defect, a virus or even an electrical power interruption, any of which could disrupt our daily routine and life and cause massive economic damage to the individual, the state and to labor economics.

The technological race is a fact and computers (in their various forms) are an integral part of our everyday life. However this is also where the problem lays: the changing pace is too fast for most of people, ignorance regarding this subject exceeds knowledge, commonly used jargon is perceived as difficult to understand – and in many cases attitudes towards the technological world is effected by a traditional, old fashioned way of thinking that isn't in line with the needs of modern times'.

Prominent victims of this reality are the representatives of the legal system– judges, lawyers and jurists. The world of justice is conservative and traditional. The judicial system relies upon laws that, on many occasions, fail to meet the scope and pace of technological changes.

Judgments have created precedents, milestones that have left their impression and set methodologies, however the method doesn't necessarily take into account the world we live in. judges, defenders and plaintiffs aren't experts in computers and technology and changing reality puts complicated issues many new and yet unanswered, before the legal system and those involved in it.

At this point I would emphasize that whilst a chronological generation is considered as twenty five years, a technological generation is considered to be in the region of just three years – and this is where the huge gap exists between law, judgment and reality.

These depressing results are expressed on a daily basis: jurists and judges are required to deal with issues combining justice and technology – and find themselves helpless. Their task should include representation, giving advice or making a judgment – however, in many instances, they lack the required knowledge or tools to adequately fulfill their tasks. A few years ago Judge Doctor Michal Agmon-Gonen declared that " courts of law shouldn't have to deal with this…", another judge admitted, during the course of a conference, that he doesn't know how to deal with technological issues and another judge asked for a computer experts opinion and announced the fact that his decision on this matter will be binding and final.

"Between justice and technology – digital evidence in practice" is about to change this reality. This book is designated for lawyers' and will be a bridge between two worlds perceived as distant one from the other – the world of justice and the world of technology.

This book incorporates a wide range of subjects, terms and scenarios and integrates the four aspects that constitute every single legal issue: factual circumstances, evidential aspects, professional data and forensic analysis.

This book was written after many years of experience and of providing advice in hundreds of complicated legal cases, civil and criminal including cases involving money laundering, rape and murder. Alongside the in depth legal analysis of previous cases, this book presents legal research conducted around the world during the past years – and mainly research conducted in the United States and England.

"Between justice and technology – digital evidence in practice" deals with the complicated issues deriving from the inevitable connection between man and technology. The idea behind this is to remove the interference that has been created between the legal world and the technological sphere, to reduce knowledge gaps and present, as much as is possible, a clear and unequivocal picture. The goal is not only to provide justice – but to provide justice based on knowledge and out of a true understanding.

This book provides detailed but simple explanations that will assist the reader in understanding the technological processes accompanying our lives. Alongside these explanations the book presents forensic analysis of the factual case, examines the issue through legal eyes – including comparative law – and proposes various alternatives for an appropriate legal solution.

This book is published after many years of study, research and accumulated experience. It is based upon a deep familiarity with the law and the legal system in the United States, England and Israel. It presents the subjects thoroughly and strictly – however it has been written in a friendly style, is convenient to use and easy to understand even for those for whom technology is a foreign language.

"Between justice and technology – digital evidence in practice" deals with various subjects and includes all technology domains, including:

Digital evidence – what is it, how is it produced and when can one rely on it.
Evidence credibility and acceptability.
Computerized output and institutional evidence.
Issues dealing with email (digital mail messages).
Laptops, tablets and Smartphone's.
Storage medium and telecommunication.
Digital evidence preservation – documentation, backup and precautions.
Communication channels.
Virtual servers.
Security cameras and closed-circuit televisions.

Computer crimes and evidence counterfeiting.
Digital signatures, contracts (agreements) and document validity.

***

Before you turn the page and become exposed to a new and fascinating world, there is one more, important thing that you should be aware of:

There are people who claim that being concerned with the technological aspects of a legal case is irrelevant. According to them, because of the fact that their proficiency domains do not include clear technological issues, they have the ability to remain completely within the areas of traditional, well known and safe law.

However in reality – whether this be accepted or not – is slightly different: the technological presence is already here and these issues aren't the exclusive property of internet laws, of computer crimes and of Intellectual Property or patent laws. Computers, as stated previously, have completely penetrated our lives – and they influence all justice domains: labor laws, family law, white collar crime and even violent crime such as rape and murder.

Whether we want to or not, computers are part of our lives – and therefore are part of the general legal system. And so long as computers continue to develop and play such a meaningful place within our agenda, we must be familiar with this domain, study and learn its influences and understand its legal implications.

As someone who has accompanied the legal system for many years and as a professional authority within the legal and technology domain, I have no doubt this book is a necessity for every lawyer and judge interested in understanding about the issues we are discussing and who wishes to be aware of the issues they are dealing with.

It is my sincere hope that this book will assist and help you find solutions to complicated legal issues, with appropriate representation and with committing fair trial.

Wishing you all productive and enriching reading,

Dr. Roffeh Ehud, Adv

CHAPTER 1: GENERAL INTRODUCTION AND REVIEW OF THE LITERATURE DIGITAL EVIDENCE

Digital Evidence

The art of digital forensics is infinitely different from traditional forensic science. Familiar disciplines such as toxicology, physics, or chemistry provide a tangible physical connection between the evidence and the crime scene - whether directly or whether on the basis of a secondary or tertiary connection. This enables the source of the evidence to be identified and cross-checked with the chain of events.

On the other hand, evaluation of digital evidence requires an in-depth understanding of the technology involved and the digital realm. This understanding is required to fulfill the threshold conditions for the preservation of evidence in its original condition, in order to study and analyze it and present it to the court in a simple and clear manner.

Characteristics of digital evidence differ from those of other types of legal evidence. This is due to the structure and sequentially of digital information storage in the form of a computer language. This language is presented as a sequence of bytes known as binary code - a series of zeros and ones. Traditional evidence includes an easily understood physical depiction and expression of evidence gathered and presented to the court. Binary code - a series of digits - is difficult for the lay person to understand.

This differences between digital evidence and other types of evidence influences all stages involved in the treatment of digital evidence, from the identification the evidence, through to its documentation and analysis before it is presented to a judge or a jury.

Digital evidence, with all its unique characteristics, has awakened the curiosity of many researchers and has led to many books and articles being published on this topic. This chapter will examine the world of digital evidence in light of professional literature, will present the core issues relating to digital evidence, and will analyze the basis, the originality, and reliability characteristics of the evidence.

The Search for Professional Literature in the Field of Digital Evidence

For the purpose of this nook, I performed a comprehensive review of professional literature in order to examine and assess the degree of understanding of the world of digital evidence shown by jurists and judges, including the technologies upon which the evidence is based.

The following sources were used as part of the literature review: computer science, criminal law, and education databases; criminal law journals, digital literature of the Association of Computing Machinery (ACM), the British Institute of International and Comparative Law, the Education Resources Information Center in the United States (ERIC), and the Institute of Electrical and Electronics Engineers (IEEE), and Internet databases, such as Google Scholar.

Unfortunately, I failed to identify any published work that examines the scope of knowledge shown by judges around the world pertaining to digital evidence. It would appear that the literary basis in the field of computerized forensics is minimal, and that, prior to 2010 (Casey, Personal Communication, July 23, 2010), nothing had been published on this topic.

During the review, I became discovered an international journal on digital evidence, a journal on digital forensics as related to the field of security, law, and justice, and a journal on the practice of digital forensics. I examined the conclusions of research discussion groups on the topic of digital forensics and the findings of the International Federation for Information Processing (IFIP) on this topic. My research indicates that these publications do not explicitly show the position of judges in relation to digital evidence.

It should be noted that already in 2008 Google was employed to search for information in the field of digital evidence. Following the search, a number of blog posts and online articles were found, but independent research studies or critical studies of research colleagues related to this field were not found or documented.

Characteristics of Digital Evidence in Professional Literature

In their book Perspectives on Learning Denis Charles Phillips and Jonas F. Soltis (2004) wrote that in the learning and education processes the individual understands new ideas and concepts because of their ability to link them and knowledge already known and understood. However, the attempt to understand the digital world based on previous knowledge accumulated over the years in the physical world may create a partial picture of the situation - and thus lead to a result that is the opposite of what is desired.

In 2006 Professor Andrew Ravenscroft and Simon McAlister from East London University stated in their article "Digital Games and Learning in Cyberspace: A Dialogical Approach"[1] that the best way to learn about the realms of virtual and digital communication is to start with no pre-conceived concepts and 'constructs' from the physical and traditional world.

Take, for example, one of the most basic and useful work aids: the document. In the 1980s, when the first graphic user interfaces became accessible, the term 'work desk' described the virtual work space. Three decades later, and the office terminology still prevails - the term 'document' describes a file on the computer.[2]

However, and as Gary Craig Kessler (2010) showed in his doctoral dissertation Judges' Awareness, Understanding, and Application of Digital Evidence[3], paper documents and digital documents are

---

[1] Professor Andrew Ravenscroft & Simon McAlister, 2006, Digital Games and Learning in Cypberspace: A Diaological Approach.
[2] Agarawala & Balakrishnan, 2006.
[3] Kessler, 2010, Judges' Awareness, Understanding, and Application of Digital Evidence.

fundamentally different. This difference influences the manner in which they are used as evidence or testimony. Paper documents are cumbersome by nature. They do not contain information about their originality and their distribution is limited; they are transferred from place to place as a whole and their security requires a lock and key.

In contrast digital documents, can simply and rapidly be altered. There is no limit to their size, and they contain information on the originality of the data. Copying is routine, their distribution is unlimited, rapid, and infinite. Simple means are required to back-up the documents, and the level of information security is influenced by the confidentiality of the information, by the standards acceptable in each country, and according to legal laws and ordinances.

Another difference between paper documents and digital documents is in their storage. Paper documents require a physical space, and therefore the storage of a large number of documents requires a large space, such as the space required for Court archives. In contrast, digital documents, are stored on a computer, and in a relatively small, physical space it is possible to store an almost unlimited volume of information.

Paper documents are, for the most part, stored in orderly and catalogued files. This is to enable rapid retrieval of a document and to identify the information appearing in the documents. In a digital environment, documents are not always stored in an organized manner and there may be no connection between the folder name and the documents in it.

It could be claimed that this disposition to a lack of organization gives the traditional storage method an advantage, which offsets space restrictions. However, this is not the case: search programs installed in computers can rapidly and efficiently analyze single words, combinations of words, or expressions and thus rapidly retrieve every document, in every format, regardless of its location on the hard drive or in the database. In this context, it should be noted that the user may consciously give different names to the digital document and the folder where it is stored to make the search difficult and delay discovery.

Another difference is the frequency of the backup. Physical documents are backed up infrequently, since paper documents do not change over time and each change in a document results in fresh copy. As long as they are stored in a proper and protected environment, they remain relatively secure for an extended period of time. Digital documents, on the other hand, can be changed with a click of a button, and are frequently backed up. Furthermore, equipment failures, such as the failure of a hard drive, may cause the loss of hundreds of thousands of files. This makes the implementation of an ordered and systematic backup system a necessity.

The backup location also differentiates between the two types of documents. Paper documents are generally stored in one or two locations, whilst digital backups can stored in a number of different places. The importance of distributed backup was proved by the 2001, Twin Towers terrorist attacks in New York.

Alongside the terrible loss of human life, companies with offices in buildings affected by the attack suffered another loss: with the collapse of the towers and other surrounding building the physical documents and the backups stored in the offices were lost - in essence, the loss of the documents wiped out the companies involved. On the other hand, companies that maintained digital backups and kept copies in another location were able to retrieve their data and thus survived.

In recent years, many organizations have been attempting to reduce the amount of paper their offices use and encourage a move to digital backup in order to save storage space and maintenance costs whilst ensuring that the document is securely saved forever. Over time we see that evidence is increasingly being transferred to a digital format with the original, concrete evidence being discarded. The digital copy becomes, in essence, the common and preeminent evidence.

Another core issue that illustrates the gap between paper documents and digital documents is the originality of the document.

Physical documents can be duplicated at a print shop or even in the office or home. Under certain conditions it is possible to create certified copies. In the digital world, however, it is possible to produce an unlimited number of copies using a variety of applications or systems for database management. This can result in multiple versions of one file. However, when a file is presented as evidence in Court, it is necessary to examine, in-depth, the issue of its originality. This is a serious issue, one that, in the end, may tip the balance and influence the entire judicial process. This topic will be discussed in the chapter, "Digital Evidence - Its Uniqueness and Acceptability".

Yet another difference between paper and digital documents is that digital documents include 'information data', namely a variety of traits and characteristics relating to each and every file (size, type, history of changes, etc.). Physical documents, in contrast, do not contain any information regarding changes, additions or past data[4].

In the matter of data transfer processes, digital documents also prevail. Physical documents are transferred by mail or courier service, and the document received at its destination is the document originally sent. It is important to emphasize that the mediator - the mailman or the delivery man - does not keep a copy[5]. A quicker way is to send the document by fax, but the original copy is retained by the sender and does not reach the recipient.

In contrast to traditional transfer methods, in the digital world it is possible to send files, in seconds, to an unlimited mailing list using email and it is also possible to read documents when not online. In addition, emails can be sent through many service providers in a number of countries, with each of the recipients or digital service providers (ISP - Internet Service Providers) retaining a copy of the message on the email servers or in the organization's backup systems for a predefined period of time.

---

[4] Casey, 2011: Kenneally, 2001a: Rothstein et al, 2007: Volonino, 2003.
[5] Anderson, 2008: Casey, 2011, Kenneally, 2001a: Volonino, 2003.

Another difference between physical documents and digital documents is the scope of information security. Information security systems for physical files includes tangible means of security, including systems to prevent water and fire damage, protection from biological pests as well as the protection of the building where the documents are stored.

In the digital environment the risk is different: the physical devices, namely the data storage servers and the backup systems where the files are stored, are exposed to attacks from external elements, elements that are invisible in terms of physical storage and whose goal is access the data via the internet and to sabotage the stored information.

Physical documents are, for the most part, kept in a room or a storage closet and are protected with a lock and key. Especially sensitive documents may even be stored in a safe. If the key or the safe combination is lost, traditional methods are available to enable access to the documents. In contrast, to protect digital files from unauthorized access or sabotage, it is necessary to encode and encrypt them. However, if the code or encryption key is lost, then it is possible that the files inaccessible even to the legal owners. In such a case, digital evidence and data retrieval experts may be necessary to crack the encryption system without harming the data's reliability.

Another essential difference between physical and digital documents derives from the evidential challenges they offer. While traditional evidence presents a direct relationship or geographic proximity to the place of the offense, digital information may be misleading, and it is difficult discover, with any degree of accuracy, how long it has been stored on a specific storage medium. In addition, when the offenders suspect that they are being followed, they can destroy or dispose of the hard drive or sabotage it thus causing the loss of some of the evidence.

Another challenge presented by digital documents derives from its information transfer path. Information saved in the drive may appear as a single block of information linked to many servers in other countries, and access to it is only possible through the Internet. Lacking all of the information saved in remote servers, the information on the original computer may, in terms of evidentiary value, be worthless or insignificant.

It should be noted that a certain type of data, such as sound and picture recordings, may suffer from interference (known as "noise") and physical disturbances alongside digital disturbances that distort the media. These distortions make it difficult to reliably analyze the data and make its reliable analysis a complicated and almost impossible task. This fact often causes a conflict between the scientific-factual data and the 'reasonable doubt' required legally[6]. While these types of evidence, namely, photographs and voice recordings, have over the years been accorded a high level of acceptability by judges and juries, modern technological ability makes it possible to, with relative ease, present falsified, misleading evidence.

Digital data sets another challenge, in the guise of the legal difficulties entailed in obtaining and analyzing the data. These difficulties are expressed in the scope of the search and seize warrant, in Court summonses, and in definitions of the goal of the search and seize process. Search and seizure entails other difficulties, due to the fact that the physical or geographic location of the information does not necessarily indicate the location where the computers or servers storing the relevant information are situated.

An additional challenge faced by digital forensic investigators is the issue of the pertinence of large data systems, namely, proving the relation between the data and the crime and the collection of the information necessary to substantiate the evidence. The processing and analysis of digital evidence are important issues for future research, but are still a difficult task to accomplish.

Differences between digital evidence and physical evidence influence the forensics process. For example, Rule 41 of Criminal

---

[6] Maher, 2009: Tibbitts & Lu, 2009.

Procedure in United States Federal Law addresses issues of inconsistency in the supervision of search warrants[7]. The law states that it is necessary to reduce the scope of searches approved by a warrant, in order to clearly set an hour and place for the search, and to define the evidence being searched for. In most cases, when physical evidence is sought, meeting these requirements is simple. However, in the search for digital evidence, the situation is different. Generally, it is necessary to seize and hold the storage media where evidence is found, namely, all the digital data, to decide which information to conduct an evidential search for. This is generally undertaken in a sterile laboratory equipped with advanced technologies that cannot be transferred to the crime or seizure scene in order to execute the warrant[8].

In this context, it should be said that the process of examining digital evidence is, because of the tremendous amount of data involved, and the fact that most hard drives can store considerable amounts of data which may not be relevant to the investigation, long and complex.

---

[7] The US Courts, 2008b.
[8] Kerr, 2005b, 2010

Prevalence of Digital Evidence

As mentioned, in the modern era digital evidence plays a central role in the courts in Israel, England, the United States and other countries. In most countries it is possible to find different types of computing devices: desktop and laptop computers, mobile phones, tablets, webcams, music players, and more. These devices, originally designed for entertainment or communications, have, over time, acquired a new use - for the documentation of evidence and recording activities, both legal and illegal. As a result, they are considered a reliable evidential source in both civil and criminal proceedings.

The advantage of digital evidence over traditional evidence and human evidence is the level of evidential precision: a computer knows to 'tell' only what was, without 'cutting corners' or adding embellishments and changing versions.

The FBI((Federal Bureau of Investigation), has stated that some 80% of the files that it investigates t involve digital evidence originating in computing devices, on the Internet, taken from security cameras, and on file sharing websites. The US Secret Service reports an even higher number of cases involving digital data. In recent years, the Secret Service and other federal agencies in the United States have established skilled and well-trained units for handling computer crimes and Internet offenses. This due to the steadily increasing amount of digital evidence collected daily by enforcement authorities. The widespread and growing popularity of digital devices, such as mobile phones, tablets and digital cameras, has made them an inseparable part of our daily life. Thus, at almost every crime scene and every criminal incident some form of digital documentation can usually be found.

Computerized forensics is also important in civil suits. An examination conducted on the topic shows that one of every four companies is required to show its email during a civil hearing, during a systematic investigation or documentation process, and of course in the framework of legal aid provided the organization.

10

It should be noted that digital devices include computerized components, and thus they are considered, in all respects, a computer. Moreover, these advanced devices use data processing and storage technologies alongside cellular, Internet, and satellite (GPS) communications. These devices are used by all sectors of the population, and thus the multiplicity of digital evidence in both criminal and civil suits.

Digital Evidence and Its Acceptability in the Courts

Among lawyers and jurists, there is agreement on the importance of digital evidence and its benefits. However, in the courtroom itself, digital evidence is still controversial and positions are often influenced by the judge's personal experience, beliefs, and professional understanding of the topic under discussion[9]. Some judges trust digital evidence more than traditional evidence because of its precision and objectivity. Other judges maintain that the value of digital evidence is limited, because of the difficulty in verifying the origin of the information it presents.

To understand the issue of digital evidence precision and objectivity , it is necessary to remember that, in contrast to traditional evidence which is open to the observer's interpretation, digital evidence is based on data stored in the form of a computer language - a series one's and zero's that comprise binary code. This computer language is a collection of instructions that the computer processor absorbs directly and without translation or interpretation. Simply put, the computer knows to say whether 'there was' or 'there was not'. The computer does not draw conclusions or make smart connections but rather presents a precise and clear picture of the situation.

Therefore, why is a computer expert necessary? The role of the computer expert is to examine the gray area between 'there was' or 'there was not'. In other words, to study the digital evidence and determine whether the evidence was indeed found. Thus, if the expert presents the Court with the original evidence after they have examined and verified it and its originality, it follows that the evidence must be accepted unequivocally as evidence whose credibility cannot be doubted.

Conversely, digital evidence has another characteristic that makes it difficult for judges in a hearing: computerized devices and the Internet

---

[9] Insa, 2006: Kenneally, 2001b

are surrounded by an aura of mysteriousness, while traditional physical evidence is well known to the courts and is easy to examine and understand. We should not forget that judges come from the world of law rather than from the digital world and hence they may not have the technological knowledge necessary to fairly and precisely implement the test of reliability in evidence law.

Section 53 of the Evidence Ordinance presents a closed list of criteria for the examination of witness reliability and oral evidence. Justice Yakov Kedmi (ret) (1990) in his book[10] addresses the four main tests that arrive from the section: impression, external comparison, internal comparison, and personality. Without delving into details, it is possible to understand that all four tests pertain to witnesses and evidence and not to digital evidence.

The lack of clarity regarding digital evidence is also apparent in American law. American Federal Rules of Evidence (Rule 702: Testimony by Expert Witnesses) addresses the abilities of experts in the field of digital forensics and gives judges broad discretion on the issue of acceptability of evidence. Judges' freedom of action is made possible in light of their lack of familiarity with the digital world - and in essence when a case involves digital evidence judges are not consistent and do not always rule in the spirit of the law[11].

Returning to Israeli law, a number of years ago, Judge Dr. Michal Agmon-Gonen stated that: "The Courts do not need to engage in this. This is a waste of time that could be used to engage in real cases that the Courts must address."

This case in question addressed the violation of copyrights in soccer broadcasts. The Israel Soccer Association asked the Tel Aviv District Court to reveal the IP address of a person who had broadcast, on the Internet, Premier League soccer games.

---

10 Part Two, Combined Version, 1991, pp. 890-901.
11 Wegman, 2005.

In her remarks, the judge said:

> "The law can do very little against rapid technological changes. This trial was conducted relatively quickly, and still my ruling was given after a year. Now an appeal is before the Supreme Court and another three to four years will pass until the ruling. Who knows whether streaming technology will be relevant at all by then?"

One judge admitted during a hearing that he did not know how to cope with technological issues, while another judge asked that a computer expert's opinion be presented to her and even announced that the expert's decision on the matter would be binding and final.

One of the goals of this work is to dispel the fog from around the world of digital evidence, to help judges examine the evidence from a legal viewpoint and to reduce the uncertainty surrounding these issues.

Digital Evidence and Its Implementation in the Court

As mentioned, judges often make inconsistent decisions. Some decisions do not meet the spirit of the law, and a few are even based on erroneous approaches. These rulings depend largely on the judges' technological knowledge when they are called to examine the nature of digital evidence or on the technology expert's degree of confidence[12].

The following cases were placed before the Courts. The judges were required to deal with complex technological and legal issues and were required to examine digital evidence and make decisions on this matter.

New Jersey v. Reid (2007)

Mrs. Reid was accused of using an anonymous email account to break into her personal manager's email account, to alter client information. The central issue was the method used by the Police to obtain incriminating evidence against the accused.

To understand the ruling, it is first necessary to understand evidence collection doctrine in the United States. Legal authorities use a court summons and search warrants to obtain essential information. While the Court summons are under Police authority and are used frequently by them, a judge must confirm a search warrant, which is used in cases where the intention is to review specific information: a company's business records, files owned by clients, personal information of value, and so on. Thus if the Police wish to find an IP address to identify the user's geographic position and obtain the name of the email account owner, then the Police will summon the Internet Service Provider (ISP) to court. In contrast, to obtain the user's email account contents or files, a search warrant signed by a judge is required.

---

12 Ball, 2008: Mason, 2008.

In this case, the Police summoned the ISP to Court to obtain the required information and link the anonymous email account with Mrs. Reid. The judge who heard the case ruled that the anonymous email account indicated Mrs. Reid's desire to avoid disclosure of her true identity and thus there is a clear expectation that her right to privacy be honored. This is similar to the Privacy Protection Law in Israel. Consequently, the judge ruled that the Police had exceeded their authority. In the judge's opinion a court summons was not sufficient, the Police should have requested a search warrant, which obligates a higher level of proof and presentation of real cause. The judge dismissed the evidence linking Mrs. Reid to the anonymous email account.

In an analogy to the world of physical evidence, the case is equivalent to a situation in which a judge rules in favor of a masked thief who claimed that the use of a mask was to protect his privacy[13] and is entitled to legal protection. This case illustrates how legal guidelines pertaining to physical evidence yield unanticipated outcomes when applied to digital evidence.

State of Israel: Sex Films and Slander

The Tel Aviv Magistrates Court determined that a film documenting consensual sexual relations between a couple and uploaded to the Internet without the woman's knowledge constitutes slander[14]. In the ruling, Judge Hana Yinon wrote:

> I believe that the publication of the film constitutes slander that humiliates and degrades the plaintiff, since the plaintiff, who is an attractive woman, a model just starting her career, is presented to all while she is making love with a former boyfriend, with her face is revealed and her naked body and private parts visible to all. In my opinion this humiliates and embarrasses her and degrading to her in public, especially in the eyes of her family and friends.

---

[13] Kerr, 2005a, 2009.
[14] Tel Aviv, 11831-03-10, Confidential (Publication Prohibited) v. Philip Koshamaro.

In comments to the ruling the judge stated that:

> The plaintiff's negligence contributes, to a certain degree, to the unfortunate incident that is the basis of the suit, since a person who documents their intimate life in films that may reach, and not necessarily in their best interests, pornographic websites on the Internet, should do so with caution. The freedom to make such films and distribute them can be considered a breach of trust on the part of the couple or those filming.

Let us examine the issue in the light of traditional evidence. Let us image a situation in which person records private sexual relations with a partner in writing and then reveals full names and identifying details and distributes the information in pornographic magazines. Does the judge's ruling in the previous case with regard the women's partial culpability still hold? Is there a difference between a detailed written recording and video films? Had this been physical evidence, for instance, an especially colorful and invasive article, would the cloud of contributory guilt still hover over the former partner? Here, too, the difference between physical evidence and digital evidence is especially prominent.

United States v. Councilman (2004, 2005)

Mr. Bradford worked in a company that sold rare books and as a part of the service he provided email accounts to many of his clients. The indictment stated that Mr. Bradford instructed two company employees to define the email server configuration so that all email messages originating from Amazon.com would be delayed and copied before they arrived at the client's email accounts.

According to US law, an email message stored in the email server and not yet opened by the recipient is considered a message in the transit stage, and the law prohibits the message from being read without permission. An email message stored in the email server or in the local computer after the message has been read is entitled to a lower level of protection[15].

Mr. Bradford was accused of conspiring to violate the Wiretap Act (1986), a law that addresses the issue of monitoring communications in the transit stage. The indictment did not address the Stored Communication Law (1986), which also grants protection to email messages stored on the email server or local computer and not yet read by the recipient.

In this case, the judge ruled that the Wiretap Act protects email messages only when they transferred via the Internet and when they were stored, unread, on the email server or computer. In essence, the Court rejected the government's argument that Mr. Bradford violated the Wiretapping Law and dismissed the accusation against him. A partial panel of the first Circuit Court of Appeals affirmed the rulin[16]; however a full panel of the Court later reversed the ruling[17].

From Mr. Bradford's trial of and the dismissal of the first decision it is possible to learn about the difficulties faced by judges when they are required to hand down decisions regarding digital evidence and the lack of expertise on the issue.

It should be noted that the Israeli Wiretapping Law (1979), which defines wiretapping, does not differentiate between listening to a message when it is conveyed and documenting it using any type of eavesdropping device and listening to it at a later date.

Israeli law determines that if an email message is found in email server or personal computer, then it can be defined as 'information' or 'computer material' as defined by the Computer Law (1995), while information in the transition stage will be covered by the directives of the Communication Law (Telecommunications and Broadcasting (1982), since the law determines that "Telecommunications - broadcast, transfer, or reception of signs, indications, visual shapes, voices, or

---

[15] Casey, 2011; Kerr, 2009.
[16] United States v. Councilman, 2004.
[17]United States v. Councilman, 2005.

information through wire, wireless, optical system, or other electromagnetic systems".

American Express (AMEX) v. Vinhnee (2005)

American Express (AMEX) filed suit against Vinhnee for more than $21,000 for invoice payments[18].

In the original hearing, the Court forbade American Express from using records and digital evidence as "best evidence" with regard to the sum of the suit. Its decision was based partially on American digital evidence regulations, Evidence Law 803 (6), which define exceptions to the matter of 'evidence by rumor' for records of regular activity[19].

According to the Evidence Law, it is possible to present business records as evidence before the Court only if it is possible to prove that they were held in real-time or near the time at which the activity was conducted. In addition, it must be proved that the source of the records, the method, or the circumstances that led to the preparation are reliable and are not suspect, namely, that they are authentic and precise. Furthermore, it is necessary to place the records in the trusted hands of the person in charge of records[20].

In this case, the person in charge of the records testified that American Express records met all the tests. Unfortunately, during the testimony, American Express offered to make certified copies of all the records. In its decision to forbid the use of records, the Court set a new rule: since the records were stored digitally, it is necessary to provide additional information to prove their originality and to accept them as having evidential value.

In a later hearing, the Court was informed that the person in charge of records was not authorized to answer basic questions in issues pertaining to hardware, software, databases, and tools that would

---

[18] American Express v. Vinhnee, 2005.
[19] United States Court, 2008c.
[20] American Express, Mason, 2008.

help produce and maintain the digital copies. Despite these limitations, the person in charge of records testified and maintained that the computer could not change numbers and data that the clients declared and preserved digitally.

The judge was not persuaded by these statements, and rightly so. The digital world offers many possibilities to change evidence, to distort it, or to make it disappear - and in essence opens up the possibility for the distortion of truth in the courtroom. When the Court was not presented with sufficiently convincing proof that the digital copies were suitable, if only in part, to the original account statements, it was necessary to dismiss the evidence in its entirety. Appeal judges later determined that the judge who had dismissed the evidence had acted with due judgment - and left the decision as is[21].

Thus, the Court acted both in the spirit and requirements of American law. Lacking proof of the originality and believability of the digital evidence, proof that American Express failed to present to the Court, the evidence was dismissed.

United States v. Boucher (2007-2009)

This suit[22] addressed a serious legal issue: the Fifth Amendment to the US Constitution and the right to protection against self-incrimination.

During questioning by Immigration and Customs Enforcement (ICE) officials at the United States and Canadian border, Mr. Boucher admitted that he had pedophiliac-pornographic contents on his laptop. At that time, Mr. Boucher turned on his laptop and the ICE officials saw the incriminating photographs.

After they saw the photographs, Mr. Boucher distracted the ICE officials' attention, typed a series of keys known only to him, and locked the laptop. This action activated a coding program called GPG[23],

---

[21] American Express, 2005.
[22] U.S. v. Boucher, D.Vt. 2007-09.

which protects the user's privacy, and thus the access to the computer in general and to incriminating files in particular.

A number of months passed, and all attempts by forensics examiners to discover the encryption password failed. The prosecutor searched for a way to compel Mr. Boucher to reveal the password. Mr. Boucher refused and consequently was summoned to a hearing. Forensics examiners testified as to the difficulty in deciphering the encrypted password and even said that the task could possibly take decades.

The judge ruled that it was not possible to compel Mr. Boucher to reveal the password, since such an instruction would violate the accused's right to protect himself against self-incrimination.

There is no doubt that this decision raises many questions and concerns. The legal system in Israel, like its parallel in the United States, frequently discusses the issue of the right to silence and protection against self-incrimination. The source of the issue appears in the Criminal Procedure Ordinance (Evidence): "The questioned person will be required to answer correctly all the questions presented to him during the investigation by the Police official, or other authorized official, apart from those questions the response to which will endanger the risk of criminal incrimination"[24].

Additional law directives addressing the right to silence appear in the Evidence Ordinance [New Version] (1971), section 47 A: "A person is not compelled to give evidence if it entails a confession to a fact that it is fundamentally an offence of which he is accused or may be accused."[25]

Indeed, the language of the legislature is clear and unequivocal. A person is entitled not to give evidence if it may incriminate him. Moreover, this right is valid, according to section 52 of the Evidence Ordinance, not only to court proceedings but also to every proceeding

---

[23] See the GPG program in chapter 14, Terms and Definitions.
[24] Criminal Procedure Ordinance (Evidence), Section 2.
[25] Evidence Ordinance [New Version] 1971, section 47 A.

in which a person gives evidence "to an authority, organization, or person authorized by law to take evidence".

The trial against Mr. Boucher examined the Constitution's Fifth Amendment and discussed issues relating to self-incrimination. However, since these are sexual films with pedophilia content from an unknown source, especially pointed questions arise. Does public good and the protection of minors take precedence over the accused's right to silence? On the same matter, is the disclosure of the network of creators and distributors of the pornographic material more important than the prosecution of a single user? Can information that the suspect provides verbally, including during the process of recording using photographic and recording devices, be considered evidence? Can the very giving of a password incriminate a suspect or accused?

Is the rule of 'the best evidence' still valid and relevant? Or has its time passed, as may be seen from the statements of my colleague Dr. Nimrod Kozlovsky: "Is the rule of best evidence - as the rule of acceptability - a rule appropriate for computer information and has the time not come for it to join the Hammurabi code?"[26]

Let us examine the question of public good and protection of minors. During the trial of Rabbi Motti Alon, who was convicted on two charges of sexual offenses against minors, Knesset (Israeli legislature) member Zevulun Orlov said: "The heart refuses to belief and wants to hug and encourage Rabbi Alon, but from an intellectual outlook it is necessary to prefer the public good over the good of the individual."

However, it is important to note that the cases are not similar. On the matter of Rabbi Alon, this is a local issue, limited in scope, and by distancing the accused from the location of the alleged offence it is possible to 'freeze' the situation until things become clear in court. Digital photographs and films, in contrast, are fundamentally different.

---

[26] Dr. Nimrod Kozlovsky, 2000, *The Computer and the Legal Process - Electronic Evidence and Laws.*

They are viral, they cross borders and continents, they are devoid of religion, sex, and race - and thus the real fear of their uncontrolled dissemination and harm of minors. We must not forget that, unlike the physical world, in which the seizure of evidence preserves the situation in situ, in the virtual world time plays an important role, and contents appearing today on the Internet may vanish or change. Therefore, in the matter of Mr. Boucher and similar cases, public good and the protection of minors should overcome the good of the individual and even the accused's right of silence.

On the matter of the incriminating password, legal experts compared Mr. Boucher's computer password to the key to a door. According to them, the disclosure of a password is like giving a key. The key itself is not incriminating, rather the contents in the room, and thus the password itself cannot incriminate. This comparison dovetails with the appeals judge's decision to instruct the accused to provide the password.

In 2009 another federal judge instructed Mr. Boucher to provide the authorities with a non-coded version of the contents of the hard drive, but this decision did not provide a direct answer to the question as to whether providing the password is considered evidence or not[27].

Other legal experts discussed the question of whether written declarations are evidence. According to this concept, had Mr. Boucher written the password on a piece of paper, then it would not be possible to force him to reveal it - since all incriminating evidence (such as physical evidence, hair, or fingerprints) is protected by the Fifth Amendment to the US Constitution.

In the end, Mr. Boucher disclosed the password in the framework of a plea bargain agreement.

---

[27] US v. Boucher, 2009.

CHAPTER 2: DIGITAL EVIDENCE, ITS UNIQUENESS AND ADMISSIBILITY

Digital Evidence and the Need for Full Digital Disclosure

From the 1990's onwards, and especially following the campaign of bombings by the Irish Republican Army, organizations, both small and large, understood the need for a disaster recovery plan or a business contingency plan for extreme situations. After the collapse of the Twin Towers in New York in 2001, the issue became even more important.

The goal of these plans is to predict situations of low frequency that have the potential to cause great damage. The scenarios described are not frequently realized, but when they do, they threaten the organization's continued existence. Although it is impossible to anticipate each and every disaster and how it occurs, general plans are essential to the organization's survival: they help it prepare in advance for the event - to define what should be done during the occurrence, who needs to act, and how to accelerate recovery – and, at the moment of truth, they reduce the degree of panic exhibited by the organization's employees.

Another type of plan presents more common situations: fraud or suspicion of fraud, offenses by employees, including information theft; slander and hate language on the Internet; computerized attacks (including from home), data theft data, and so on. These actions endanger the entire organization, and reality shows that legal implications may be severe and that some organizations that were forced to deal with these situations vanished from the business arena never to return. However, it is important to note that most organizations that experience a business crisis are forced to cope with these situations for only a few months, and only a few of them experience such events on a daily basis.

As with all contingency plans, it is possible to prepare in advance for these situations. A comprehensive and quality legal plan will attempt to identify credible evidence that may support the organization's position when necessary, for example, when the organization is required to meet the requirements of full disclosure within the framework of civil legal claims, to assist legal authorities in the investigation of crimes and counter-terrorism, to respond to accusations of inappropriate behavior on the part of an employee, or in controversial transactions where it is necessary to respond to accusations of neglect or breach of contract, to support the claims of insurance after loss, and so on.

What happens in more complex scenarios, which suit the modern, often virtual, business reality? In the world of the law, there is a tendency to label hi-tech crimes as "other" crimes, different from other types of criminal activity. In reality, the situation is different. The boundaries between the traditional world of crime and the world of digital crime have blurred. Most people and businesses in the modern world use computers, mobile phones, and other digital devices and most traditional criminal investigations necessitate the collection and examination of digital evidence. This constitutes part of the investigation process in a broad range of offenses such as murder (for example, the murder of the Meoz[28] couple in Jerusalem), drug trafficking, sex trafficking, pedophilia, terror, and more. The presentation of digital evidence as a part of the traditional legal process is seemingly a purely technical action but because of ignorance on this issue, it is important that the organization's decision makers understand the process and take pains regarding supervision and control throughout the entire process.

We see, therefore, that this reality necessitates setting a high threshold when dealing with digital evidence, including evidence that originates from the Internet, laptop computers, handheld computers and tablets, mobile phones, mobile and desktop media components, and communication systems owned by large corporations. For this reason many organizations have developed a legal plan, an orderly and

---

[28] State of Israel v. Meoz - Severe Criminal Case 54877-09-11.

detailed doctrine for implementation in extreme situations.

A legal preparatory plan is not intended to protect potential digital evidence, but the organization itself. As a rule, digital evidence will never become meaningless as a result of contamination or corruption of computer systems. The organization is the body expected to face a difficult dilemma during the investigation: whether to turn off essential systems in order to preserve digital evidence and protect them - and at the same time incur business losses due to the shut down systems - or to accept the limited ability and to present digital evidence in a version faithful to the original and thus to increase the risk of a legal failure.

The chances of winning a legal civil or criminal suit depend largely on the accessibility of reliable and compelling digital evidence. In the digital world there are digital traces and from these traces it is possible to learn and draw conclusions regarding the intentions and actions of the parties involved. Moreover, since more and more businesses are run digitally - by commercial corporations, private individuals, public sector organizations, and government authorities - the best way to prove their existence is through digital evidence.

Nevertheless, despite the increasing use of digital evidence, there are few organizations that address the issue of digital evidence in their emergency planning. Many organizations have contingency plans for fire, flooding, electricity outages, communication failures, terror actions, and even war - but only a very few have prepared detailed plans for the identification, collection, and preservation of digital evidence, as well as for meeting the standards and rules required to maintain credibility and reliability in the Court.

However, in the proposed Israeli Evidence law it states that: "Section 41 B gives computer output that is an institutional record the status of the original"[29] but let us ne clear: in most cases an institutional record is <u>not</u> digital evidence. This topic will be discussed at length later.

---

[29] Proposed Law to Amend the Evidence Ordinance (Number 15) (Source and Copy as Evidence), 2006... 248.

Following some of the large financial scandals that occurred in the United States and in Israel at the end of the 20th century and the beginning of the 21st century, a clear trend developed regarding legislation that compelled corporations and businesses to maintain, over time, a broad range of business records. One of the known examples in the United States is the Oxley-Sarbanes Law of 2002[30], which imposes punishments for the intentional destruction of certain vital files. Israeli law also addresses the topic, and section 2 of the Computer Law discusses the "disturbance and/or disruption of a computer or computer material". This issue also will be discussed later.

The Basel II Committee which engaged in the regulation of international capital and supervision of banks required companies in the financial services industry to perform a comprehensive risk assessment and to painstakingly manage their financial risks. Consequently, the Israeli Bank Supervisor published a circular, and in chapter 3 addressed bank's supervision activities for 2004. The subchapter "Financial Reports Unit" stated that:

> It is necessary to emphasize the central reporting instruction that was developed by the department in 2004, which obligates providing separate personal declarations by the CEO and the head bookkeeper regarding the efficiency of disclosure controls in banking corporations' quarterly and annual reports, as per section 302 of the Sarbanes Oxley Act[31].

The British Freedom of Information Act of 2000 determines that all organizations in the public sector must provide the information required within twenty business days and that the information must be "reliable". In this matter, digitally produced information is considered reliable.

In 2007 and 2008 a number of governmental divisions in Britain suffered severe security problems. These issues led to the loss of

---

[30] Sarbanes-Oxley Act of 2002.
[31] Chapter 3 - Activity of the Supervision over the Banks for 2004 …. 127.

computers, memory cards, and CDs, as well as the loss of 25 million records[32] that were stored on two CDs. Following these failures, a number of reports were written and the joint conclusion was that it is necessary to form an official policy that addresses the issue of information security, changes in the corporate culture, and more painstaking examination of security routines.

In 2010 the British government combined the Online Computer Security Office with the Central Office for Information Security and established a single entity - the Office of Cyber and Information Security. Consequently, the status of digital evidence improved, the issue of the evidence's originality was accorded the importance it deserves, and agreement was reached regarding the need for full digital disclosure.

In civil law full disclosure is a procedural process in which the sides in a suit provide each other copies of documents that they hold and that are related to the legal proceedings. Both in Israel and in the United States the principle of full and fair disclosure is upheld to ensure that all sides are aware of all the circumstances and receive equality of opportunity in the Court. The process of full disclosure is not subject to choice but is anchored in law. The absence of full and fair disclosure may even be legally detrimental to the side that violates this obligation.

The process of full disclosure has two stages. In the first stage, the sides provide each other with a detailed list of all relevant documents. In the second stage, the sides allow their opponents to examine the documents they hold, with the exception of documents for which the law provides confidentiality.

It is accepted that in the second stage all sides examine the original documents or copies. The word 'documents' has a very broad definition and can include email messages, CDs, tape cassettes, video cassettes, computer files, computer software programs, and additional digital materials.

---

[32] MRC – Poynter Recommendations – ICO Audit Executive Summary Version 1.0

In October 2010 the British law added a practical and focused directive[33] on the matter of full disclosure. The directive includes a concomitant questionnaire the completion of which enables all the information stored digitally to be circled and noted. It should be noted that a considerable portion of the requirements appearing in the directive are in no way trivial and maintaining them will prevent 'leg dragging' and will reduce legal red tape. Thus, for example, the sides are required to conduct a reasonable search within the documents and concurrently to cooperate in all issues pertaining to technological means that may facilitate the examination process. This includes agreeing formats for providing materials, methods of storing information, and other technical data.

Indirectly the questionnaire is intended to help senior managers in the organizations and their legal consultants to understand issues of strategy and management. The questionnaire predicts the requirement for full digital disclosure and the potential need to provide digital evidence in certain cases and therefore sets normal management rules for these cases. In addition, the questionnaire includes a review of the types of digital evidence and presents problems and concomitant issues, including that of the admissibility of digital evidence.

The success of the full disclosure process in particular and of the digital evidence collection system in general depends largely on the organization's and management's level of preparation. Frequently the organization is required to make a significant decision: whether to properly and safely save the digital evidence and thus to shut down main computer services for a lengthy period of time or to continue to operate the business but to risk the loss of digital evidence. This decision must be made by the corporation's senior managers or the business and not by outside consultants or computer technicians who are hired ad-hoc and are not aware of the entirety of the organization's considerations.

Every corporation and business should develop an official policy to preserve its documents, as a part of a legal preparation plan.

---

[33] Practice Direction 31B – Disclosure of Electronic Documents

'Documents' include, as stated previously, materials in digital format, and it is the organization's responsibility to save the data in a manner that facilitates control and intra-organizational examinations and also ensures that saved documents meet tests of admissibility and that their originality not be contestable.

A review of technological terminology

The first stage of the computer forensics process and the collection and documentation of digital evidence is making a precise, legally acceptable and uncontestable copy of all evidentiary materials. To ensure that original digital evidence will not be damaged in any way, it is necessary to produce an exact copy of the storage medium - namely, the computer, the server, the mobile phone, or any other digital storage means. Examination of the evidence, analysis of the digital medium, the legal examination - all these are always performed only on an exact copy.

At the end of the evidence duplication process, the duplication device provides a printout of its activities. This is done in order to show that the evidence duplication was performed completely faithfully and that the duplicated evidence is a mirror copy of the original. The printed output should be attached to the duplicated hardware and the digital evidence. Thus the duplication process is documented throughout, and if an error message is received during the process, this indicate a technical problem with a piece of the original evidence. This requires a different approach when being addressed.

The legal copy of the evidential medium is known, in professional terms, as a 'mirror image'. This term is familiar to computer experts and forensic examiners, and it indicates an exact copy which is faithful to the original. In the physical, traditional world, this term has the opposite meaning: a mirror image is the reversal of things as seen by the observer, since the mirror reflects a reversed picture of reality. Therefore, to prevent a mistaken understanding of the term and lack of clarity before the Court, the exact copy is referred to as a 'bit to bit' copy.

With regard to simulations performed as a part of the process to prove the integrity of the original data, this precedes the final duplication. Segments are marked virtually and segments of equal size are duplicated to the test equipment for examination. Each duplicated segment is separately validated.

As previously mentioned, at the end of the imaging process a printout is produced, which indicates that the copy is exact and true to the original. However, the size of the copy may be different from that of the original. This discrepancy is due to various imaging formats that use different compression algorithms at the end of which the duplicated material may take up less space than the original evidence. The fact that the copy of the original evidence, the 'bit to bit' copy, may not be identical to the original evidence in terms of file size can induce a certain degree of confusion[34].

I would note that the production of a copy that is faithful to the original, namely a legal copy of the evidentiary material, is the sole physical science used in the examination of digital evidence as part of the process of examining digital evidence on a computer alone.

As processes that present valid information with evidential value, these processes must meet the test of reliability[35] and prove that it is possible to reconstruct them again - namely, two different authorized technicians who use identical hardware and software can product copies that are faithful to the original digital evidence, namely legal copies identical to the original evidence.

Despite that previously stated and in extreme cases, it is possible that this will not be sufficient. Let us assume, for example, that the hard drive containing the original evidence was damaged for an unknown reason during the initial duplication process. In other words, the drive includes a damaged sector that cannot be read another time.

Explanation

The component where data are stored on the computer is called the 'hard drive' or 'hard disk'. The hard drive consists of digital rings made of aluminum or glass. These rings are covered with magnetic substances and are connected to one axis. The hard drive is the fixed memory device, non-volatile, and its digital head writes data on the

---

[34] Ieong, 2006: Kenneally & Brown, 2005.
[35] Daubert, 1993: Kerr, 2005a.

rings and stores them in sectors. As needed, it is possible to extract the desired information from the sectors on the hard drive.

We can compare the hard drive to a CD. We all know what happens when there are scratches on a CD - the audio material 'jumps'. In the same way, when an accredited computer investigator attempts to extract digital evidence from a hard drive of a crime suspect and the hard drive contains damaged sectors - 'scratches on the CD' - the attempt may fail.

Nevertheless, the investigator has at his disposal advanced software which can be used to 'bypass' the algorithm and reconstruct the damaged sectors. At the end of the reconstruction process, the software will report that 'the damaged sectors were reconstructed successfully' and the skilled investigator will be able to extract the required information from the new copy created.

Reconstruction of damaged sectors does not leave traces, and it is impossible to know which files were reconstructed. This fact may create a problematic and often common situation. The computer expert accesses the hard drive, and finds files that include numbers which he uses to continue the investigation. However, on occasion, the reconstruction of damaged sectors creates a reversal of numbers in the reconstructed sectors without leaving traces, and this may shift the investigation's direction and lead to erroneous results.

After the accredited technician or investigator creates a faithful copy of the original hard drive, it is possible that for some reason a sector may be damaged and is no longer readable. Thus, when another technician attempts to create an additional legal copy of the source hard drive, the new copy will not be identical to the original copy, because of the damaged sector, despite the fact that the expert performed the exact same process. Sometimes the difference between the copies is minimal and sometimes great.

Given a situation in which there is a printout attesting to the accuracy of the first copy, then additional copies may be made from the original copy and they will also be seem as legal copies in all respects.

A problem arises when there is an error message in the first copy that indicates flawed sectors in the original hard drive. In other words, all copies will reflect this flawed sector and it is possible that the contents of this sector may never be known. I will address this matter in the chapter "The Admissibility of Evidence, Its Authenticity and Its Weight".

In most of cases where the computer expert creates an image of the hard drive, he removes the drive from the computer or the server. However, under certain circumstances it is essential to copy the drive from the working computer, such as when information from a coded drive is required and may be impossible to reconstruct after the system is shut down or when the shutdown of an organization's server may disrupt regular activity across the entire organization. Sometimes computer investigators are concerned that suspects will notice the disappearance of the server from the Internet and will disrupt the investigation process and therefore copy the drive from the operating computer. This process - the imaging of a computer system in action - is called in professional terms a "hot copy". A hot copy may lead to a situation in which files belonging to open applications will not be saved in the hard drive - and thus the original evidence will change before the copying process is completed.

Explanation

An open application, or in popular terms, an open file, allows a single user to modify and save changes to the file. Only when the file is closed can other users edit and change it. This issue frequently appears in large organizations, when a number of workers are required to use one file. This is also true in our matter: when the file is open, when the application is working, it is impossible to copy it.

A hot copy provides an opportunity to produce a legal copy of random access memory (volatile memory) - or in professional terms, RAM. This memory serves as a means of storing data on the computer and requires a constant supply of electricity so that the information t will not be erased. Since the imaging program must be loaded into volatile memory to copy it, some of the volatile memory's original content will be overwritten before the copy is produced. In such a case the Court must be made aware of the fact that this is hot copy and be convinced that the information lost in the process included an equal amount of incriminating and exculpatory evidence. Thus, the presiding judges can provide an appropriate balance and reach a fair legal result.

When recording of the copying process is not done in full, it is necessary to add a clear explanation and reasons for the partial recording. In addition, it is necessary to support the evidence with additional digital evidence.

An additional digital investigation process is that of online forensics on the internet and mobile networks using a program that collects the data directly. These programs use a method known as "packet sniffing" and have a variety of goals: to supervise network performance , to solve communication problems, to solve network data transfer problems, and so on. The software is also very popular amongst hackers, who use it for the illegal collection of information from the Internet and mobile networks, to prepare an infrastructure for computers and mobile phones and to trap personal data such as passwords, IP addresses, online protocols, and so on.

In essence, the legal world's lack of familiarity with the world of digital evidence makes it difficult to manage cases in the Courts, since a lack of technical understanding may prevent the judges from reaching the correct decision. However, we must not forget that the final product produced from the digital evidence is computer output, and its goal is to 'translate' machine language into simple, easy to understand language. The role of the digital evidence expert is to provide judges with the same reliable and original computer output and thus reliving them of the need to be technology aware.

Rules of Digital Evidence

To create an evidential infrastructure admissible in the Courts, the digital evidence must meet three basic rules: belonging, reliability, and an adequate amount of evidence that has continuity and a direct relationship.

- Belonging. For the digital evidence collected to be relevant to the legal process, it is necessary to prove the existence of a concrete relationship between the evidence and between the accused and the defendant.

- Reliability. The precise definition of the issue of the reliability of digital evidence changes from one judgmental authority to another, but in most cases the digital evidence is considered reliable if it indicates the chain of events.

- Adequate amount. The digital evidence collected must be in a sufficiently large quantity so as to enable examination and cross checking of the data with all the information obtained during the investigation.

In addition, it is necessary to make certain that digital evidence collection will be undertaken according to local rules and arrangements of the local authority. It is possible that the computers or the servers will be located different places in the world, and therefore it is important to be sure of global cooperation. It is also critical to ascertain that all processes used in the collection of digital investigation materials will be validated legally before they are used - both in the country of origin and in the target country - to eliminate the possibility that the Court or the opposing side will argue the illegality or inadmissibility of the evidence[36].

Digital Evidence Collection and Rules

Many business and legal scenarios necessitate the collection of digital evidence. In each and every case, it is necessary to examine the expected process of evidence collection by a number of parameters: the need for digital evidence, the quality of the evidence, the precision required for data analysis, service rehabilitation, and the financial investment required for the collection. Since every case is different, it is necessary to determine ahead of time processes and priorities, to differentiate between the different needs - and to focus on evidence whose quality will lead to a precise reconstruction of the evidence.

---

[36] International Standard ISO/IEC27037

The stage of the deciding priorities is intended to reduce the chances of losing potential digital evidence - and thus raising the future evidential value of the collected evidence. This process includes evaluation of existing raw material, as well as the development of rules regarding the order in which evidence will be collected.

Rules

There are a number of fundamental rules that must be followed in the stages of digital evidence collection:

The collected material must be related to the event. It is necessary to prove that the collected material is relevant to the topic of the investigation, that it includes information of value to the investigation, and that there is sufficient reason to obtain it.

The expert performing the collection process must explain and justify the series of actions required for collection and describe in detail the decisions that led to the collection of the required material.

All actions required for the collection or reconstruction of evidence must be subject to inspection and reconstruction. In other words, it must be possible to perform the same actions and achieving the same results that led to the creation of the evidence. This means that the process is subject to inspection and the evidence is proved to be believable.

For the investigation to be thorough and appropriate, the computer investigator must collect an adequate amount of digital evidence, and it should be collected from a number of different computers or servers. This arises from the fact that there are systems which create a distortion in the issue of admissibility of evidence - as will be described in the chapter of "Reliability of the Digital Evidence" and in the chapter of "Technology Against Digital Forensics".

The computer investigator must use a control system to measure the amount of material collected. In addition, he must examine the processes used so as to determine whether the type and amount of material is satisfactory.

At the end of the collection process, it is necessary to transfer the materials to a forensic computer expert, whose role is to present the evidence, convince the court that the evidence constitutes an adequate evidential infrastructure, indicate the relation between it and the rest of the findings in the case, and prove that the evidence does not fall into the trap of 'technology against digital forensics'.

An explanation regarding a number of phrases used previously.

'Can be justified'. The computer expert needs to explain and justify all the actions and methods used to extract digital evidence from the raw material. For this purpose, he must present proof that the decisions he took were correct for the obtaining the digital evidence, for its successful reconstruction, or for the providing validity to his actions.

In the civil area, it is the duty of companies and organizations to train an authorized examiner to address digital evidence, and he must have technical skills and meet requirements of international standards. The training of an expert will ensure, as stated, the correct and proper management of all the processes required when addressing digital materials, as well as the handling future digital evidence. In this way, digital evidence that may have value in the future will be saved.

'Subject to inspection'. The computer examiner or computer expert must appropriately document all actions that led to the creation of the evidence placed before the Court. The goal is that every licensed expert and every authorized examiner acting on behalf of the defendant in civil proceedings and on the part of the accused in criminal proceedings can evaluate these actions.

The examiner or the expert must be available for independent evaluation so that it will be possible to determine whether the correct method or scientific process required to prove the admissibility of the digital evidence was used.

'It must be possible to perform the same actions'. It is necessary to prove that, if the examination is performed again in the same way, using the same measurement method, with the same examination tools, and under the same conditions, then the results obtained will be identical. It is important to note that the determining test is that of results rather than method. Even if the reconstruction is performed in a number of different ways, the result of every reconstruction must be identical to the results obtained through other reconstruction methods.

The success of the reconstruction process is examined according to a number of criteria:

- The ability to produce identical results from the use of the same measurement method.
- The ability to produce identical results when using different tools in different conditions.
- The ability to execute a reconstruction at any given moment after the evaluation of the original examination.
- The ability to facilitate the reconstruction using at least three different reconstruction programs.
- The ability to obtain identical results in each and every reconstruction.

If two different results are obtained, then it is necessary to examine the credibility of the reconstruction program - and simultaneously to search for additional reasons for the differences. If the findings are not unequivocal, then it is necessary to repeat the entire examination and to add another examination program. In every case in which the reason for the discrepancy between results is not found, it is necessary to update the forensic computer expert and note this openly in a detailed report to the Court. This enables the Court to examine the nature of the evidence as a whole and attribute relative weight to the evidence presented or declare its disqualification.

If the process documentation for the collection of raw material indicates that, during the process, a physical failure is discovered, then it is likely that a repeat examination will not lead to identical results. In this case, the additional computer examination must ascertain that the process of collection and documentation of the materials is undertaken in a reliable manner. This will ensure that the raw material is not destroyed because of the failure, and that the possibility of recurrence is not impaired. In addition, it is mandatory to examine the processes quality control and documentation procedures.

Data reconstruction procedures change from one judgment area to another and with them also the requirements and rules for execution. The computer examiner performing the reconstruction process must be aware of the specific requirements of every area of judgment and accordingly manage the reconstruction process.

Reconstruction Programs

In essence, the process is the reverse of the data backup process and is performed by an integrated system that includes both hardware and software.

The term "backup" refers to creation of copies of data so that they can be used to reconstruct the original information, from the storage media, in the event of its loss or corruption. Backups have two main objectives. The first is the reconstruction of information as a part of the recovery process following a 'disaster', and the second is reconstruction of information that was erased or corrupted.

As a part of the process of sending data to the storage system, it is necessary to separate the files intended for backup, namely, to remove them and even change their structure, including adjustment, of coding, registration in the backup system's archive, compression, encryption, redundancy elimination, and so on.

The complexity of the backup process has led to the development of many methods for data verification and for kevel of the system's credibility. In general, it is important to know that the system that created the backup files on tape or on another hard drive is the system that is able to perform the most precise reconstruction. This requires the execution of a number of reconstruction evaluations and tests using a variety of systems as test results rather than test methodology is what determines the precision of the results and their credibility.

The problem arises when the backup system and the original reconstruction is no longer available for reasons related to the investigation or due to rapid technological development that has overtaken the backup's technology and does not provide a means to restore the data. In such a case, the forensic computer expert must disassemble the digital media's case and combine new hardware and software that is able to retrieve the data from the digital media.

The Process of Handling Digital Evidence

Digital evidence is fragile by nature. It may change, be corrupted, be damaged, or disappear due to bad or inappropriate handling or incorrect examination. The result is evidence that is not admissible in Court. For this reason, it is important that experts who handle the raw material and the digital evidence be certified and skilled and able to identify the risks and manage them.

The process of handling digital evidence sets four fundamental principles, and the forensic computer expert must act according to them in order to ensure the integrity and the reliability of any potential digital evidence.

- The digital evidence experts must reduce, as much as is possible, the handling of the original digital components or the potential digital evidence.
- The digital evidence experts must provide an explanation for every action and for every change made in the original digital evidence or the potential digital evidence. This explanation must be detailed in order that other experts be able to form an opinion regarding the reliability of the evidence.
- The digital evidence experts must obey local laws relating to evidence and avoid any action that detracts from their abilities or deviates from the authority granted to them.
- The digital evidence experts must preserve and document all their findings, and primarily when they are required to conduct an investigation into any instance of unavoidable change to digital evidence..

Digital evidence has two aspects: physical and logical. The physical aspect is the means, the equipment, in which the evidence is stored, while the logical aspect is the virtual representation of the data within the hardware component. The process of handling the evidence pertains both to the physical aspect and to the logical aspect and includes four stages: identification, collection, production, and preservation. We will examine the meaning of each one of the stages in the following sections.

Identification of Digital Evidence

The identification process looks at physical digital media and the processing components that may include potential digital evidence. The process includes, amongst other things, setting priorities for the collection of evidence on the basis of its degree of volatility. The examiners of digital evidence must identify the level of the data's volatility so as to determine the correct order of collection and thus reduce, to the greatest possible extent, threats of possible damage, the disappearance of potential digital evidence, and to attempt to obtain the best digital evidence.

It is important that the examiners of digital evidence search thoroughly for physical items that may include potential digital evidence. It is necessary to take into account that this evidence can be concealed or merged with seemingly unrelated materials. In addition, they must be aware of the existence of concealed digital evidence. They must further know that all digital means of storage can be identified easily and simply, for instance, an environment of remote servers and cloud servers (NAS and SAN, see the chapter on terms and definitions). These and others make identification difficult and add a virtual dimension to the process of physical identification.

Digital Evidence Collection

After the identification of digital components that may include potential digital evidence, the forensic experts are required to decide how the material will be collected in light of specific circumstances.

The first stage in the collection process is the removal of the components from their original location and their transfer to a laboratory or other controlled environment. There, at a later stage, the data stored in the components will be analyzed. This stage includes documentation of approach processes and packing of the components before they are moved.

At the collection stage, the components may be found in one of two states: a state in which the operating system works, in other words, it is connected to a source of electricity, or a state in which the system is turned off. The preferred state is determined by the component type, the component state, methods and tools, types of hardware and encryption systems, any and all of which may which may create a situation in which after system is shut down it is no longer possible to open the data and examine it, as in the case of Mr. Boucher[37].

Simultaneously with the collection of the digital components, the evidence examiners must collect all the material that may be related to potential digital evidence, such as printed documents that include passwords, hard drives, and electrical connectors of system components. The obligation of the evidence examiners is to adopt the best collection method as required by the circumstances and the constraints of time and cost and, of course, to document the issues that guided them in the choice of the collection method.

If the evidence examiners decide not to collect some of the digital components, they must document their decision and provide an explanation that meets the requirements of the relevant judicial authority.

Production of Digital Evidence

The third stage in the chain of action is that of producing the digital evidence.

In every digital device on which it is possible to store information (such as pictures, files, lists of contacts, and so on) there is a hard drive. To produce the potential digital evidence, the digital evidence

---

[37] U.S. v. Boucher, D.Vt. 2007-

examiners must examine the integrity of the original hardware and then create a faithful copy of the hard drive that contains the evidence. In professional language, this copy is known as "copy hard drive bit by bit" (see the chapter on terms and definitions).

At the end of the copying process, a faithful copy of the digital hardware is created, and all the relevant and required tests are performed only on this copy leaving the original untouched and in its pristine state. A search for network channels that can indicate the existence of additional digital or virtual components will be conducted only on the duplicated component.

The copy obtained must be validated against the original hardware using original proven and tested verification functions. This is intended to indicate the precision and integrity of the copied materials, as well as to prove to all judicial and legal factors the reliability of the findings.

Under circumstances in which it is impossible to conduct the verification process, such as when there is a hardware failure or when the original hardware includes damaged or erroneous sectors, the digital evidence examiner must use the best method at his disposal and justify his choice. When it is impossible to verify the copy in its entirety against the original hardware because of errors in the original, it is possible to verify the copy against those parts in the original that can be read - and thus provide the verified evidence greater weight than that of evidence that was not verified due to failure of the original hardware.

An international standard determines that in cases where the original is too large, the evidence tester may copy only the relative part required, or, in other words, to produce a partial copy that is faithful to the original. This is also true regarding previously determined formats or when it is impossible, for instance, to copy erased files or unallocated sectors in the hard drive. This is true in all other cases where, according to the standard, this copying method may be effective or when task control systems are working or active and it is impossible to turn them off[38].

---

[38] International Standard ISO/IEC27037

It would appear that this is a flawed process: it denies the accused or the defendant the possibility of defending themselves, since the presentation of a partial copy of the drive is comparable to the disclosure of a small part of the evidence and the denial of the accused's or defendant's right to look at the entirety of the evidence. This process denies one of the sides a fundamental right granted to him by law - the right to due process - and thus damages one of the principles that guides the legal system in Israel.

As an aside, it should be noted that today, the United States also recognizes this fundamental right. The Sixth Amendment to the United States Constitution protects the accused's right to a fair trial in criminal proceedings and determines that the trial will be held in front of a jury and not a judge or government official.

Preservation of Digital Evidence

The preservation of digital evidence from harm or corruption is an inseparable part of the process for the care of digital evidence. The preservation of digital evidence is a paramount consideration throughout the entire life cycle of the evidence - from the identification of the digital components that include the potential digital evidence, through the collection of evidence, to the production of evidence.

The digital evidence should be saved to ensure the effectiveness of the investigation. By saving the digital evidence we provide protection both for the digital evidence itself and for the digital components related to the digital evidence, such as date or time stamps. One of the roles of the digital evidence tester is to prove that the evidence was not altered or, if there were unavoidable changes, to provide an explanation for the change and documentation of the actions that leading to it.

Reliability of the Digital Evidence

The challenge to the precision and reliability of the digital evidence becomes steadily more complicated, even more so because of the fact that digital evidence, by nature, is found in a 'gray area', which the majority of people are not conversant with.

It will become clear that the arising difficulties and doubts do not pertain to familiarity with computer components, but rather to the ability of the digital evidence expert to identify the exact data he is searching for - the data that will, at the end of the judicial and forensic process, provide the judges with a clear, accurate and credible picture of events.

Among many in Israel's legal community and that of the United States, the accepted approach is that if the Court accepts the digital evidence and confirms it, then the evidence is considered to be original and reliable. Conversely, as this book will explain, mistakes in the legal copying process, differences in content, and technological knowledge gaps between different experts influence the reliability of digital evidence, its precision, and its integrity. These characteristics raise serious questions regarding digital evidence and suggest that it may be unreliable. One of the main problems contributing to the lack of reliability of digital evidence relates to time stamps, which are linked to files and give them an element of authenticity over time.

Time stamps are a collection of data related directly to a file, documented by an operating system, and saved in the digital component. They note the date and the hour at which the file was created, the data and the hour when it was last opened, and the date at which changes were made.

The use of time stamps is common in the logging of computer operating system events or in logging of relating to different software: alongside every documented event there appears a time stamp that indicates the time of the occurrence. Time stamps are also used in internet communication protocol logging o and when sending and receiving email messages. Data is synchronized between the time stamp of the message sent and the time stamp of the message received - and in the world of digital evidence, this can be critical evidence.

An additional use of time stamps is in the field of computer security and cryptography. Time stamps appear alongside information security digital signatures and algorithms, for instance, to prove that a worker attempted to retrieve information from the company's system outside of work hours.

In a another analogy, the various caching mechanisms use a system of time setting for the purpose of defining cached information items and to determine when the cached information expires. Time stamps of digital files are important evidence. They enable the digital evidence experts and forensic testers to build the time line of the occurrences, namely, the order in which the events occurred, and hence they can significantly influence the interpretation and solving of the events.

An especially fascinating issue is that or erroneous time stamps. Sometimes digital evidence experts extract mistaken or imprecise information from time stamps and thus the trustworthiness of the information in its entirety is cast in doubt. In addition, not all computer programs update time stamps at any given moment and consistently, and therefore it is possible that the files system will present conflicting time stamps. One such example is the presentation of impossible information, according to which the changes in the file were supposedly performed at a date prior to the file creation.

In contrast to the physical world, the time stamp in the world of digital evidence has a life of its own. - For this reason a unique process of verification that ascertains that the times of the events are fully commensurate with the physical time dimension is necessary. This is clarified in the following example: more than once the question of a time stamp of a Word document attached to an email message is brought before the Court. The following question arises. Are the Word file characteristics attached to the email message reliable and is there a change in the date of the file's last update or in the date of its creation?

The Time Stamp in Word Files

Word is a word processing program developed by Microsoft. It is included in that company's Office Software Suite.

The 2003 version of the software supports a variety of languages (including Hebrew) and enables the integration of text and pictures. The accepted format for the saving of Word 2003 files ends with .doc. The names of the Word files in advanced versions of the software, namely 2007 and 2010, end with .docx. In these versions, as opposed to .doc, it is possible to integrate passages of software code and to create personal extensions and even to write and include viruses in the Word file.

Every Word file includes information about the data it contains. This information, 'data about data', is known as meta-data. Some of this data, such as the date the file's creation date and the last date it was saved, are automatically updated. However, this data is not always precise: when a Word 2003 file is sent to a computer where the Word version installed is belongs to the Office 2007 and upwards suite, the meta-data are corrupted - and this leads to mistaken parameters regarding the document's originality, creation date, and last modification date.

Email Messages

Email (electronic mail) software is a digital system for sending messages and transferring them from one computer to another through the Internet and computer servers. It is possible to send an email message using a simple text format or HTML format, and it is possible to attach files in different formats, including pictures and compressed files.

Today there are hundreds of email software programs. These programs offer comfortable interfaces for reading, writing, sending, receiving, and saving email messages. Some are provided as a free service available to all. These free services include: Gmail, Yahoo, Walla, and so on. The common denominator of all the email programs is their compatibility with network protocols (protocol 25 for sending email messages, known as SMTP, and protocol 110 for receiving them, known as POP3), as well as the stability of their development language. These traits provide a trustworthy interface for companies and individuals that use these email services during the workday and in during leisure hours.

The difference between the various email programs is in the structure of each and every program, in the database, and in the additional applications installed in the software. These applications include databases, lists of contacts, a calendar, information backup to an external file, an activity tracking log, opening and sharing of private and public folders, connection to different peripheral devices, such as mobile phones, handheld computers, laptops, and remote cloud servers (servers that are distant from the user's location), search engines, and products offered by a third party.

The most widely used email software in Israel is Outlook, from Microsoft. The software file found in personal computers, also known as a PST file, is similar to the OST file used as the main email server in organizations and companies. Therein lies the problem: in many cases the digital evidence expert is given a computer with email software installed other than Microsoft Outlook. More than once, due of lack of knowledge or lack of expertise of other software, the expert quickly attempts to convert the file to the PST format so that he can view the messages using the Outlook program - and in essence, by this act the expert himself distorts the evidence.

The conversion of a file from its initial format used when it was first created creation due to the lack of compatibility between companies that created the email software, whether intentionally or not, distorts the contents and the characteristics of the file and leads to a situation in which the data received are not necessarily correct or precise.

It is mandatory to examine whether this is the original email software through which the email messages were written, sent, and received. If this is not so or not known, then it is possible that the data presented will be distorted and that this, in turn, could lead to the disqualification of the digital evidence or reduce its importance relative to other evidence presented in the case.

PST File or Export of OST File

Another issue relating to the issue of the reliability of digital evidence is the process of file export and import.. Files are intended to save only data that the programmer defined, and this is the root of the problem. The files in Microsoft email software do not save data from the past, with the exception of those that the user defined to be saved. In other words, if the user erased email messages before exporting the file, then documentation pertaining to the message erasure will not be found in the export file.

It should be possible to find the data regarding the erasure of the email message in the computer or in the email server. My recommendation is that whenever there is doubt relating to email messages, it is necessary to present the user's computer for examination or the status of the email server in real time or close to the date at which the activity actually happened.

Given the lack of a copy faithful to the original computer or the server hard drives from which the data were collected in real time or near the date when the activity actually happened, this email message should not be seen as admissible evidence, in other words, it should not be considered a copy faithful to the original that can be used in the legal proceedings.

From the proposal to amend the Israeli Evidence Ordinance, it is possible to learn that the legislator's desire is that there be an obligation to keep a copy of the computer hard drives faithful to the original[39]. This copy must be from a date close to the date of the documentation. The aim of this requirement is to ensure that there always to be a possibility of examining and validating the originality of the information documented as computer output and to be presented as evidence as a part of the legal process. As a part of their role as guardians of justice, the judges must determine the reliability of the reports and data collected in the process of digital evidence extraction and the legal identification[40].

---

[39] Amendment of the Evidence Order (Number 15), 200, p. 248.
[40] Jones, 2009: Kenneally, 2001b: Kerr, 2005a

Over the years, commercial companies have developed software programs for the collection and documentation of digital evidence based on accumulated knowledge and on research and development. The leading names in this field include FTK software developed by AccessData, the Autopsy software program developed by the Brian Carrier Company, the EnCase software program from Guidance Software Company, and the x-Ways Forensics software.

In general, results obtained from these programs and presented as output are considered trustworthy and admissible before the courts in the United States. In Israel there is still a void on this matter: less importance is ascribed to the type of software program or the tools the expert used to collect the evidence as opposed to the findings and professional testimony. On this matter, in my opinion, we are moving carefully forwards, towards the formation of an orderly list of programs, which, after they have been examined and assed, they will be considered as providing reliable and admissible evidence.

In the United States, judges are entitled, by law, to cast doubt on digital evidence and even to disqualify it if a specific version of software used for the investigation and collection of digital evidence - no matter how reliable, subject to verification, devoid of mistakes, and thorough, like previous versions that the Court accepted - was not examined and assessed by recognized forensic laboratories which then confirmed the reliability and admissibility of the said software's findings. .

Only when the new version is validated will its findings be admissible in a legal process. I would note that judges are not obligated to understand the process of technical examination or to engage in an in-depth comparison between the present version and the previous version of the software.

Digital Anti-Forensic Techniques

Another factor that influences the reliability of the digital evidence is specific attacks on the process of legal computerization, including programs for the collection and documentation of digital evidence

The system that causes these attacks is known as MAFIA. It includes unique applications that can penetrate other systems, change information regarding the a file's time stamp , hide information in the empty space in data files, and change information about the data identifying the format of the content as a part of the file characteristics.

These tools act on a deep level and necessitate a considerable understanding of the concealed processes in the computer works. Lacking this understanding, it will not be possible to properly evaluate what occurred, the nature of the collected evidence, or whether may or may not produce information of great value to the legal proceeding.

It is always necessary to take into account that experienced digital evidence investigators and legal computerized examiners are not always those who collect the data from the computer. More than once, criminal investigators understand that a computerized crime may have been committed only after a routine check in the organization looking for suspicious or irregular activities reveals criminal or civilian activity which consequently leads to the opening of a professional legal investigation. During the initial process, the organization may have conducted random, data collection using unprofessional personnel and/or procedures, and this makes it difficult for the investigators to prove the completeness and reliability of the data[41]. Moreover, it is possible that the initial collection harmed the originality of the evidence and their originality and reliability will be cast in doubt.

For these reasons and for many additional reasons, in my opinion the 'rule of best evidence', which requires the court to present the source of every document[42], will develop into the 'rule of best digital evidence'. The reason for this lays in the statement of Honorable Judge Heshin on another matter: "only the source indicates the truth about itself, only the truth, and all the truth"[43]. Lacking the source in its entirety that can testify about itself, I will accept the rule of best digital evidence, with reduced importance, and in direct analogy to the rest of

---

[41] Lathoud, 2004: Losavio, Adams & Rogers, 2006
[42] Evidence Ordinance (New Version), 1971.
[43] Civil Appeal 6205/98 Unger et al. v. N. Ofer et al.

the evidence presented in the Courts.

As an aid, and in order to reduce the 'grey area" that exists in matter of the originality and believability of digital evidence, I that a parallel examination be executed using a number of the programs mentioned in this chapter and that the information from each of the programs be examined and cross checked by an expert.

The technology uses the defeat digital forensics can be defined as a variety of processes intended to 'confuse' data. These are sophisticated methods that include integration between technological methods and the human factor.

One of the issues that troubles digital criminal computerization investigators is the constant development of software programs that are designed to hinder or even make impossible digital forensics. The investigators must examine the digital evidence in depth so as to ensure that it is not harmed when it is integrated in the collection of legal material.

This chapter addresses the formation of a policy and clear procedures designed to defeat activity aimed against digital forensics. This is part of the digital forensics framework in general, including use of ineffective reconstruction processes, which maintain the uniqueness of potential digital evidence through the implementation of mechanisms that prevent possible distortion of the evidence.

In general, within the framework of digital evidence collection, it is necessary to re-use the collected raw material, so as to prevent the use and instigation of processes and mechanisms designed to hinder a digital forensic investigation. Hence, there is the need to conduct, already at the initial stage, an in-depth examination and to attempt to monitor these mechanisms.

Recently there has been a rise in the number of mechanisms that hackers use to bypass the systems of discovery and disclosure during the investigation. Moreover, the mechanisms that the digital forensics investigators use do not necessarily provide an in-depth analysis of the data. This fact casts doubt on the authenticity of the digital evidence, since we are obligated to identify every possible distortion or suspicion of data loss during the computerized investigation[44]. Lacking proof regarding the admissibility of the evidence, it is very doubtful whether it is possible to use the data.

As I understand it, there are a number of issues related to the disruption of the criminal identification process. I will focus on three issues that required the implementation of processes against digital criminal identification: erasure of data, concealment of data and blurring of 'traces', and computerized attacks against data processing and database processes.

The destruction of digital files can hinder and even cause great damage to the investigation. The concealment of the files is, in essence, a malicious act that removes data from clear view making it difficult to identify and use as evidence even though, in most cases, it is possible to reconstruct the data.

The most problematic factors are the human elements, the dependence on mechanisms, and physical and logical limitations. The term 'dependence on mechanisms' hints at the fact that investigators depend on mechanisms that are subject to attacks, and therefore flaws in the results may be created. 'Physical limitations' pertain to the storage format of the investigation, and 'logical limitations' include limitations of a specific storage place, as well as limitations of time and money.

I would note that the role of anti-forensics software programs is to identify when use is made of software for digital forensics, from the moment of its activation by the digital evidence examiner. This anti-digital forensics software then attempts to obscure the data relevant to the investigation. The operations of the malicious software programs can be divided into a number of stages, and as well as the obscuring of the data there is also disassembly, concealment, and self-destruction of the malicious software. In this way, the source of the confusion is

---

[44] Boddington, R., Hobbs, V. J., & Mann, G. "Validating Digital Evidence for Legal Argument," The 6th Australian Digital Forensics Conference, 2008

concealed from the examiner's eyes.

The classification and precise documentation of a cyber-attack are relevant for the purpose of evaluating damage and the recovery from it. This action is performed through the documentation and blocking of malicious applications originating from the Internet and which constitute possible channels of attack, as well as through the use of tools for analyzing and understanding these applications. Thus, it is possible to monitor the human and technological attacker in an attempt to block present and future attacks and also to prevent further corruption or destruction of data.

In today's technological world there are a number of methods and mechanisms that help protect the data and that perform ongoing examinations in an attempt to identify internet based security gaps and hacks (IDS). These systems include a deterrent mechanism and tools that take action in order to reduce the ability of malicious applications to analyze data in a concentrated manner, and to defeat the attack.

In 2010, a research study was conducted in the United States that addressed techniques of coordination and tracking towards the goal of developing a similarity based approach for hacking analysis. In the framework of the research, cases were characterized and divided into two categories: the first was based on the attacker's signature and on the statistical analysis of the data, while the second was based on a technical comparison between known attacks, on security policy themes, on types of attack defense systems, on undesired situations, and on appropriate configuration definitions[45]. Coordination techniques include a series of characteristics that were painstakingly chosen and intended to identify patterns of behavior in the various cases.

As a rule, the process of digital forensics that acts against attack systems uses software that looks for deviations from the norm, so as to match aspects of data obtained as a part of information security

---

[45] Qishi Wu, Yi Gu, Xiaohui Cui, Praneeth Moka, Yunyue Lin. "A Graph Similarity-Based Approach to Security Event Analysis Using Correlation Techniques," GLOBECOM 2010

activities and those outside of it. This technology, known professional language as Digital Anti-Forensic Techniques (DAFT - see the chapter on terms and definitions) aims to compensate for improper technical behavior and for improper human behavior that may cause the destruction or distortion of data.

Preventative Technology against Digital Forensics

This chapter examines the main goals of technology designed to prevent attacks on digital forensics from the perspective that addresses the merger of data. As mentioned, there are five basic components[46]. These include collection, analysis of data, presentation of data, deterrence, and initial data.

Collection of the Data

The stage involving the collection and documentation of digital evidence is the first stage, which involves determining the quantity of the evidence. This topic is examined and analyzed at a later stage. The mechanisms used in the collection of information may provide data on the components of the computer and network being used and thus present a broad picture of the process of investigation and identification of digital evidence.

Systems for information collection were intended to solve one of the main problems in the data collection process: the human factor, which is required to cope with the multiplicity of digital data from a variety of computerized systems, such as firewalls, servers hosting Internet websites, information servers, routers, and so on.

At this stage initial data processing is conducted to ascertain that the collected information is free of flaws, incomplete or otherwise compromised. In this process, a comparative system, 'bit after bit', of the hard drive where the comparison is held, in random intervals is

---

[46] Satpathy, S. and Mohapatra, A. "A Data Fusion Based Digital Investigation Model as an Effective Forensic Tool in the Risk Assessment and Management of Cyber Security Systems, "The 7th International Conference on Computing, Communications and Control Technologies", 2009

used. In this way, already at this early stage, it is possible to evaluate the situation and estimate whether or not activity designed to thwart the criminal forensics has taken place.

Data Analysis

Data analysis systems are parallel to data collection systems. The systems operate in real time and analyze the data discovered so as to identify information regarding hostile activity.

The use of parallel systems in real time may yield information from a variety of sources. It enables the processing of the data, the cross-checking of the data, the in-depth examination of the data, and the implementation of adjustments until significant digital evidence is obtained. The analysis of the data is an active action undertaken as part of the computerized forensics process, to differentiate from the collection of the data, the goal of which is to document and preserve the data. The analysis of the data obtained from the database enables comparison of the data, 'bit after bit', with the data on the original system - this issue will be addressed later.

Observant readers will argue that in the database, which is used as the basis for the comparison, there are frequent changes, resulting from everyday business activity and also from the very nature of the information systems used in the organization. Hence, the effectiveness of the data analysis system in monitoring and identifying hostile activity is in doubt.

Explanation

Systems of data analysis operate in a number of dimensions, some technical and some statistical. The statistical part regularly examines the organization's conduct and creates a database. The system knows to examine the database and to analyze routine behavior versus hostile behavior. In other words, if the percentage of statistical change is greater than the organization's standard, then it can be assumed that counter-forensics activity is occurring or has occurred. If this is the case, then the system will shift to the stage of the technical analysis of the data.

Data Presentation

The goal of the data presentation is to report results of the investigation, whether there is data on hostile activity or whether the results are normal. In other words, the systems were examined and a security breach or attempt to penetrate the organization was not found.

Some maintain that we must present data regarding the correctness of the system before all the employees in the organization. The aim is to provide all employees confidence in relation to possible malicious activity and the system's capability of identifying it. This has serious social impact[47]. In essence, the counter-systems that serve as the social guardian provide a sense of reciprocal activity against hackers and cyber-attacks alongside a range of perceptual aspects related to the way in which society uses technology.

From the World of Law

The issue of 'presentation of data' returns us to the legal world and to the test of data admissibility when presented as evidence in the legal process.

The Supreme Court of the United States addressed the issue of medications and expert evidence [48] and found that federal regulations on the matter of evidence indeed created unfair preference. After in-depth study, the Court explained in its reasoned ruling that the purpose of rule 702, 'evidence of experts', must be based on appropriate scientific methods, well-anchored, believable, and based on accepted principles and devoid of speculations.

By analogy, according to the "Fruit of the Poisonous Tree" doctrine, a legal term in the United States that describes evidence

---

[47] Newsham, T., Palmer, C., Stamos, A., & Burns, J. "Breaking Forensics Software: Weaknesses in Critical Evidence Collection," Retrieved from Slides.BH2007.pdf, May -www.isecpartners.com/files/iSEC-Breaking_Forensics_Software 2007
[48] Supreme Court of the United States. Daubert v. Merrell Dow Pharmaceuticals

obtained illegally and any information deriving from it, there is an analogy between the legal term and the legal inference regarding scientific, believable issues based on accepted principles, devoid of technological interpretations.

Digital evidence is fragile and by its very nature subject to interpretation. Therefore, it is the duty of those presenting digital evidence to show extreme caution. The Fruit of the Poisonous Tree doctrine is intended to deter the use of illegal means to achieve evidence. Criminal law in Israel has also adopted the Fruit of the Poisonous Tree doctrine: evidence obtained illegally receives less weight, although it is not necessarily disqualified.

In addition, in 2006 the Supreme Court determined in a precedent-setting ruling[49] that it is possible to disqualify evidence obtained unlawfully - this in contrast to what is considered admissible in the American Court, which determines that this illegally obtained evidence **must** be disqualified.

Thus, I pose the following question. Has the time not come for the Israeli legislature to determine clear procedures on the issue relating to the handling of digital evidence, on the issue of who can be considered expert, and on the question of how it is necessary to submit to the Court the entirety of the evidence? With regard to the Fruit of the Poisonous Tree doctrine, and since digital evidence is so sensitive, is there room to formulate another dimension through the doctrine and to establish clear rules on this issue? Has the time not come for technological interpretations to reach the ears of the Court and thus we will be able to maintain the judge's focus on the relevant issues.

Deterrence

Deterrence is a tool for social education. It creates a correlation between the motives, the reasons that lead the hacker to attempt access the system, and provides the impetus (education) that may cause him to

---

[49] Criminal Appeal 5121/98 Private (in reserves) Raphael Yissacharov v. Chief Military Prosecutor

cease his actions.

Learning the hacker's pattern of behavior enables the organization to develop and plan a deterrence policy in of the event of unauthorized access from inside the organization, both in internal cases and in external cases. Deterrence means must be regularly and constantly updated to address all potential and conceived situations of vulnerability, whether the source of the vulnerability is technical or human.

In addition on the issue of deterrence, I will present one of the most problematical phenomena – that of a "zombie computer". A 'zombie computer' is a computer that is connected to the Internet and has taken over by a hacker, virus, computer worm, or Trojan horse. Generally the computer is hacked as part of extensive activity that creates a network of 'bots' (robots – automatically executing code) which is used to organize and execute large-scale attacks by the hacker who remotely controls the affected computer.

Network of Bots or 'Zombie Computers' (Botnet)

A 'bot' is a computer that has been remotely taken and has been transformed, with malicious software, into a robot, and which is then used to disseminate malicious software that in turn transforms additional computers into robots controlled from a distance. This phenomenon is known by the popular term as a 'zombie computer'.

In essence, this operation causes the infected computer to perform automatic tasks on the Internet without the user knowing. For the most part, criminals use the bots to infect a large number of computers, and these computers create a network - a botnet. Thus, it is possible to send spam messages, distribute viruses, attack computers and servers, and perpetrate crimes such as fraud and theft[50].

From the World of Law

.[50] http://www.microsoft.com/security/resources/botnet-whatis.aspx

The Federal Court in Seattle sentenced Mr. Christopher Maxwell, aged 21 of California, to 37 months imprisonment and three years parole after he was convicted of hacking into millions of computers by creating a network of systems which were centrally controlled, known also as a 'bot network'. The automatic attacks that Maxwell instigated and led harmed a hospital in West Seattle, the Ministry of Defense, and the Colton District United School.

Representatives of the district attorney's office of the West District of Washington in the United States in the said, with regard to this matter, that bot networks have become a popular tool among online criminals in their attempts to take control over computer systems and to perform hacking attacks, send spam mails, and perform fraud and scamming offenses[51].

In the framework of a plea bargain signed with Maxwell, he admitted to conspiracy to defraud and to the causing of damage to the West Seattle Hospital, as well as to computers in military installations in Germany and in the United States. The phenomena observed in the hospital included doors of operating rooms that did not open, pagers that did not work in times of emergency, computers in the emergency care unit that were disrupted, and a variety of mishaps that led the hospital to use its backup systems for the continued care of the patients. The 'bot' software infected more than four hundred systems in the control division of the security department in Germany, including the information management system in Fort Carson in the State of Colorado. The damage was estimated at $138,000.

The Court in Israel

To the best of my knowledge, until now, the Courts in Israel have not been required to hear a case that addressed the issue of a bot network or a 'zombie computer'. The closest example is that of a Trojan horse[52], a harmful software program that penetrates computer

---

[51] "Based on evidence discovered during the investigation, we know that this bot net affected over a million computers", Assistant U.S. Attorney Kathryn Warma said in a recorded statement posted to the Web site of the U.S. Attorney's Office for the Western District of Washington. "The damage suffered was worldwide"

in the guise of an innocent program. The intention of the original software is to spy on the attacked computer and to extract personal data, such as credit card numbers.

Like a 'bot' net, Trojan horses also create permissions for an outside user, thus allowing them to remotely enter the attacked computer. This action is also known as 'installing a back door', and it enables the computer to be transformed into a 'zombie' by using the Trojan horse software.

The research staff at Pace University in the State of New York[53] developed an innovative strategy that helps monitor the flow charts of a 'bot' net. The development includes management of a simulation of the net load and investigation of topology, namely, the lifecycle of a 'bot' net. Analysis of 'bot' net behavior and of the databases enables the organization to clearly define what is considered acceptable use and what is not - in other words, are the processes within the scope of what is permitted and what is reasonable? If, then it is necessary to reduce user access permissions and to increase the security requirements for processes that cause changes in system files. This information helps the organization in the finalization of deterrent procedures and policies. It is possible to implement this process among organizations with the aim of preventing the use of processes and mechanisms against digital forensics.

The Process

The process of implementation is divided into a number of stages. The first stage is that of data analysis, which begins the prevention of digital forensics process. As stated previously, we analyze the data regularly to prepare ourselves for their submission at a later date. When the required information is available, the warning/deterrent mechanism is implemented.

Following this first stage, a base line must be established. In other

[52] Criminal Case 40061/06 (Tel Aviv District), State of Israel v. Ruth and Michael Efrati
[53] Massi, J., Panda, S., Rajappa, Gl, Selvaraj, S., Revankar, S. "Botnet Detection and Mitigation," Proceedings of Student-Faculty Research Day, CSIS, Pace University, 20.

words, the version of the comparative examination of all activities captured which is then disseminated in the organization or the digital forensics software. We can compare this system to the recurring illegal information capture process. The investigators are required to maintain the confidentiality and secrecy of the final information obtained from the system regarding techniques against digital forensics.

Issues of Computer Clock and Network Servers

Often the issue of the computer's internal clock as opposed to the Internet clock is the central foundation for questioning the admissibility of evidence in the legal proceeding. This is one of the clearest issues for every person who has ever asked themselves 'what time is it' and then looks at their watch, and sees the answer.

In the world of computers and the Internet, the answer, which is so clear to us in the physical world, is subject to interpretation.

Explanation

Computers have an internal clock that provides a date and hour that is a derivative of the computer's physical, geographical location. The clock is accessible to the computer user and can easily be set for any time and location that the user chooses.

The computer's operating system uses an internal clock to document three time indicators for every file: its creation date, its access date, and its modification date. The data is documented and saved as an integral part of the file using meta-data tags that receive the data from the computer's operating system.

The data's presentation is an expression of the technical examination of the computer system and/or network, the goal of which is to provide a human investigator with a description of the nature of the activities that occurred in the specific system. This process consists of logical data produced by system, such as end users or main server data, files, applications, etc.

This information contains much evidence that indicates historical activity as recorded in the system logs, which document events on the computer's hard drive, as a part of the computer files. The core of the problem lays in the fact that this information may include inconsistent and even conflicting data.

This chapter examines the reasons for this inconsistency as it pertains to computer times and their impact. Three types of inconsistency in the schedule are examined:
1. Inconsistency that derives from the regular behavior of the computer system.
2. Inconsistency that derives from the transfer of files via email and/or from a world-encompassing organizational structure, with servers (service computers) located in different time zones around the globe.

3. Inconsistency that derives from an intentional sabotage attempt on the part of a suspected party.

As mentioned previously, inconsistency in the recording of times leads to lack of adjustment in the area of digital evidence, and thus lack of coordination with the flow of the computer system's historical events. This can lead to the imprecise reconstruction of the computer's physical history.

In essence, the most common time inconsistency in in relation to issues of digital evidence is the result of the computer's regular activity, or in other words, inconsistency that does not result from malicious sabotage. Sometimes the reason is a computer event and/or online event such as an electrical outage or other hardware and/or software flaw which resulted in the file or its time marker not being recorded. It is even possible that the file rewritten during the computer's regular operation or as a result of data being reconstructed.

Lack of consistency can even result from data that is, by its very nature, erroneous or imprecise - perhaps due to hardware characteristics, erroneous software configuration, or any other failure. These and other reasons for the inconsistency create difficulties for the digital evidence investigators, even if they are not the result of intentional actions on the part of a suspect.

I would note that where computer clocks that are connected to a specific case create time stamps, there is real concern that the computer's hardware clocks will cause an inconsistency between the different time sources. Therefore, time stamps created by local computers are considered to be data whose degree of precision is not reliable.

As mentioned, in investigations that include a single computer, the distortion of the time data will cause inconsistent time stamps in digital evidence. The fact that there is only one clock providing time stamps in the investigation may result in the creation of time lines that are constructed so as to mislead. In extreme cases, when the time is reset as the result of a system reset and/or another incident, the new time registered by the computer may be set to a time that has already passed. The 'return in time' creates a misleading mix between events that occurred in the original time frame and new events, which are supposedly recorded for the same time frame.

I would also note that alongside the inconsistency, damage is caused to the integrity of the digital evidence's structure. –This presents yet another challenge for the investigators. One example could be a lack of integrity in the continuity of digital evidence caused by routine and normal activity of the computer system.

Take for example a computer system that logs, in its basic data files, information about the connection and disconnection of users over the past six months. The system's computerized profile is, in fact, a file created some months ago and will appear as if it was created outside of the user time frame. . A human investigator can find an explanation for this phenomenon, but along the time line, the creation of the file may appear unusual.

The problem arises when computer records are changed or altered with the goal and concealing illegal activity. This creates inconsistency in the structure of digital evidence. For instance, a computer user who downloads illegal material from the Internet may attempt to blur this fact by erasing the browser's history and storage caches and also erasing the event log records that show the user accessing the files, including the erasure of records showing the opening of and disconnection from the browser. Experts in this matters are well aware of other means of achieving the same results, but it is not our purpose to provide help to those seeking hide their tracks.

So, whilst, as a part of the investigation process and computer seizure, the illegal material is revealed, the user may have succeeded in blurring the time recording data. In such a situation, they could argue that the illegal material discovered on the computer was downloaded outside of the time lines when they, the user, was using the computer and that no blame can be attached to them.

Identifying Time-Line Inconsistencies

The identification inconsistencies in the time-line addresses three main situations: an encounter between the user and the computer, during which the user produces a document and does not attempt to blur his actions; an encounter between the user and the computer during which the user produces a document that includes original information that is intentionally misleading, while maintaining the time-line, and an encounter between the user and the computer during which the system journals and time-lines were changed.

The aim of collection the time stamp is to build a time for all the processes that are attributed to the user profile in the computer system[54]. The time line is a series of events that are documented over time from all of the events recorded on the computer. The series of events should be examined regularly, and if a failure is found, then it should be documented on the appropriate time line. This is an indirect approach to the issue of time stamps, which may lead to the fact that events outside of the series, whether they were removed manually or whether they were simply not recorded, are returned to the time line as an event which is documented outside of the relationship in which it was actually held. It is necessary to add to this pattern an examination to identify and deal with situations where there is a data inconsistency.

Another limitation is the issue of time stamps provided by the local computer clock. Lack of precision in the time stamp is 'natural', or in other words, derives from the regular and normal working of the computer system. The solution for this issue, which has been proposed and documented in professional literature, is to note the time point on the computer clocks under investigation, while examining the difference in time in comparison to the actual and determining the lack of compatibility between these time points[55].

This solution is not relevant to the issue a clock deviation that changes over time prior to the examination of the computer system. The difference may lead to situations where the time line is imprecise.

---

[54] A. Marrington, G. Mohay, A. Clark, and H. Morarji, "Event-based Computer Profiling for the Forensic Reconstruction of Computer Activity," in AusCERT Asia Pacific Information Technology Security Conference 2007 Refereed R&D Stream, Gold Coast, 2007, pp. 71-87
[55] R. Nolan, C. O'Sullivan, J. Branson, and C. Waits, "First Responder's Guide to Computer

On this matter, I would examine the series of events documented on the time line in the computer itself, including information reconstruction in different segments and throughout the computer's life. Thus we will create a series of events from which we will derive the time line.

In practice, it will be necessary to formulate a clock hypothesis for every moment throughout the computer system's history. The techniques described are intended to assist in the identification of situations of internal inconsistency on the time line, which can help the investigator form the appropriate clock hypothesis.

Identification of Events outside the Clock Sequence

As mentioned, certain events can occur only after another event. This issue of relation is called 'happened before'[56]. For instance, it is not possible that a user created a file before he entered the computer system.

After the construction of a time line and the execution of an adjustment process between the computerized profile and the series of events, it is possible to implement an evaluation of the time stamp and, if necessary, to correct it. In other words, if a certain event occurred before another event, but the time stamp indicates that the second event occurred before the first, then it is possible to correct and define a new series of events, based on chronological logic from the physical world.

The process of identifying lack of consistency, alongside the construction of a new time line, obligates the definition of laws that will describe the relationships between 'happened before', the chronological series of events, and the reasons that led and/or can lead to the disruption in the time line, for a variety of types of events.

Certain events, which 'happened before', before the first event, are

---

[56] L. Lamport, "Time, Clocks, and the Ordering of Events in a Distributed System," Commun. vol. 21, pp. 558-565, 1978,ACM

a prerequisite for the occurrence of the second event. In relationships of this type, the existence of the second event unavoidably hints at the time of the first event's occurrence and the correct chronological sequence.

In the legal world, the 'prerequisite condition', constitutes a circumstantial relationship, which places an event that 'happened before' in the time line in its proper position. In essence, there is a reciprocal relationship between the 'prerequisite condition', which is fundamentally the circumstantial relationship for the identification of missing events and the circumstantial relationship that fundamentally creates the correct time line.

Another prerequisite condition is an event that occurred and does not exist in the event recording system and/or in a system of events deduced from the computer's artificial intelligence processes. Such an event is considered a missing event.

'Missing events' were given this name because they were never recorded in the computer's system logs, and they were never documented on the basis of object relations. They are also known as events that originate from the drawing of conclusions, but it is necessary to differentiate between events discovered following the use of the object relationships approach and other deduced events.

The identification of missing events is a process of identifying and monitoring evidence that mistakenly vanished or was intentionally erased from the system logs. The process enables the construction of an entire time line and gives the investigator a profound understanding of the computer system as a whole.

The process is implemented using monitoring and automatic examination of specific points on the time line. The examination, which is intended to identify events that were not documented or whose recording was erased will provide the investigator with a complete picture from which he will be able to earn why the logs are missing. If the logs were intentionally erased, then this may indicate that the user attempted to conceal suspicious activity.

In many cases, missing events may be created as a result of regular computer activity. The investigators must integrate deduced events and events documented in the system logs, so as to provide as complete a time line as possible. It is also necessary to take into consideration that, lacking complete information on the issue of the time line, the investigator's evaluation in all issues pertaining to events considered suspicious, is cast into doubt and it becomes necessary therefore to ascribe reduced weight to this type of digital evidence.

The Computer Clock around the World

Time regions are defined according to global lines of longitude. Therefore, computer clocks are set according to the local time region where the computer is being used. This may, sometimes, result is a difference in the time stamp of the computer that created a specific document or message and that of the receiving computer which is in a different time zone. This is true regardless of the means used to transfer the document/message from the source to the receiving computer.

Additional variables must be added to this fact, such as the organizational structure of the global businesses, using servers (server computers) located in different time zones around the world and/or businesses that, for the sake of convenience, use 'cloud computing' technology. The 'cloud' is, in essence, a server that provides different types of computer services through a remote computer. In practice, the user connects to the designated server through the Internet, from a remote location.

In most cases, the person purchasing 'cloud services' is not at all aware of the fact that their files storage location is in a foreign country. The reason for this lays in the economic considerations of the service provider. For instance, Google (google.com) servers and of GoDaddy (GoDaddy.com), both multinational conglomerates that provide computer and website hosting services to all, are found in many different locations around the world and the issue of the server's location is not relevant or a topic of discussion.

There are two solutions that can address the issue of this lack of coordination between time records. The first involves the synchronization of the organization's computer clocks with the local clock used in the target country and the creation of a global presence as a part of the local organization. The second is the use of a communication protocol that enables clock synchronization and is based on a time server connected to an atomic clock through a GPS receiver or any other accurate time device.

I would note that there are additional variables which make the process of the monitoring and evaluating differences in computer events in a global environment difficult. For instance, different versions of operating systems, geographical distance and locations and technological junctions, the difference between application versions such as Office 2003 and Office 2007 which perform, in part the same actions, software used to send email messages in different versions, proxy servers (see the chapter on terms and definitions), and so on.

The computer forensic investigators must be aware of these variables, must examine and document their implications on the issue of data authenticity when the data is presented within the framework of digital evidence, and be able to explain the source of the difference on the time line in relation to the facts and data to which they are exposed.

In addition, computer forensic investigators must perform critical monitoring and recording of all the processes performed as part of the time line creation process as this relates to digital evidence, so that an independent third party can examine the processes and reach the same result using the same tools.

The Best Digital Evidence

As a rule, digital evidence must include all the characteristics of physical, material, that make the evidence admissible. Evidence derived from the computer presents a large number of challenges to the courts and as a part of legal proceedings in general.

To conduct an in depth examination of these issues, it is necessary to address the definition of digital evidence in physical terms. Evidence is a part and/or type of testimony presented to the court with the goal of persuading the court to reach a certain understanding in relation to events that may be controversial. The evidence must be physical, like an object - output in the form of a printout, a movie clip, or any other means that can be used to illustrate the matter under discussion to the court.

Unlike digital evidence, the testimony of an individual who is not an expert witness, who was present at the time of the event, or who was directly related to those involved and from whose memory details have been retrieved and verified with the evidence, such as business records of any type - if the witness's credibility is proven, then it is possible to examine the content of the evidence upon which he based his testimony.

Regarding a technical examination, if an authorized forensic technician performed processes involved in the retrieval of original digital evidence and brought about certain results, then his evidence, with regard to the digital evidence being presented to the court, does not have the same validity as the evidence of a legal expert on issues relating to digital evidence. This expert, known in legal parlance an 'expert witness', has skills derived from his undisputed expertise and from his experience in a specific field. The expert witness brings to the court, in his testimony, his expertise on the specific topic that the legal claim addresses. An expert witness focuses on the meaning of the facts derived from the digital evidence presented to the Court.

At times, in order to illustrate how it is possible to draw certain conclusions, the court is presented, as a part of the evidence, with byproducts that were produced from the first, original evidence, such as diagrams, video clips and/or voice clips, printed copies of email correspondence, and/or any other correspondence facilitated using a digital device.

The evidence and testimonies presented to the court must meet the tests that will assure their admissibility in two critical categories: their reliability and their weight given the circumstances under discussion. Hence, I return to the issue of best evidence. First, I would note that the original provider of the evidence is a computer, a camera, a recording device, and/or a cellular phone. As a result, I shall examine this issue from the perspective of the device.

From another point of view, I would ask the following question. Is it possible to see a computer printout, regardless of its format, as evidence that can be in the list of the exceptions regarding hearsay evidence, statements by a deceased person and/or statements of those who are dying or think that they are dying and who therefore elect to speak their minds? This when the source of the evidence vanishes as a result of the logical and/or mechanical distortion of computer data or the digital device has been deliberately concealed or thrown away.

To differentiate from a person, digital devices lack emotions and/or are devoid of any ulterior motives   that can be directly attributed to the moment of their disappearance or disruption. Therefore, we must isolate those areas that meet the test of emotional manipulation, since digital devices, by their very nature, was are only able to provide facts rather than interpretations.

With regard to the gray area between 'there was' and 'there wasn't', the role of the computer experts includes being able to identify and locate digital evidence, as the computer (or other digital device) is unable to reveal its "feelings".

In the Bidder ruling[57], four accumulative conditions were set down. The statement contains a conflict of interests and the requirement for awareness of conflict of interest, since digital devices, by their nature, are devoid of interests. The requirement for awareness of the facts and the circumstances of the statement do not awake suspicions of software credibility. In this respect, as already noted, digital devices by nature are only capable of showing the truth.

Simply put, it is possible to say that there is an analogy between a ruling that refers to an individual who sees themselves as being under

---

[57] Civil Appeal 601/68 Bider v. Levy, Court Ruling 23 (First Part) 597

threat of death and digital output, retrieved from a digital device the moment before it vanished. In addition, the ruling also discussed the issue of the deceased's statement at the time he was performing his function. The rationale is the assumption that if this is undertaken while filling the function, apparently it represents the truth.

The conditions required for confirming the validity and credibility of the statement are that the statement must be made during the fulfillment of the function and that the details of the statement address an activity already performed as opposed to future activity. With regard to these conditions, there is no doubt that digital device meets the requirements. Another condition is that the circumstances under which the statement was given must not cast doubt on the content's truthfulness. In an analysis of the statement, the intention is that it is possible to assume to a level of reasonable certainty that the statement was indeed made within the framework of the role and not from the deceased person's individual interest.

It is obvious that the digital device does not have any personal interest, and thus it is necessarily to establish the relationship between the digital device's 'statement' and the circumstances. Given an analogy between the two, it is possible to see the output as 'best digital evidence' and/or within the framework of the 'secondary evidence rule'[58], as customary in the State of California.

In the United States, the best evidence rule is anchored in laws 1001-1008 of the Federal Rules of Evidence[59]. By law, a copy faithful to the original or a reliable copy of all the digital evidence is required. This copy must have been examined and found to be faithful to the original, namely it must meet the standards relating to evidence given to a legal examination of substantive law.

Rules 1004-1007 are the exception. When the original evidence is not accessible, the content - whether printed, recorded, and/or photographed, is admissible if the original documents have been lost or

---

[58] California Code of Evidence, Section 1521.
[59] Federal Rules of Evidence Rule 1001.

destroyed, not by the accused or the defendant who has been found to be above suspicion. When it is possible to obtain the original evidence through a technical process or from another legal proceeding, or when the original evidence is outside the accused's control, then, in these situations and given the failure to present the original evidence, and providing that the evidence meets the cumulative standards of the law, then the 'secondary evidence rule' will be admissible.

However, let us not be mistaken. The United States legislature recognizes the importance of original evidence and yet refers to situations in which, for the reasons stated above, it is not possible to access the original. For instance, sub-section (2) indicates a situation in which the original at the disposal of an individual, namely a third party, cannot achieve what is required. In these situations, and after the examination of all the variables, rule 1008 give judges the power to determine whether, given the lack of an adequate faithful copy the evidence presented as output is credible, and whether it is possible to submit said output to a jury.

The United States legislature was correct when it left the decision on this matter to the judge's subjective judgment. In a situation in which the source of the digital evidence is not found, it is doubtful whether we can know with certainty that the evidence is reliable. More than once the question has been raised whether it is possible that the same technology, based on mathematical data (when in mathematics there is no doubt about the result), creates faults that cast the admissibility of the evidence obtained from these digital devices in doubt, and which are presented before the Court as a part of the legal proceedings?

As a result of technological development, approximately every three years a new computer generation and/or new technological generation is created. This fact casts doubts on the volume of the legal precedents from which it is possible to learn and to infer with regard to the admissibility of digital evidence prior to the introduction of these new technologies. Moreover, it casts in doubt the issue of technological relationship between previous versions and the newer versions, and thus the matter of the test of legal precedence.

The legislature must apply the rule of 'best evidence' in an upgraded constellation as a legal criteria for the virtual world and thus recognize the advantages of digital evidence, as well as its disadvantages.

The Best Digital Evidence: Credibility, Admissibility, and Weight

The revolution in computer, cellular, and Internet technology that has taken place over the past twenty years is expressed in of the ever widening scope and form of digital evidence. This is an area of frequent and rapid change which has a tendency to leave the legal world light years behind.

Chapter 4 in the Evidence Ordinance [New Version] and legal rulings addresses the issue of the weight to be placed on evidence[60]. From this, the following question arises. Is it possible to attribute legal blame on the basis of a 'DNA' test of computers being submitted as the sole source of evidence? We shall examine this topic as a derivative of legal jurisdiction and authority and as in relation to United Kingdom laws relating to admissibility of evidence.

The Law of Fairness in the Acquisition of Evidence, which gives judges authority wide reaching discretionary power, enables information obtained to be disqualified as evidential material[61], if such material is found to be in violation of the boundaries set by the law.[62]. The Evidence from Rumor Law is the indirect evidence law, according to which when printed documents are placed before the court as evidence, it is probable that a connected individual be required to testify in relation to said documents. The Business Documents law certifies documents, such as an institutional record produced within the routine business framework as being admissible. [63]

In the United Kingdom it is possible to use content purely for intelligence purposes, namely, it cannot be presented as evidence to the judge[64]. However, there is a trend according to which, in extreme cases such as serious crime and acts of terror, the barrier will be removed and it will be possible to present such evidence as part of the legal process.

In the United States, federal evidence laws facilitate the definition of 'admissibility' within the framework of judicial authority, by institutionalizing the issue of authorized testing software programs, so as to cope with the issue of the admissibility of new scientific digital evidence[65].

---

[60] Evidence Ordinance [New Version] 1971.

[61] Police Law, 1977 (England).

[62] Evidence from the Police and Criminal Evidence Law 1984.

[63] Criminal Law 2003, S117 and S9, Civil Evidence, 1995.

[64] Regulation of Investigatory Powers Act 2000, see also p. 60 below.

[65] The Daubert tests – Daubert v. Merrell Dow 509 U.S. 579 (1993) provides the following tests: (1)
Whether the theory or technique can be (and has been) tested; (2) The error rate associated with the

In most European countries, an investigating judge is the one who controls the criminal hearing. Laws of admissibility do not exist and/or are not recorded in a case in which it is possible to create a correlation to the computer, cellular, and Internet world. In British criminal law, the judges can use their judgment to disqualify evidence obtained unfairly.

The weight given the evidence is, in essence, a derivative of its importance in the legal proceeding as a whole. In order to meet criteria and requirements for a physical analogy, it is possible to attribute the ability to persuade and the value of the evidence to its overall weight, while in the final analysis, 'weight' is not a scientific concept.

In the physical world there are a number of characteristics that teach about the original, namely, that include elements that show the relationship to the circumstances, to people and precision - lack of doubt in all that pertains to the quality of the procedures that guided the collection of the material, which, after its analysis will meet the required standards and can be presented before the Court. In addition, it must be produced by an individual who is a professional tester who can explain clearly and exactly the steps were taken and the methods used. If use is made of a legal method, then it must be 'transparent'; or in other words, it must be able to be tested openly by a third party expert.

With regard to printed computer outputs that include written declarations, the issue of 'precision' must also include the content. This requires putting the evidence to the 'test' of admissibility to ascertain its originality by a legal computer expert, so that the findings will be accessible to criticism and to the process of cross examination.

The source of the evidence must be complete, subject to technological circumstances and/or findings retrieved by the digital evidence investigators. In other words, digital evidence output tells 'in its own words' what it knows and details the circumstances and/or

---

method; (3) Publication in a peer-reviewed journal; and (4) Whether the technique has gained widespread acceptance

events surrounding the issue. On this matter, I would note that the legal computer expert 'helps' the digital evidence in presenting to the Court what the source of the digital evidence 'experienced'.

At this point another element is added, that of the 'continuity of evidence'. In the United States this element is known by the name of 'chain of custody', a term derived from the possibility of reporting what occurred from the perspective of the digital evidence, this from the moment the digital evidence was obtained and through to its presentation before the Court as digital evidence admissible in a legal proceeding.

Hence, in physical illustration, we document what a knife undergoes when it is found at the scene of a crime. The 'continuity of evidence' is based on and achieved through police reports, photographs, 'storing and labeling' the knife in a labeled polyethylene bag with a numbered abel, eye witness statements, and documentation of the findings, declarations of forensic scientists who searches for blood or fingerprints, DNA, etc. at the scene of the crime and in a laboratory, including documents relating to the care of in which evidence was 'bagged and labeled' and additional statements and evidence from forensic scientists. The process is intended to minimize or completely eliminate opportunities to make mistakes, accidentally or intentionally, or to identify the time at which the mistake occurred.

Despite that stated previously and in order to differentiate from the physical analogy, in the world of digital components there are also many other variables that differentiate digital evidence from physical evidence. Much physical evidence is documented only through photography. This is different from evidence taken from the digital world, where there are many different types of hardware and software programs that link between types of hardware and operating systems, network systems, and synchronization processes with cloud servers and remote email accounts, as well as synchronization with tablets and different cellular devices.

As a result of improper handling of hardware components and digital evidence, the components may be very 'temperamental'. For this reason and for many others, there may be considerable difficulties in the process of authenticating the content and in the time needed to produce the digital evidence.

Computer data can be changed easily without leaving a clear indication that any changes have been made. In general, printed output such as journals and accounting books are harder to modify or to forge, since it is easy to see whether a page has been destroyed or removed. Having said that, those who maintain that there are many examples of the forging of printed or handwritten documents are generally correct. However, with digital documents it is much easier to fake or to alter without leaving traces.

Even though there are technological systems that frustrate certain unrecognized changes in computer files, unlike handwriting or paper-based accounting methods, in computers there are few 'standards' that set a clear measure of expectations.

Change and distortion of computerized material: One of the main problems with which computer testers are faced with is the fact that, unlike DNA tests where samples taken from the will also show identical results, with computers the situation is different. In the process of collecting and examining digital material to be produced before the courts as evidence, it is possible, whether mistakenly or intentionally, to change the computerized material with ease.

Different legal tests carried out by computer testers may distort the data, and this is a fact that we should be aware of. Merely by turning on the computer or opening an application and/or file could result in changes being made to the files or the system even if these changes were not intentional. Furthermore, these changes, in the event that they occur, may not be immediately apparent.

As is known, those lacking the technical skills or training will find it difficult to clearly read and understand the majority of the digital evidence, in its original, raw state, taken from the computer. Real objects are often derived from the entirety of the evidence, presented far from their point of origin.

For the purpose of illustration, this is the moment at which raw digital evidence becomes a physical 'product', in the form of a recording or document that was produced by a computer. There is no uniqueness in this process. The unique identification mark changes after the evidence is produced and is no longer the same mark but a representation that helps 'analyze' the data.

Digital evidence includes a large number of potentially 'precise' items, which are retrieved from the computer and can be presented as part of the legal process. In actuality, this is a hard drive that includes a large number of folders with files of different types, while to the Court only a limited number of supposedly precise printouts may be presented.

The great variety of software programs that produce files in different formats and which constitute digital evidence in their original version, makes it very difficult to develop global 'standards' such as those developed for individual DNA charts. As a result, the possibilities for improper representation are greater. Evidence derived from the computer force the Court, in almost every instance, to make a series of inferences before they reach a conclusion on this matter.

It is the nature of computers to be the creators of records, which can, at the end of the process, also be presented as evidence. In the world that preceded the computer era, accounts were paper based and consisted of sheets of paper with hand written or printed records. Supporting calculations, or in legal terms 'appendixes' were also executed primarily manual, even if a simple calculator was employed for some stages of the calculation. However, in computerized accounts the process of inputting of the original data is manual and all the remaining processes are performed by the computer, without human intervention.

This fact often makes it very difficult to monitor the process that led to a given result. In general, we tend to accept the computer's results as a final, indisputable fact. However, it is important that we remember that the computer and the computer software that calculates the data did not create themselves, they are the result of human development and invention. Therefore, we have a duty to examine, in depth, the admissibility of results obtained from the same data manipulation program.

There are many examples of computers that 'collect' data, documents, perform calculations and then present them when there is a demand to produce a document, whether in digital format or as a paper printout. Examples of this are the supermarket printout of our bill, a credit card statement, bank account printouts and more. The majority of people will examine these documents in order to ascertain if the data does, in fact, accurately mirror reality and the facts as we know them. Thus, it is our responsibility, and even duty, to examine the authenticity of the printed data, namely to examine whether the software program that created the output met the appropriate tests, used ascertain the admissibility of software in the United States. Remember, the output of the calculation should not be accepted blindly. It is our duty to examine the authenticity of the data, subject to economic and/or any other subjective considerations.

The term ICT (Information and Communications Technology) addresses topics relating to technology of information absorption, for instance, digital broadcasting of information. This term is analogous to the term 'information technology' but primarily refers to the importance placed on the methods of communication and their implementation for the purposes of gathering or producing information.

In the world of ICT there is an interaction between the different types of hardware, such as laptop computers, tablets, and smartphones and the operating systems that are software programs installed on the hardware components. These operating systems also include application programs (professionally known as 'applications'), and communication protocols, which, through the Internet and cellular networks, create a global interaction.

The vast majority of physical forensics addresses concealed and unchanging physical, biological, and chemical findings, although, over time, new techniques for the analysis of these findings have been developed making for more accurate examination. In the world of technology, information, and communication, the pace of changes is exceedingly rapid and can be measured in time periods of days, weeks or months.

The Internet, in its original version as a consumer 'product' to be used by all, existed from 1994-1995 and changed and continues to change at a meteoric pace. Digital forensics experts are forced the cope with an unparalleled pace of innovative changes, but they still aspire to work according to the same standards of painstaking authentication derived from the areas of traditional law and subject to the laws of the country where they are found.

Digital Evidence, Sequentially and Continuity

The 'sequentially and continuity' are underlying terms relating to the start of an investigation. The terms relate, not only to physical evidence, but also to digital evidence. Certain types of 'computerized' evidence are clearly physical objects such as personal computers, CDs, hard disks, mobile phones, external drives for backup, and so on. These are placed into a bag or a box, sealed and are labelled in the same way as objects taken from the scene of a crime.

It is possible to present evidence in the original version or in the digital version as evidence that was not examined providing that, at an earlier stage, the evidence was subject to a 'digital fingerprint' - the making of a copy that is faithful to the original. In other words, the file or the drive was subject to a mathematical process that created an output of letters and numbers.

When the file or drive was copied using the same mathematical process, then, in essence, a copy faithful to the original was created which can produce exactly the same output that can be compared to the original 'digital fingerprint' to successfully compared the two sets of data.

Another meaning of the concept of sequentially and continuity in digital evidence is that most of the material presented in the Courts is produced from material obtained from the original (in its raw form), in other words, the source of the material, the computer itself, is not presented. Frequently what is presented before the court is a printout, computer output of original digital material. The output must prove a clear sequence demonstrating the uninterrupted the chain of events, including proof that it is whole and reliable and must also provide evidence regarding the identity of the person that produced it.

Let us move on to another stage: The human mind cannot 'digest' a complete log file in its entirety and therefore computer testers use software tools to search for patterns of activity that are, in their opinion, more significant, subject to the directives of the forensic computer expert. This action is also undertaken in all the other data bases, found as is to be expected at the heart of the businesses - documenting orders obtained, merchandise sent, receipts and invoices produced and creating a general log that documents all business actions.

Only after the filtering and removing all relevant material from the database is it finally submitted as evidence to the court. There is no reason to expect a judge to feel comfortable and at ease when he is presented with an actual computer as evidence. Therefore, the tester's role is to analyze the data, to search for files and other patterns, and to extract the relevant material and present it to the court in a manner that is easily understandable.

Sequentially refers to providing the defense team with the possibility of moving back in time to review digital evidence and the raw materials from which it was produced. . The aim of this process is to ensure that digital evidence remained unchanged and was not tampered with during its processing, to ensure that mistakes were not made in the data analysis procedure and to prove that the accused's basic rights was not denied or withheld, a situation in which the defense could argue that certain choices and analyses may lead to very different results from those that were, in fact, obtained.

There is considerable practical significance in the way in which digital evidence is submitted in the judicial process. Every item must be accompanied by an explanation regarding the location of its origin. In the case of a file produced from a hard drive, for instance, it is necessary to document the full path from which the data is retrieved.

Digital Investigations in Organizations

The main reasons for the existence or non-existence of digital investigations are the high costs entailed by the investigation, alongside the limited resources available, in direct analogy to the victims of the computerized crime that attract the attention of the global media.

These are the same events, some low level internalintra-organizational on the low level, such as issues involving work contracts, documentation of time clocks, etc. If these events are not addressed properly, it is possible that they will cause significant direct and indirect losses to the organization.

Statistics show that one or more events of this type will most probably occur in organizations during the business year, and that the reasons for these occurrences can include suspicion of and attempted fraud on the part of a worker or a third party, arguments and accusations centering around the duty of care, misuse of the Internet or email programs, online defamation of character - namely, harm to the employer's good name or that of another employee, sexual harassment, and so on.

Another type of digital offense includes the obtaining and storage of pornographic and pedophiliac materials, theft of confidential data, theft of data, and industrial espionage, theft of original code, and pirating of software programs, illegal access of workers, illegal access of people from outside of the organization, including illegal penetration of a computer or Internet site, illegal alteration of data by viruses, Trojan horses, and the theft of corporate computerized resources for private exploitation.

Additional relevant events are included in the definition for the use corporate resources and computerized sources as part of a complex crime in which a third party is the intended victim. As stated in section 5 of the Computer Law 1995: "...accessing computer material to commit another offense": failure in the organization's computer systems , which in turn results in harm to third parties and encourages legal claims due to breach of contract or neglect, including failure of computer systems to the extent that the organization is encouraged to sue providers for breach of contract; blackmail attempts, whether through physical threats or whether through simulated attacks, such as a prevention of service attack; duplication of an existing Internet webpage to create a false presentation and to encourage surfers to provide their banking details or any other confidential data, including Internet passwords.

In professional jargon, this phenomenon is called 'phishing' (see more in the chapter on terms and definitions). Another offense is a denial of service following which the organization cannot function, thus leading to loss of income and a situation in which the organization is exposed to third party claims.

The criminals or the hackers may be amateurs or professionals, who seek to promote an ideological agenda, or criminals who attempt to wield their power through blackmail.

Technological developments enable the long hand of criminal organizations to reach cyberspace and expand 'protection money' operations and attempts blackmail. Crime organizations may hire the services of computer experts and succeed in developing a virus that performs a unique encryption process and thus locks computerized documents. The owners of computers infected by the encryption virus do not receive the key to open them until they pay ransom. After payment, key code needed to access the encrypted documents is provided the computer owner. In a similar case, in a different analogy taken from the world of 'traditional' crime, past experience shows us that crime organizations installed hacked into gaming websites of legally operating casinos and installed malicious software designed to disrupt operation. Casino owners were then contacted and told that, unless they paid a monthly protection fee, the software would be used to disable (crash) the site.

Traditional disaster recovery programs prepare citizens for events that contain a high potential of injury, but with low frequency or likelihood. More frequent disasters are those that occur in the field of ICT, and therefore we must prepare primarily for events of this type.

Often organizations find themselves pulled into computerized investigations against their will. In civil suits, the sued side is sometimes entitled to full disclosure or disclosure of the materials produced through the computer. The Court may order the disclosure of documents that facilitate the legal hearing between the two sides.

As a part of the criminal legal process, the organization may be a victim or, in another case, a totally innocent bystander. It is possible that the defendant's legal team will file a request for full disclosure from the computerized system. The processes of investigation that include digital materials often fail due to mistakes made in the early stages, as a result of the disappearance or destruction of material, improper handling of digital materials, or compromise on the part of the organization's managers, who decided not to end ongoing activity.

When it is necessary to begin an investigation of this type, the victim, in this case, the organization, may suffer a crisis. Following are some of the principal questions that we will need to address and answer at a later stage:

- To whom should initial suspicions be reported and who manages the investigation in the organization?
- Who needs to be involved, how should the investigation be managed, and according to which procedures is it important to act?
- What are the characteristics of good digital evidence, and which stages are essential in the identification of the digital evidence from the moment of its identification and how should it be saved reliably?
- What are the organizations legal obligations and what avenues are open to third-parties demanding full disclosure?
- How can the investigation be conducted effectively without interfering with the everyday activity of the organization and without encouraging a crisis of trust that may cause even greater harm than a failure to achieve justice?

I would note that all that has been written regarding the handling of digital evidence in general to this point is also true regarding the behavior of organizations that were suspected of an offense. In addition, I would note that in the lifecycle of the digital incidents and investigations that may follow, planning is impossible without evaluation of the organization's activity. It is important to note that the process and events assist the investigator in developing an understanding of the variety of management tasks required during the event, so that it may be possible to identify possible conflicts and solve them ahead of time.

Risk scenarios that the organization may face are open, so that it is possible to characterize them and predict them. In this process, there is a correlation between information security data in a digital environment and analysis and planning of security for events in the physical world. The aim is to characterize possible scenarios and to develop means of prevention and/or detection tools, some overt and some covert, with which it will be possible to explain the types of digital evidence collected, should this be needed.

On this matter, I would note that in the Tali Isakov affair[66], in the Rani Fisher affair[67], and in the Tiberius municipality affair[68] clear principles were determined that address and defend the issue of the employee's right to privacy in the workplace, and it was determined that the employer must meticulously maintain these principles.

Regarding the issue of protection of privacy, the following was determined:

> ...It would appear to us that the rule suitable within the framework framework of work relations - unless it was agreed otherwise between the sides - is that the worker is entitled to make private use, at a reasonable level, of the digital email box placed at his disposal, and is entitled - as a rule - to privacy in all that pertains to this correspondence. Conversely, the employer has their own right to supervise the use made of digital mail for private purposes, this by examining the scope of private use of the digital mail box. However, this must be facilitated without viewing or copying such private messages (including printed copies or recording telephone conversations). . With regard to the examination of said content - the fundamental rule is that it must not be permitted in light of the damage caused to the worker's right for privacy. However, since the right to privacy, like any other fundamental right, is not absolute but is relative, it should be balanced

---

[66] Elections Appeal (Tel Aviv) 10121/06 Tali Isakov v. Official in charge of the Women's Labor Law

[67] Elections Appeal 1158/06 Water Channels et al. v. Rani Fisher

[68] Arrests File 46/06 Tveriya Municipality v. Binyamin Eliyahu (unpublished, October 22, 2007)

against the employer's interests and thus examination is permitted when the employer has, according to the three tests of proportionality, and depending on the specific circumstances of the case, significant specific interest that justifies this[69].

Following the formulated principles, a collective agreement was written and signed between the General Workers' Union and the Economic Organizations Coordination Bureau. The following are the central principles of the agreement:

- The principle of legitimacy determines that justification is required to allow infringement of the employee's right to privacy.
- The principle of proportionality determines that it is first necessary to employ alternative, less invasive, means.

Explanation: The individual is, by nature, an emotional being, they may be influenced by the facts disclosed to them. This differentiates a human being from a machine, such as a computer, which performs all tasks assigned to it, no more and no more less. Software that searches the computer or the servers is only following the precise definitions provided it and intentionally ignores all other information. Thus, the worker's privacy is maintained, alongside the employer's right to find the relevant data.

- The principle of adherence to the goal determines that the information collected will be used for the purpose for which it was collected - and this purpose alone.
- The principle of transparency determines that the employer must inform the employees clearly of the rules regarding the use of the equipment belonging to the employer in general and in particular, relating to computers, network equipment, and cellular devices. The employer must provide clear and precise rules and conditions of use of the organizations equipment and inform the employees of those circumstances under which the employer will monitor the activity of digital devices and the

---

[69] Elections Appeal (Tel Aviv) 10121/06 Tali Isakov Inbar, 15, paragraph 2.

manner in which use will be made of this information and follow up activities. In this context the employer must act in good faith and with integrity.

Finally, the general characteristics of 'the best digital evidence' and the special problems involved in the handling digital evidence are taken into consideration when examining the weight, uniqueness, and quantity of the evidence and the sequence of events.

These considerations and many others create the standards that must be developed and implemented in order to prevent any possible scenario that could be created during the organization's day to day, regular, activity. Tis is also true when the organization fails to characterize a specific standard, or, in other words, failed to take into account the types of digital evidence that would reasonably be required.

It is, therefore, the duty of managers and senior staff to formulate a broad array of corporate planning actions, that are applicable for the entire organization, and to attempt to predict all possible scenarios, including risk analysis, management goals, writing reports alongside the development of procedures and methodical tests that should be assimilated and conducted within the organization.

These management targets and the variety of events mentioned previously, with which managers at all levels cope, go beyond the routine activities of most organizations. The regular and normal balance between continuation of business activity and reduction of damage and media exposure may create an internal conflict within the organization and an unanticipated crisis.

From an organizational perspective, the nature of the crisis is the loss of income and harm to the organization's good name. Computer investigations generally arise following a crisis; however, very quickly, such an investigation can develop into an investigation in its own right. When the organization's management makes a decision to deal ahead of time with future threats, namely with the different issues pertaining to the setting of the level of applicable resources alongside the level of required information security, it is necessary to prepare for these expected scenarios in an appropriate manner.

The organization must be willing to accept the financial expenditure required for equipment, security systems, and work teams and also be aware that these are resources and expenses that it may never have to use (hopefully). Conversely, the very establishment of procedures and information security systems within the organization may, by itself, prevent the need to implement the systems and thus minimizes future expenditure that would be required sooner or later.

I would note that no importance is placed on the cause of the damage - whether this is a flood, a fire, an act of terror, or a failure in the computer and Internet services. The disaster plan, which includes sections on recovery, describes certain situations and illustrates the actions that should be undertaken so as to minimize, to the greatest possible extent, the harm and to allow for the continuation of ongoing business processes without disruption to the rest of the departments in the organization,.

The basic aspiration of the organization is to survive so that it can continue to serve its clients, to meet its commitments to lenders, banks, workers, the general public, and the country. In addition, and naturally, the commercial organization also seeks to generate revenues and profits for its stockholders.

Different arrangements in place within the organization at a time of crisis are also potential weaknesses, since they may eventually lead to the loss of data or potential evidence. These are arrangements that are designed and put in place to enable the organization to continue in its main activity and thus rapidly recover and reach full operational status. Recovery includes the restoration of computerized systems to normal activity, restoration of the organization's endangered assets, handling insurance claims alongside legal suits against third parties, meeting commitments to third parties and helping enforce the law in potential criminal issues. Computerized investigations are amongst the hardest that any organization may face. This is due to the complexity of computer systems, the fear of adversely impacting the number of hours that employees are able to work which could affect customer services. Managerial goals could also change the more that the impact of specific scenarios is known.

In this matter and in situations of crisis, there exists a significant conflict between the need for organizational continuity and the requirement to reliably collect digital evidence from the machines and computer systems that enable the organization's continued operation. For this purpose, the organization needs a managerial and executive operational framework in which decisions can be made in a time of crisis.

In many organizations there is a recovery plan in place to address and recover from disaster scenarios such as fire or a flood, bombing, kidnapping, or malicious handling of a product. It is necessary to clearly differentiate between recovery plans in cases of physical disaster and plans that relate to the recovery of computer and internet based systems. Thought processes, handling, and recovery are different, and therefore a separate plan, different from a physical recovery plan, to recover from a computer disaster plan is required.

We can illustrate this if we take, for example, the terrorist attacks that led to the collapse of the Twin Towers in New York City. As have previously mentioned, apart the loss tragic loss of human life, companies that had designed, developed and put in place disaster recovery plans which were, following the attacks, then implemented, were able to continue or resume the organization's operations from outside of the destroyed structure and were thus able to reduce the degree of damage sustained by the organization.

In addition, the organization will need an operational arm. This may be a security planning unit or a completely new unit established specifically for this goal. The organization must accept the decisions of this body and implement them according to its needs.

The Life Cycle of Digital Evidence in the Organization

In the world of digital evidence, there are no two identical computerized investigations. However, the time line provides general parameters for investigations, which include complexity alongside the period of time that may be required to complete the various tasks. Meeting these time restraints with the managerial framework is essential, and it is possible to draw conclusions and learn about behavioral patterns within the organization.

The essential details may change considerably. By understanding all of the elements that exist in the evidence life cycle, it is possible to perceive and understand the range and scope of management decisions that may be involved during and after the computerized investigation.

In this section we address what occurs during the 'incident'. However, some of the characteristics of the time line will also be in effect in other circumstances, for example, if there is an unexpected demand on the part of a governmental investigation to produce various types of digital evidence.

In practice many of the tasks listed so far will be implemented concurrently. The use of the word 'incident' refers, primarily, to the use of the computer and can illustrate, in a neutral manner, the labeling of events that may occur accidentally or as the result of intentional malicious activity. The following shows the life cycle of a digital incident, stage after stage.

Discovery. Following a dramatic event, such as a blackmail demand, a clear failure of main servers, routine intra-organizational criticism, discovery of irregularities, or suspicion that arises following unusual behavior.

Report. Organizations need a defined point at which the reports are made, whether by corporate security, online personal computer security, auditing of accounts, by company's secretariat, the human resources department, or a legal adviser.

Initial assessment of findings. Persons, with the appropriate and required skills, experience and resources, receiving the report will evaluate what possible outcomes and provide initial guidance regarding the way in which the organization needs to handle the problem.

Managerial actions based on initial assessment. At this stage it is necessary to act according to procedures defined ahead of time for specifically for events of this type, while informing the relevant managers and activating the staff in charge of specific tasks.

Evidence collection. This is one of the earliest and most important stages. The goal of this stage is to identify and determine the relevant point of time of the event, to identify and seize the evidence, and thus prevent it from 'vanishing', and at the same time to collect and document the evidence under controlled conditions and save the raw digital material.

Assessment of the problem's source and situation analysis. Initial assessments may be mistaken. From the collection of digital evidence in its raw form, there is a move to the evaluation of evidence, a stage that has a great deal of influence of the perceptions of the team addressing the various aspects of the problems being dealt with. In most of the crises entailing computers and information systems, the initial evidence is achieved with the aid of computers. Very quickly, the ongoing assessment process shifts outside of the organization's boundaries and collects evidence and testimony from people and businesses, including documents and physical evidence.

Managerial actions based on the assessment. This is a process that takes time. As the source of the problem becomes clearer, the organization's managers are capable of defining their goals in a more certain and clearer manner. After the immediate risks that harm the integrity of the computer and database systems are blocked, the goal of the organization is to focus on the long-term. On the time line, the action of the managerial task team does not cease until the end of the process, when conclusions are drawn and lessons are learned.

Restoration of the organization to full business activity. When computer systems function partially, business is disrupted, and there may also a public crisis or loss of assets and income.

The organization and its managers must act to restore all the affected systems to full operation, and as fast as is possible in order to reduce negative impact. For all intents and purposes, there is no difference between damage that derives from fire, flood, or theft or from digital/virtual sources. The process of recovery is, from the public's perspective, identical. Experience shows that recovery from the catastrophic collapse of computer systems will usually take longer than expected. Typical tasks at this stage include re-booting/starting of computer systems, restoration of lost assets, and to engage in public relations. The organization will be required to manage and execute these tasks for a number of months, and only over time will it be possible to estimate the overall degree of damage caused to the organization.

Corrective, repair and restoration activities. This stage includes drawing conclusions, preventing the recurrence of the event, implementing new management and accounting processes of and new security engineering facilities. However, it is impossible to learn lessons from the event unless an in depth investigation into the event has been carried out. Lessons and the conclusions may exceed the boundaries of the immediate events and expand to include problems in the organization's corporate culture and management structure.

Civil legal action. This stage includes insurance claims, restoration of assets, claims for damages, neglect, breach of trust, etc. Civil legal activity entails demands for full disclosure of the material, which may influence the outcome of the litigation process, if such is held.

Activity of the Police or other body responsible for law enforcement. Law enforcement activity has a number of possible stages: initial investigation, collection of digital evidence and collection of affidavits, repeat visits for the continuation of the investigation and the search for additional physical evidence, preparation of the materials collected, and their transfer to the prosecution, and preparation of materials in order to meet the requirements and obligations of full disclosure, if required by the defense.

It would seem that dealing with digital evidence as part of the recovery and recuperation plan only takes part towards the end of the process and after all immediate actions have been taken. However, but this is an illusion. To be truly effective, it is necessary to begin the identification and collection of digital evidence even before the event occurred. In other words, it critically important to develop and implement clear procedures and systems of examination and protection, both inside and outside of the organization. These systems should document, collect, and save data within the organization - like a 'big brother'. Thus, it is possible, at every given stage, to reconstruct, to examine, to learn what was, and primarily to return to the former state.

CHAPTER 3: PRESERVATION OF DIGITAL EVIDENCE

How digital evidence is preserved is the relatively 'safe part of the processes that address digital evidence. This refers to the preservation of the original digital evidence, in its original version, and to the creation of a copy, faithful to the original, onto another hard drive that had passed examination in a digital forensics laboratory and found to be in working order prior to the copying of the data. The copied data will be encrypted and a number of identical copies made, each saved at a separate location.

In general, these are simple processes, but we must not be mistaken: examiners of digital evidence must conduct a series of procedures that will ensure that the evidence is properly preserved. The following are the main principles from the *Good Practice Guide for Computer Based Electronic Evidence* written by the Association of Chief Police Officers in the United Kingdom (ACPO)[70].

1. Law enforcement agencies and/or their representatives and/or all other computer experts who have access to the original media are absolutely forbidden to change and/or distort data stored on a computer or on other storage media which may subsequently be relied upon in court.

2. In unusual circumstances where an accredited computer examiner decides to access original data stored on a computer or on storage media, the examiner must be competent to do so and capable of giving evidence explaining the relevance and the implications of these actions.

---

[70]

http://www.7safe.com/electronic_evidence/ACPO_guidelines_computer_evidenc e.pdf

3. An audit trail or other record of all the processes performed on the matter of the original digital evidence should be kept, so that an independent third party will be able to examine those processes and achieve the same outcome, using the same instruments.

4. The person in charge of the investigation is assigned serious responsibility; the person is responsible for ensuring that the law and these principles are upheld.

The guide continues and states that computer-based digital evidence is no different from a printed document. For this reason, digital evidence is subject to the same rules and laws that address the documentation of evidence. In other words, the prosecution has the responsibility to show the Court that the evidence produced has not been changed or altered from the original as it was at the time of its collection by the Police.

Copying Partial Information

In cases where the amount of data is too large and copying of the information is impossible, there exists the possibility of copying the information in part or selectively. This alternative is effective and generally not recommended but still possible. In such situations, those in charge of copying the selected or partial information have an increased responsibility, alongside the duty to adhere to the four previously mentioned principles.

Experience has shown that this is not a good alternative, from the perspective of the defendant. The investigating organization which retrieved the digital evidence believes it holds the proof it sought. The accused and their defense believe that possible evidence which may, perhaps, have presented the picture in a different light has been removed.

It is my opinion that the issue of the 'copying of partial information' is a serious subjective topic. Approval of actions of this type should not become widespread or common; partial extraction of digital evidence must receive the Court's approval, and then only after it has examined all of the implications.

Accessibility to the Original Evidence

In rare cases, for diverse technical reasons that are primarily related to the structure of the hardware, the types of controllers, network structures, and so on, it is impossible to obtain the desired data through the use of a recognized imaging component. Under these circumstances, it is possible that it will be necessary to obtain the evidence again. It is the examiner's duty is to review and document the event and to give evidence before the Court.

It is necessary to objectively present to the Court both the continuity of the digital evidence and their integrity. In addition, it is essential to show how the reconstructed evidence was obtained, while presenting all of the processes through which it was achieved. The new evidence must to be preserved so that a third party can repeat the same process and reach the same outcome as that presented before the Court.

In the G8 committee, a standard was proposed to address the issue of the exchange of digital evidence among international organizations. The standard proposes an array of principles on the matter of processes for the preservation of digital evidence as established evidence in the digital world[71], similar to that presented in the *Good Practice Guide for Computer Based Electronic Evidence.*

1. After the digital evidence is captured, the actions taken must not change the evidence.

2. When the need arises to access the original digital evidence, the person given responsibility for this must have the legally accepted and appropriate competence and training.

3. All activity linked to holding, sanctioning, storing, and/or transferring digital evidence must be undertaken with full documentation that meets all accepted rules.

---

[71] G8 Proposed Principles for Forensic Evidence

4. The person in charge of the digital evidence in the organization is responsible for all the actions adopted in all that pertains to digital evidence when the evidence is held by the organization he manages.

5. Every organization that is responsible for holding, obtaining access, storing, and/or transferring digital evidence must implement these principles.

On this matter, see the guidelines of the United States Department of Justice[72] and the ISO 27037 Standard *Guidelines for Identification, Collection, Acquisition, and Preservation of Digital Evidence*[73].

---

[72] U.S. Department of Justice, Office of Justice Programs National Institute of Justice, Forensic Examination of Digital Evidence: A Guide for Law Enforcement
[73] International Standard ISO/IEC27037, First Edition 2012-10-15, Information Technology — Security Techniques — Guidelines for Identification, Collection, Acquisition, and Preservation of Digital Evidence

Chain of Custody for Digital Evidence

In the investigative process in general, and in digital investigations in particular, forensic examiners and the authorities must be able to explain and describe the data and the various elements collected from the scene of the crime and from other locations, and which are held in their custody. The documentation and record of the chain of custody is a document that identifies the movement of the evidence in general and the handling of potential digital evidence in particular.

The process of documentation begins at the stage of the capture and collection of the digital evidence and includes the documenting of the situation in which the evidence was found and its present location. The record of the chain of custody is held in a series of linked documents detailing each and all of those individuals who were responsible for the care of potential digital evidence, whether in the form of digital data or in other formats. The goal of the record is to maintain the chain of custody as a whole and to enable identification of potential digital evidence and to facilitate access to it at any point of time.

There are a number of types of custody documents, for instance a document of capture and documentation, records of the digital data, hardware components, manner of saving and movement of the component, record of copies including creation date and proof the copy is faithful to the original , process of analysis, and so on. The record of the chain of custody is supposed to include information on the unique identifier number, the details of the person involved in capturing and collecting the digital evidence and/or digital evidence examiner, the date and place where the evaluation was performed, the processes involved in the examination, both overt and covert, the manner in which the investigations findings were preserved, and the date of the examination. In addition, it is necessary to document the reason for the examination, the goal of the examination, the authority that grants approval, and every unavoidable change performed in the original, potential digital evidence. I would further note that it is mandatory to document the name of the person who is responsible for any such changes and the reason for the change in the original digital evidence.

The chain of custody documents, like the digital evidence itself, should be preserved throughout the entire period of the legal proceedings and for a certain period of time after the end of this period. This is, of course, subject to local laws concerning the preservation of evidence. This period of time is set by the local judicial authority which has jurisdiction over the collection and application of digital evidence. It is mandatory to uphold these rules from the moment of capture and collection of the digital components and/or potential digital evidence, and the issue of the length of the period must not be compromised.

Processes of Preservation of Digital Evidence

Works Stations and Personal Computers

As I have already mentioned, it is mandatory to create a precise copy, faithful to the original, of all the hard drives in the seized computer, so as to ensure that every examination will be performed solely on the copies and that the original will be preserved in the same state as when first acquired, namely, no further use will be made of it.

The copying of the drives is performed precisely and will include both open and concealed areas; in other words, not only the visible files but also the hidden partitions of the hard drive. From these areas it will be possible to reconstruct and produce evidence, even if at the beginning of the process they appear empty.

It is the duty of forensic computer investigators to make a copy faithful to the original and to copy and document the entire process, from the moment that the digital device is acquired. It is also their duty and responsibility to refrain from and to prevent any damage to the original digital evidence. This process is known as 'forensic imaging'.

To successfully realize the process, unique technical devices are needed that can examine the integrity and working order of the original hard drive and copy it in full. The authorized examiner's duty is to follow the instruction and processes defined as a part of the duplication chain. He is also required to painstakingly fulfill the recording and documentation stage, so that any other digital evidence examiner 'will be able to repeat the process and examine the originality of the copy.

I would note that there are a variety of software products that can copy a hard drive. These software programs are intended primarily to assist in the reconstruction and recovery of data after a hardware failure and/or after data loss. These programs do not meet the criteria of the legal arena, since they can copy and reconstruct visible files, namely the 'live' part of the hard drive, but are unable to copy the concealed sections of the hard drive, sections from which we will reconstruct and extract concealed digital evidence. Another reason why the copies produced by these software programs are disqualified for use as copies faithful to the original and as legal evidence is that, as a part of the replication process, the software adds data and thus voids the originality of the copy.

People working in the field of computerized forensics today use unique software products, for example EnCase, FTK, and others. These software programs and others have identical functions, alongside the unique added value that each individual program offers, and they complement the array of devices at the disposal of the authorized computer examiner.

The uniqueness of these software programs is their ability to conduct a test of originality and copy a single file that will be an exact and faithful of original as part of the examination process. This is seen as 'taking a digital fingerprint' from the original file and dragging it to the copied file.

As noted, not all imaging software can cope with all the operating systems in use by digital devices. It is possible that some of versions of imaging systems, the most familiar ones, will not succeed in capturing all the digital evidence on the hard drive. This is where the human factor comes into play. Talented, expert computer examiners will succeed in linking the lost sections and partial results produced by the imaging software and so be able to complete the process and present the entire picture.

After seizure of the hardware, it is necessary to ascertain that the device was not booted (powered up), since in the boot process new data will be written on the hard drive. Therefore, after capture of the digital device, it must be turned off and not connected to a source of electricity. The legal computer examiner will remove the hard drive from its original mounting and connect it to a professional work station. This work station will use professional imaging software programs and a hardware defense component t prevent any additional data being written to the seized hard drive[74]. A hard drive will be

---

[74] A hardware product, an 'anti-writing protection' component. This component is

connected to the work station where it will be possible to store the imaged files before they are copied onto a CD and/or any other storage media. This action is valid also for laptop computers.

In the case of different types of hardware, from which it is difficult to remove the hard drive and/or when unreasonable physical intervention is required, such as disconnecting soldering and/or damage to the original hardware interface that constitutes an inseparable part of the motherboard, the device will be activated using an alternative or external operating system, from a CD/DVD drive. The special CD/DVD disc includes imaging software and can document the linking of the links.

The copied digital device is linked through a network cable to the examining computer, which is responsible for all the processes and procedures and collects the data into an image file through the network cable. I would note that the communications network is composed of only two computers, namely the computer being examined and the examining computer and that the network cable must be a 'crossover' one[75]. Imaging through a network cable is for the most part a long and continuous process, since the data must pass through the cable slowly relative to the transfer rate of a direct connection between one hard drive and another.

Forensics experts often arrive at a scene where there are computers and/or other digital devices which are still operating. The digital evidence experts must use their judgment and decide upon the optimal method required for the seizure whilst taking into consideration the type of hardware and its components.

If the suspect is a regular user, then a note of the active software programs, alongside a screen shot of the desktop, is sufficient. If the suspect is an expert in the field of technology and information and/or a

---

connected through a unique cable or a similar method to the hard drive or the computer. The component enables the data on the hard drive to be read but blocks any attempt to write it.

[75] A 'crossover' cable can transfer data from the sending device to the receiving device but not from one sending device to another sending device.

computer communication employee, then it is possible that software for the destruction of evidence is installed on the computer and turning the computer off may erase and/or destroy the digital evidence, in part or completely.

If there are open connections to a remote computer or server, then the computer must not be turned off. It is essential to involve an expert computer technician who is conversant in the legal field before any attempt is made to disconnect and remove the device. This action can provide a variety of opportunities for the identification and capture of additional digital evidence, and it is essential in order to prevent destruction of data.

Another problem arises when a personal computer or server contains a number of hard drives intended to work together, as in a RAID system[76] (see the chapter on terms and definitions). These computers primarily operate in locations where rapid data processing is required, such as companies, offices, and video editing work stations. It is impossible to perform imaging of the disks connected to such a system separately – the assistance of a hardware components expert is required to decide upon the best method of copying the connected disks. The legal computer expert is required to document the hardware components expert work method, which will be presented as part of the declaration relating to the digital evidence and/or its presentation at a later stage.

It is further required to examine the imaged computer's time clock. As mentioned previously, computers have a built-in clock, sometimes referred to as a BIOS clock[77] (see also the chapter on terms and

---

[76] RAID – Redundant Array of Independent Disks. In this method, a number of hard drives are united into one logical unit, which is managed by a hardware component, a controller. The unification enables access to a number of drives simultaneously and thus improves the work speed and reconstructs information that was lost as a result of a failure. There are different methods to manage RAID. These methods are called RAID levels, each of which has its own advantages.

[77] BIOS – Basic Input Output System. This is an integration of the hardware and software system engraved in the hardware and used to boot the computer, to support the input and output software, and to maintain consistency of the internal computer clock. For this purpose, the BIOS has a lithium battery, similar to that of watches.

definitions). Accessing this clock, time stamps showing the days and hours of computer usage can be ascertained. . The timestamp has, as stated, a vital impact on the issue of showing the chain of events at a later stage, and therefore it is important to determine the extent to which the clock time of the computer has deviated from real time. It is possible and even desirable to photograph the computer clock alongside a real clock, with a digital camera or a mobile phone with a built-in camera.

Many legal imaging software programs are intended for personal computers (PC[78], see also the chapter on terms and definitions) using Microsoft's Windows operating system (in it various versions). These software programs also work with other operating systems such as versions of Linux[79] and in some versions of UNIX[80] (see the chapter on terms and definitions). Experienced legal computer examiners frequently prefer to use technological tools based on Linux to examine hard drives using Microsoft's Windows.

Another player in the field of operating systems is that of the Apple Macintosh family, which, for the most part, are not suitably supported by commercial legal tools. The EnCase software program 'learned' the format of Mac drives internal divisions and sectors and today, there exists a range of tools that specialize in the field of Mac operating systems, such as MacForensics Lab[81] and Black Bag[82]. The Mac operating system is supported by BSD Unix, and hence the need for the use of unique tools, based on UNIX, for imaging and analysis.

---

[78] PC – Personal Computer. This is a comprehensive name for the personal computers intended for the use of individual or individuals.

[79] Linux is a family of professional operating systems. Today Linux is used in many areas, from computer-embedded systems to super computers. Linux is an important example of the development of open software and open code; the original code is accessible for free use, modification, and distribution.

[80] The UNIX operating system was first developed as a noncommercial system by the AT&T Company. Over the years the system became the basis of different study programs for operating systems and many knew its original code.

[81] http://www.macforensicslab.com (of the SubRosaSoft Company)

[82] http://www.blackbagtech.com/software_mfs.html

Explanation

Apple Mac operating systems are run by Intel processors, incorporating an EFI (extensible firmware interface), which bridges between the software interface, the operating system and the computer hardware. It significantly improves the accessibility of the BIOS (basic input-output system) and creates a short and rapid bridge to the activation of the computer operating system.

With regard to the issue under examination, this primarily influences the manner in which the computer boots and connects to the hard drives and the computer's inner partitions. Legal analysis tools from the previous generation can 'see' only the symmetry of the inner partition and do not allow access without the technician's manual intervention.

Legal Issues

Seized computers and communication equipment will be considered original and admissible digital evidence and as a part of the legal proceeding. However, the extraction of the contents of documents found on the computer may necessitate separate confirmation, especially in a situation in which it is necessary to reconstruct and/or examine the admissibility of the computer clock. Separate confirmation will be required in a situation in which more than one person had access to the same computer. According to British Law, computer investigators must prove that they are authorized and permitted to access the contents of the computer for the purposes of examination, as stated by law[83].

In general, authorized judicial examiners and their agents are authorized and licensed to access seized computers in their possession. However, approval is given for the purpose of copying and duplicating digital evidence and not for the detailed examination of work contracts.

The examination of document contents is performed by the previously mentioned and other software programs, which can read the content of files of any type, whether open or concealed, subject to the

---

[83] www.legislation.gov.uk/ukpga/1990/18/contents

predefined search definitions. Those authorized to open the files are professionals, such as lawyers, accountants, or other experts, whose job it is to examine the nature of what the documents contain, the sequence of events, and the relationship to the offense. In general a "test of least harm" is performed, which is a fundamental right, anchored in section 7 (A) of the Basic Law: Human Dignity and Liberty, where it is stated that, "Every person is entitled to privacy and confidentiality."

The "test of least harm" is also associated with the principle of proportionality, and on this matter the respected Judge Aharon Barak wrote[84]:

> Since the *Knesset* established the basic laws on the matter of human rights, we use the standards determined in them to interpret the governmental authorities given by legislation (primary or secondary),. This whether the legislation was enacted before the basic laws or the legislation was enacted afterwards, whether he matter of harm to human rights 'is covered' by the two basic laws on human rights and whether the matter of harm to human rights is not 'covered' by these basic laws … we always determined that the purpose of legislation that harms human rights includes general purposes and specific purposes … The general purposes are the values of the State of Israel as a Jewish and democratic state. The specific purposes are 'appropriate purpose' in the limitation of the ruling. The principle of proportionality that is set out in the basic law is another expression of the principle of reasonability according to which we acted, in the past as well, to interpret all legislation.

The honorable Judge Dorner also addressed this matter, as she wrote in the Supreme Court Ruling of Miller v. the Minister of Defense[85]:

---

[84] Supreme Court 5016/96 Horev v. Ministry of Transport, Court Ruling 51 (4) (following: Horev Court Ruling), p. 43.

The paragraph regarding the limitation is effective only on authorities whose rights are derived from laws enacted after the legislation of the basic law. However, by the power of inference, the main tenets of the law should be applied to the issue of the duty of government authorities. By force of section 11 of the basic law, it is also effective with regard to authorities that are based on laws preceding the basic law. There are two reasons for this: first, the defense of basic rights in Israel should be performed on the basis of similar standards, whether the legal norm whose validity was examined is law or whether this is another legal norm. Second, the arrangement set in the limitations paragraph – which differentiates between the purpose of harm righto rights and the degree of harm – is suited in its basis to the constellation of legal norms and not only laws.

The honorable justice Dorner focused on the distinction between balance and human rights, the balance of human rights and the balance between human rights and public interest[86].

Standards in the ruling of limitation and especially in the principle of proportionality do not suit the balance between the two human rights. The goal of the horizontal balance is to reduce harm to the two rights and this, as mentioned, through reciprocal surrender that enables the realization of both, even if not fully. However, if there is no possibility of maintaining the two competing rights, then the right for which the result of harm to the individual is

[85] Supreme Court 4541/94 Miller v. Ministry of Defense, Court Ruling 49 (4) (following: Miller Court Ruling), p. 138.

[86] 1514/01 Gur Aryeh v. The Second Authority of the Television and Radio, Court Ruling 55 (4) 267, pp. 284-285.

more severe will prevail.

As known, digital evidence that constitutes professional legal material is confidential in civil issues. The situation frequently arises in 'search and seize' warrants such as Anton Filler[87] orders and others. The owners of the seized computer and/or digital hardware of any type can protest citing invasion of privacy and can object to the review of the information being sought and/or immediate review of the data held by the devices as material not relevant to the case. Another argument addresses the issue of the commercial confidentiality of the seized material alongside commitment to protect the data.

From a technical perspective, it is impossible to edit part of the computer's hard drive and/or any other digital hardware and present it as evidence in a legal proceeding. The editing harms the credibility of the evidence and the ability of any third party to examine the originality of the evidence presented and to validate the sequence of events. Under these circumstances, the solution is the appointment of a receiver for all digital evidence that will be seized in the framework of a 'search and seize' warrant, who will hold a copy that is faithful to the original f.

The receiver, a lawyer or retired judge, must be independent and must use their discretion in all issues that pertain to relevance and full disclosure. In the case of disclosure of materials taken from the array of digital evidence in its raw form, the receiver must have personal technical expertise that enables them to translate legal judgments into appropriate practical technical solutions.

---

[87] The Anton Filler warrant is the name of a warrant of the Court in a civil proceeding that enables the prosecution to seize electronic evidence and material of the defendant, if there is the concern that the defendant will cause them to disappear during the course of the trial. On this matter see the chapter of concepts and definitions.

Digital Evidence and Surveillance of Typing Actions

From a technical perspective, systems that track typing activities are hardware systems and/or software programs that capture every key press performed on the computer. The key log generated by the hardware and/or software enables the data to be reconstructed. Hardware versions link between the keyboard and the computer itself. Generally this is a small component, so that it is difficult to discover it in a superficial inspection.

From time to time, the investigator collects the data and examines it their own computer. Hardware systems that track typing can only capture data actually typed into the computer, in other words, computer activity displayed on the screen, including mouse movements, will not be captured by the hardware. In addition, any computer activity when the computer is used remotely or when a touch screen is used will also not be captured.

Software versions offer a broader range of possibilities. They can document mouse movements, even if the computer is used remotely, as well as actions using a touch screen. Generally all software programs are implemented discretely from a remote source, that is to say, the computer user does not know of their existence.

As mentioned, software programs that track typing are applications which enable remote monitoring, inspection, and control, either through a communications network and/or the Internet. This will be possible as long as the digital hardware is connected physically or wirelessly to a communications network.

These systems are intended to uphold the rule relating to the 'test of least harm', namely the authorized computer investigator defines ahead of time the expressions that create suspicion of an offense that will be searched for. , The surveillance software program reports, in real-time, key strokes made and also records the data. The software then sends alert to investigators if certain key words are typed.

Evidence Collected during Unauthorized Entry into a Computer

An interesting issue arises when an investigator wants to secretly access a suspect's computer through a communication network and/or the Internet.

Technically, this is a relatively simple task. Identify and/or create a breach in the suspect's computer, insert a 'back door' software program along with software allowing for remote management, and the goal is achieved. In addition, systems that track typing are also installed to capture every key press. In addition, screen shots are taken regularly and frequently. All the information collected is then consolidated into a full and detailed report of all actions carried out on the target computer.

Remote tools for criminal forensics are a type of hacking (accessing a computer system without permission), and to operate them special authorization is required as well as high security classification. When a corporation hires a computer investigator to implement such an action, there are significant legal risks. Every entry into a computer without permission from the computer owner is an offense according to the laws of the United States, Britain, and Israel.

To make things clearer, I would note that even if the computer is owned by the employer, the computer user has an expectation of privacy and the employer has a duty to inform the user ahead of time that he intends to use a tool to examine and monitor the computer. For law enforcement agencies, the situation is different. They can obtain a search warrant, if there are circumstances justifying such an action.

In addition, there is the problem of the reliability of digital evidence Police investigators do not have the source of the raw evidence and they are operating in a gray area. The dilemma is finding the means to satisfy the Court and ensure that the evidence on the computer and that was presented to the Court was not distorted? Moreover, how can an objective third party repeat the same processes and obtain the same result?

From the moment the investigator access the computer, the guarantee of the fairness and integrity of digital evidence produced, of any kind, is voided. This is the situation in which it is impossible to unequivocally determine that there was no damage to the digital evidence and/or no use was made of it. Therefore it is necessary to balance the weight of evidence presented as a result of this process within the hierarchy of general evidence as strengthening evidence that carries reduced weight.

It is the duty of the defense council to demand a copy of the digital evidence that is faithful to the original digital materials and thus negating any possibility that the evidence presented to the Court was obtained by illegal or unauthorized access to the computer in question.

If the district attorney's office did not transfer to the defense counsel was all material required, there is real suspicion that the defense's client was indeed the victim of such an invasion on the part of law enforcement agencies and/or another agents. In addition, if the prosecution is based on evidence that lacks a digital source, it is possible that the defense will be able to present strong arguments that the evidence is inadmissible and that the Court must disallow any testimony based on the tainted evidence in the indictment.

Legal Issues

In a situation in which the investigator, at his employer's direction, installed systems that track typing, the legal considerations are similar to those that exist in another type of employee based investigation. Thus, the concern is for potential harm to the employee's privacy. The employer's duty is to maintain the principle of transparency and the principle of good faith.

Under different circumstances, in a criminal investigation, Police investigators who install system components, whether hardware and/or software, will need to obtain the Court's approval and to act according to a warrant that allows them to install such components. In British Law the topic is controversial. The 1997 Police Law[88] Part 3 states that

---

[88] http://www.legislation.gov.uk/ukpga/1997/50/contents

the Police are not permitted to use such components, as it is stated in Section 10 of the law that the misuse of computers, provides defense against unlawful access.

The United States federal government enacted laws against the clandestine use of systems that track keyboard typing[89]. The reason for this derives from the fact that the systems are based on a mechanism that intercepts digital information. This means that the clandestine use of systems that track typing so as to spy on a spouse and/or to track employees is a violation of federal law, since it fundamentally entails the interception of digital communication. Moreover, individual state laws and regulations set additional punishments on this matter.

In criminal proceedings, the defense counsel's duty is to request a copy, faithful to the original, of all the original digital materials and thus, negating the possibility that the source of evidence presented to the Court results from unlawful access to the specific computer or computers. If the prosecuting attorney fails to provide the defense the required material, there exists a real suspicion that his client was the victim of such an act on the part of the law enforcement agency and/or another agent.

If the district attorney argues this issue behind closed doors, then the defense must demand that the source be presented to the Court and thus negate the possibility that this is evidence taken in a process involving remote, unauthorized invasion of the computer. If the district attorney and/or authorized investigative agency do not present to the Court the source of the evidence in its raw form, then the defense will argue against the admissibility of the evidence.

Email Correspondence

Copies of different types of email messages can be found in the personal computers of both the sender and the recipient, on mail servers, and on the different service providers' servers. In addition, it is possible that copies may be found in in different formats in archived. If

---

[89] USC § 2511 - Interception and disclosure of wire, oral, or electronic communications prohibited

the sender of the email or the recipient uses a mobile device, such as a mobile phone or handheld computer, then copies of the message may also exist on these devices. A simple printout of the email message is the most preferable form to present such evidence. However since it is possible to use a word processor to easily change, edit, and forge email messages, a more sophisticated approach is needed for the original message, namely, meeting strict standards regarding the issue of the admissibility of evidence.

The key to examining the originality of the email message is the way in which the organization ensures the originality of and access to copies of email messages, which are supposed to be stored in a secure location that is not accessible to everybody. This is true for every provider of email services, even if the service is free. It is not unreasonable to assume that suspects will attempt to erase an email message from their personal computer and thus it is important to save alternative copies.

Clearly, every additional copy of the email message found at different locations and on different computers raises the degree of uncertainty regarding the originality of the message and increases the importance of verifying its validity. To this must be added metadata elements, an issue which we addressed earlier, which enable to cross-check data regarding the time the message was sent, the identity of the sending server and the receiving server, and the identity of the users themselves.

In other words, an email message sent through the Internet and/or while using protocols similar to the Internet bears 'headers' that include information on the original locations of the email and the path it took to reach the recipient, whoever that may be. Although it is possible to forge the 'title', it is possible to provide a higher level of verification by crosschecking a number of messages.

On the matter of processes involved in the preservation of digital evidence, it is possible to divide email software programs into two main types. The first is local software, which can be found on personal computers that are used to send and receive email messages. These programs include, for instance, Microsoft Outlook, Outlook Express, Eudora, and others. The second type is collaborative email software programs installed on servers, which act as a focus for the exchange of digital mail among people in the organization and with the outside world. Server based software programs include, for instance, Microsoft Exchange, FTGate, MailTraq, and others.

Most organization use the IMAP protocol (Internet Message Access Protocol)[90], through which they save copies of email messages on other, remote servers for extended periods of time. Email messages are stored in a file structure linked to the digital email application, and the technician and/or legal computer investigator know what type of files and file structure is used by the relevant programs and where they are stored.

In older and simpler email programs, it was frequently possible to read digital mail files directly, using a basic text editor. In newer programs, email messages are held on a structured database and it is only possible to read them from the email program itself.

A file from one type of software must <u>not</u> be converted into a file of another type. Frequently this conversion damages the structure of the message's Meta labels, which indicate the originality of the email, and thus blur message's the basic data.

The advantage of a structured database is that it allows the forensic investigator to search for individual email messages and track them, according to the sender's name, the recipient's name, subject, content, date, and so on. The disadvantage is that all email messages are found in a structured database, thus making it difficult to examine the content of every message separately.

This shortcoming has further significance. A series of email messages from the mail program's database may include material that is not relevant to the investigation but which is impossible to separate

---

[90] IMAP is an Internet protocol for access to electronic mail found on a server distant (remote) from the local computer.

from the rest of the data. Thus, these materials are 'pulled' into the investigation, assume volume, burden the examination systems, and primarily are subject to the legal jurisdiction on issues relating to defense of privacy and human rights laws. Under these circumstances, and primarily in civil proceedings, it is possible that it will be necessary to reach an arrangement so that an independent third party will serve as the official supervisor on issues relating to digital evidence, in parallel with the guidelines associated with search warrants and Court directives.

Another type of email service is accessed through the browser interface. The service is provided to private individuals as well as to companies and organizations. Such services are provided by Internet service companies such as Hotmail, Yahoo, and Gmail. The Internet service providers offer a service based on the use of browser applications such as Microsoft Explore and Google Chrome which, in turn, use the internet. Thus it is possible to obtain access to mail correspondence regardless of the point of origin, through a computer and/or a connection application on a mobile phone and/or internet connection available at a public place such as a bar or restaurant.

Digital email services such as Microsoft Exchange and others that are used in large organizations enable employees to access email messages through the Internet, while using a browser application. Under these circumstances, the personal computers owned by people who are suspected of a crime will not record the email messages sent and received. What is required will be found on the email server – and only there.

Legal Issues

In Israel, the employer must inform employees, ahead of time, that they intend to monitor computer activities, including the monitoring of the Internet. In Britain there are a number of general limitations on the employer's supervision of employees, which are applicable to email messages, telephone conversations, surfing the Internet, and so on.

After we have overcome the legal obstacles on the matter of the lawfulness of the process, email messages that are obtained from the employee's personal computer are admissible as business records and/or real digital evidence. Therefore, it is compulsory to act according to all applicable laws and regulation, local and national, and to obtain all the required approvals for supervision and monitoring ahead of time. When the computer is a personal computer, the computer owner and/or other authorized person must express their agreement in writing; otherwise the monitoring can be classified as an offense. In addition, such a case will lead to the unavoidable situation in which the information obtained unlawfully will be disqualified.

The honorable Judge A. A. Levy addressed this matter, when the Court convened as the Supreme Court of Criminal Appeals the, in case 4988/08[91]. On the basis of section 32 of the Privacy Protection Law, which determines that:

> Material obtained while harming privacy will be disqualified for use as evidence in the Court, without the consent of the harmed party, unless the use of this material is permitted by the Court, and for the Court's stated reasons, or if the party responsible for the infringement of privacy, which was a party to the process, had protection or exemption according to this law.

The ruling stated that:

> It was found that according to the rule, evidence obtained by infringement of privacy is to be disqualified. However, the rule of disqualification is relative and this means that, subject to the consideration of the Court, the acceptance of evidence for the Court is possible, despite any infringement of privacy (Civil Appeals Authority 1917/92 Skoler v. Jerabi, Court Ruling 47 (5) 764 773 (1993). The purpose of the rule of

---

[91] http://elyon1.court.gov.il/files/08/880/049/o06/08049880.o06.htm

disqualification is to provide a balance between the right to protect privacy and the social interest entailed by doing justice (Family Appeals Request 3542/04 Anonymous v. Anonymous (not yet published, 20.6.05).

The Court discusses a series of events of the type of considerations that will be taken into account when it goes to examine whether there is room to instruct the disqualification of evidence, according to the rule of disqualification set out in section 32 of the law of the defense of privacy. It was determined that there is room to consider the probative power of the evidence, the degree of harm to privacy, whether damaged was caused innocently or maliciously, the extent to which it was possible to achieve the evidence without harming the aforementioned, and last – the severity of the offense (And see: Supreme Court 249/82 Vaknin v. The Military Appeals Court, Court Ruling 37 (2) 393, 436 (1983); Criminal Appeal 480/85 Cortam v. State of Israel Court Ruling 40 (3) 673, 690-691 (1986), Criminal Appeal Authority 1917/92 Skoler v. Gerabi, Court Ruling 47 (5) 764, 774, (1993).

This is similar to section 78 of the 1984 British Police Law[92] that addresses criminal evidence which states that evidence collected unlawfully will be erased.

Email messages found on a server are divided into two groups. The first group consists of email messages that were sent and/or received; they will be admissible and will serve as evidence for all purposes. The second group consists of email messages that were not sent to their destination. In the majority of cases, the reason for this is a technical failure and/or a communication and/or email server overload. These messages may indicate the sender's intention but not necessarily

---

[92] http://www.legislation.gov.uk/ukpga/1984/60/pdfs/ukpga_19840060_en.pdf

the willingness of the intended recipient. It is necessary to take pains to differentiate between the two groups, and it is mandatory to examine the sequence of the correspondence and thus to learn about the relationships and their legal weight.

One of the skills involved in search for evidence in the form of digital email is the avoidance of those potential sources for email messages that may become inadmissible and thus may place in doubt the entire sequence of events.

Following are ways in which it is possible to extract digital evidence from email:

- In a situation in which the email message arrived from a software program installed on a single personal computer, it is compulsory to seize the computer and make duplicate copy, faithful to the original, of every hard drive in which the software is installed. It is necessary to perform reconstruction and examination processes in the attempt to track previous backup files, which may possibly contain different data regarding the specific email messages. In addition, identification of the software program will be undertaken in stages, to capture and preserve the email program's support files and databases of.

- If the email messages arrived from a server based program, then it is necessary to crosscheck the data from the server and the data obtained from the support system. In addition, it is necessary to examine the suspect's access to the main email server: if his access is limited, then the files can be seen as original. If the suspect has a broader access to the server as a part of his everyday work, then it is necessary to hold the evidence as 'something in addition' and crosscheck with as much data as possible.

- If the email server is owned by a company providing Internet services of the previously mentioned types, if a warrant is issued by the Court instructing the company to provide the original file, the company is legally required to provide a copy of the original email that is faithful to the original. The user has no access to the company's database, and even if one or more messages were erased using the browser interface, reconstruction of data from the backup system will restore the erased files. These files will be seen as admissible evidence in legal proceedings. This is true also on the matter of cellular companies email servers, for example, iPhone, Blackberry, and others.

Handheld Computers (Tablets)

At the beginning, I would note that handheld (or tablet) computers, including cellular phones, despite their small physical dimensions, include all the components of a computer, and thus they should be seen as a computer in all respects. They can store personal data, diaries, documents, pictures, data on surfing Internet and connections to remote servers, email correspondence, multimedia elements using a touch screen, software files, and more.

In relation to the capture of digital evidence, handheld computers include hard drives, which are similar in their shape to a digital component such as a disk-on-key and soldered to the device's motherboard. Therefore, it is necessary to make a copy of the hard drive that is faithful to the original, this is the same as copying hard drives that were seized and taken from different data storage media.

In addition, digital evidence examiners must be able to prove that the process of data collection did not cause any changes and/or distortion to the data, just as in the parallel process with conventional computers. I would note that sometimes the simple action of a non-intrusive examination (taking a look) may cause a change and distort data.

In most handheld devices, the hardware components include two types of memory: internal memory and external memory. The external memory is generally found on a storage card known as 'flash memory'; it is relatively easy to work with a memory card of this type, since it is possible to disconnect it from the device and read the data that appear in it separately. In contrast, it is impossible to remove the internal memory from the device or to read without using in some way the handheld computer. Moreover, some handheld computers lose data if their on-board batteries discharge.

If the handheld computer is supposed to serve as a central piece of evidence, and in light of the fact that it is necessary to enable a third party, at any given stage, to repeat the actions taken for data retrieval and that the results must be identical, then it is necessary to employ a different method of preservation, which will ensure the originality of the data and enable its retrieval.

On this matter, there is a wide ranging and useful review carried out by the United States National Institute of Science and Technology (NIST)[93]. I would note that technical processes change between handheld computer 'families' , due to different development processes, the complexity of the application, and technological development between earlier and later generations of devices.

To differentiate from conventional computers, and since these are hardware components that are often interconnected, both on the hardware level and the software level, there is greater likelihood of human error. Therefore, I would recommendation preparing and writing a full and precise report to document every stage in the process, including the most basic stages, and to film, on video, all stages of the process involved in the handling of digital evidence.

In addition, handheld computers are often connected to a remote personal computer to synchronize logs and backup files. Therefore, one of the first tasks of the authorized computer investigator is to ensure that there is access to the linked hardware, so that it will be possible to crosscheck data and verify its originality.

As mentioned previously, there are many types of personal pocket computers, handheld computers, and mobile phones that are used for a

---

[93] http://csrc.nist.gov/publications/nistir/nistir-7250.pdf

vast range of purposes[94]. The widespread distribution of such devices, alongside the multiplicity of mobile communication companies plus increasing access to wireless networks has led to a situation in which it is possible to transfer information between the mobile component and the personal computer and between the handheld computer and many different and varied social networks through Internet websites. Given these circumstances, it is possible that it will be necessary to use a broader technique to capture vital, critical information, including a very real need for cooperation with social content websites.

The central problem that digital evidence investigators face is the fact that it is possible, through any internet connected computer and from any location, to use the virtual chat rooms that are freely available on many websites. It is the investigators' duty, through legal means, to deny the user access to the social network, and thus to ensure the presence of the digital evidence for the purpose of comparison to the data in the handheld computer.

The legal instruments that help in the examinations and search for digital evidence in handheld computers include software programs such as EnCase Neutrino, through which it is possible to examine all versions of the iPhone, ITouch, FTK, and Oxygen Forensic[95].

Today many handheld computers operate with the Android operating system[96]. The system is distributed by Google in cooperation with the Open Handset Alliance. This operating system was developed especially for mobile phones based on touch screens and for handheld computers. Towards the end of 2010, Android was crowned the most widespread operating system in the world of smartphones. For more on this issues, see the section on operating systems, in chapter 15 "General Explanation on the Structure of Computers and the Internet".

Legal Issues

The legal issues on this matter are similar to those concerning

---

[94] http://www.iwar.org.uk/comsec/resources/nist/pda-forensics-sp800-72.pdf
[95] https://viaforensics.com/android-forensics/
[96] https://viaforensics.com/android-forensics

personal computers in terms of the admissibility of the evidence taken from the handheld computer and/or admissible original evidence for all purposes. However, there are many obstacles before of the investigator or examiner is able to gain full legal access to the handheld computer in cases where the owners refuse to cooperate and/or the handheld computer is personal and private property rather than the property of an organization or business. In such cases n unlawful invasion and access to the device in question may be considered a criminal offense, and it is possible that it will entail issues pertaining to the protection of data and human rights.

Cellular Phones / Smart Phones

Today the mobile phone is far more than a cellular communications device. Modern cellular phones provide a broad range of services, like a computer and/or handheld computer, independent of place; namely, it is possible to use the device to connect to the Internet from almost any location in the world.

As mentioned, cellular devices include network and hardware components, as do handheld computers, and include contacts, diaries, stored files, photographs and videos from the built-in camera and of the ability to synchronize with personal computers. All of these functions are in addition to the devices ability to make and receive telephone calls. Many cellular phones are also capable of sending data and connecting to the Internet, both to surf the web and to receive and send digital mail.

In addition, almost all internet service providers accessible from desktop computers and laptop computers also are accessible from the modern cellular phone - a rapidly increasing, worldwide trend. Today's cellular phones include hardware components that allow it to connect to a local wireless network, thus making it more difficult to identify the IP address and the precise position of the wrongdoer.

Cellular devices usually include another hardware component, Bluetooth, which permits connection of wireless ear-buds to the cellular phone and communication with other, nearby, Bluetooth devices. Using Bluetooth the telephone may be in one location while the scene of the crime is in another. This creates a situation in which the device's location does not necessarily indicate the suspect's location. Cellular phones may also include satellite navigation systems a many smart phones have GPS software and make possible the installation of different types of navigation applications.

The variety of smart cellular telephones and their complexity cause the authorized computer investigator many problems. If all of the previous technologies that the investigator is required to understand and deal with where not enough, new cell-phone models enter the market constantly. Additionally, and unlike personal computers, which for the most part use operating systems from Microsoft or Macintosh (Mac OSX), some manufacturers of cellular phones develop private operating systems for their devices.

There are a number of different cell-phone operating systems in use today. Because of rapid technological advances, many of systems include a number of versions as manufacturers of cellular devices change frequently the operating systems and adjust them to meet the needs of a new device or model[97]. This necessitates a real investment on the part of the investigators and computer experts, since they must acquire and maintain considerable equipment, without which they will find it difficult to work. This equipment includes various connectors and adaptors, and electric cables and software for a variety of models.

Because of the number of available operating systems and the different versions available for and used by cellular phones, the wide variety of hardware that connects to different types of networks, the digital evidence experts face serious questions, such as what is the best way to extract and preserve evidence, how is it possible to ensure that the data that exists in the telephone will not be rewritten or lost, and how is it possible to extract all the data from the devices and the systems.

---

[97] On the matter of types of operating systems for cellular phones, see chapter 15, Operating Systems for Cellular Phones.

I will address this matter in chapter 6, "Digital Evidence in Mobile Devices". In addition, I will also refer to the *Guide for the Collection of Computer Based Digital Evidence*[98] and the legal guide for the handling of mobile phones of the United States National Institute for Standards and Technology[99].

A cellular phone that is seized when it is turned on is considered a telephone ready to receive conversations and messages. On this matter I would point out that device, if it is operating, should not be turned off until it has been examined and the possibility of damage to or destruction of data from powering down the device has been negated. Additionally, some cellular phones are protected by smart encryption. This locks the device the moment it is shut down and turning it on and restoring to full operation will not be possible without the owner's cooperation.

In certain cellular phone models of there is a volatile memory hardware component. Any data stored in this component and not saved will be lost when the device losses power or is turned off. Mobile phones with a volatile memory component should be kept in a working situation so as to maintain the data stored in the volatile memory. It is also important to block incoming calls. The correct procedure involves placing the device, while it is turned on and connected to a secure and stable power source, into a metal box or cage. This prevents the penetration of electromagnetic signals and block incoming calls.

Blocking incoming calls is a vital operation that address issues of data originality as some devices. New data and calls received after the seizure of the device could raise questions as to the date and time of seizure. Additionally,, some devices, by nature, erase old data and exchange it for new.

We shall now examine the basic functions of the cellular phone, namely incoming and outgoing calls. Cellular phones can be identified in two ways. First through a SIM card or a subscriber identity module[100].

---

[98] http://www.7safe.com/electronic_evidence/ACPO_guidelines_computer_evidence.pdf
[99] http://csrc.nist.gov/publications/nistir/nistir-7250.pdf
[100] USIMs are the equivalent for UMTS or 3G services.

This component identifies the device and its owner to the cellular network and also provides the means of payment according to the registered payment plan. The second method involves the identification of the cellular equipment on the international network. This is a hardware element that identifies every component separately. Known professionally as an IMEI component, this will be discussed in chapter 6 "Digital Evidence in Mobile Devices" and tin he chapter on "Terms and Definitions".

Most cellular phones include four elements containing unique information which, if relevant to the investigation, can be saved:

- The SIM card, which includes information regarding the telephone number.

- The IMSI, which is used for the identification of the device's position and also saves contacts and messages and international the technical code number identified with the device model.

- The telephone body, which includes hardware components, a hard drive which is used to store data, including details of contacts, messages, photographs, and Internet browsing data and details about incoming and outgoing telephone calls, including unanswered calls.

- Secure digital (SD) memory is a type of hard drive that can be used for the storage of any type of data and is inserted into designated slots in many cellular devices. The full name of this memory type is Secure Digital High Capacity Memory (SDHC)[101].

Thus if we need to seize and impound a cellular phone to access potential digital evidence, it will be necessary to get appropriate professional help at a very early stage, in order to ensure that the process of seizure and preservation will be executed in a manner that makes it possible to extract digital evidence, if found, from the device

---

[101] On this matter see chapter 15, definitions and terms, cellular devices.

and to ensure that the findings (the evidence) will constitute admissible evidence in legal proceedings.

Because of the unpredictability of the aforementioned topics, it is important to keep careful and precise records, with timestamps, during the preservation process. These records indicate, for example, whether the cellular phone was on and at the time it was seized. Based on these records it will be possible to decide whether to leave the phone on or to turn it off and why the selected action is to be taken. The aim is to ensure that the battery will last until the transfer of the device to the laboratory.

It is necessary to photograph the device from all sides and also, upon delivery to the laboratory, to inform the technician if calls and/or messages were received from the moment of seizure to the moment it arrived at the laboratory. Another directive that addresses this matter is that of the American National Institute of Standards and Technology (NIST) for the United States Department of Homeland Security[102].

Most cellular phones include a synchronization program provide by the manufacturer. This is a software program that backs up the phone's data on a personal computer. On this matter I would note that there is a considerable difference between the various programs. Some backup key definitions, some provide synchronization with well-known personal computer applications, such as Microsoft's email software program, and enable the transfer of data such as contact list details, diaries, memos, and 'tasks' from the telephone to the computer and vice versa.

If the phone is connected to a network, whether cellular of physically connected to a computer, then imaging and preservation of data is executed. As I have already noted, the computer investigator must deny the suspect access to the synchronizing computer and determine its location in order to seize it as well. This action data from the mobile cellular device to be crosschecked with data found on the computer used for data imaging and backup. This ensures reasonable

---

[102] http://csrc.nist.gov/publications/nistpubs/800-101/SP800-101.pdf

certainty regarding the reliability of the digital evidence.

I would note further that the cellular device's different hardware components should not be disassembled and/or separated until the device is in the examining laboratory. The disassembly of the hardware may cause loss of data and/or exclusion of the data as a faithful source in the legal proceedings.

Analyzing the Position of the Cellular Phone Device

As a part of the investigation process, law enforcement agencies are able to track the movement of the cellular phone by using signals sent from the cellular device as a part of an ongoing call or in general. Given that the device includes a Bluetooth hardware component, it is necessary to examine whether this component was used and to examine whether the suspect's position is identical to that of the cellular device.

In general, the cellular phones system relies on the existence of a large number of local base stations. These link the cellular telephone to the telecommunications network. Every cellular telephone supplier knows, at any given time, the precise position of each of its clients, namely the clients who carry active cellular phones. This enables communications to be facilitated through the closest base station. I would emphasize that the cellular devices are programmed to synchronize with converters (reception antennae distributed throughout the country), or in other words, to broadcast short transmissions from the cellular device to the reception antennae, while recording the position of the device in real-time.

Many cellular devices have miniature batteries, which are designed to maintain clock calibration in real-time and to save data and additional user definitions. In extreme cases, with a court order, it is possible to identify the position of the cellular device even when it is turned off. The cellular company saves the recorded data of the cellular device's position and can provide the data to law enforcement authorities, given the appropriate justification.

On the same matter, I would note that it is possible to assemble all of this data and to track the movements of the telephone over time, namely it is possible to obtain a precise 'picture' of what has been done. The level of precision depends on a number of factors, including the number of reception stations in the relevant area, lack of erroneous data readings, transmission breaks as the result of high buildings and other characteristics of the area, data transfer loads on broadcast antennae, and so on.

In Britain this data is saved for twelve months. In the European Union the law differs from country to country with data being saved for sixth months to two years[103]. We will address American law extensively later on. At this stage, I would note that until four years ago there was no law regarding the obligation of cellular providers and/or Internet providers to save data[104], similar to the instructions to save data contained in the European convention.

In the United States, the FBI requires Internet and cellular providers to save data for a period of at least eighteen months[105]. It should also be noted that in some states it is the duty of cellular providers and Internet providers, to save data for at least 24 months.

As we know, the wheels of justice turn slowly, and the loss of this type of data may be critical to the investigation process. These are data of serious importance, which can decisive in establishing whether the accused was present at the scene of the crime or proving the argument of 'I was in another place'[106], which is the accused right under Israeli law.

---

[103] Directive 2006/24/EC of the European Parliament and of the Council of 15 March 2006 on the retention of data generated or processed in connection with the provision of publicly available electronic communications services or of public communications networks and amending Directive 2002/58/EC". Official Journal of the European Union. April 13, 2006.

[104] Akrivopoulou, Christina; Psygkas, Athanasios (2010). Personal Data Privacy and Protection in a Surveillance Era: Technologies and Practices. Idea Group Inc. p. 257. ISBN 978-1-60960-083-9. "These civil liberties organizations also highlighted the absence of such a data retention obligation for ISPs in the US..."

[105] http://news.cnet.com/8301-13578_3-10448060-38.html .FBI wants records kept of Web sites visited

[106] Section 152 (3, 4) of the Law of the Criminal Code [Integrated Version], 1982.

The main limitation of this technique deals with the protection of privacy. In contrast to law enforcement investigations, data regarding the position of the cellular device will only be provided if there is Search and Seizure order under the auspices of a law enforcement agency or a court order. This remains true unless the owner of the cellular telephone agrees to being tracked. Private services of this type are available in a number of European countries and in Israel. Typical clients are parents who are anxious about their child's fate or businesses for which it is essential to know the workers location.

In Britain and in Israel the law demands the worker's explicit agreement in advance for the tracking the movement of the cellular device he owns. Through its map service, Google developed an application for cellular phones that provides a 'Where am I?' service which is based on a global positioning system - GPS. It should be noted that services based on GPS are far more precise for identifying the device's position than the providers' cellular antennae.

Regarding the many legal issues arising from the complexity of the cellular device and in light of the fact that this is, today, the most widely used communications device, and due to the many functions that it provides such as, photography, web surfing, file transfer, messaging, devices for satellite reception, and so on, a later chapter is devoted to this device..

Additional Storage Media: Photographs, Disk-on-Key, Media Players, and Other Mobile Media

Over the years and in light of technological developments, the dimensions of storage components have shrunk, and today they are smaller than ever before. Information storage cards, digital cameras, compact flash, disk-on-key, CD, and/or DVD can save and hold any and every type of file and data.

Alongside technological developments and the increase of storage volume, the price of the hardware has drastically declined. A disk-on-key that connects to the computer through a USB connection and has two gigabytes of memory cost about $150 in 2005; today a disk-on-key of this volume is often provided free, sometimes as part of a marketing campaign to promote a business.

At the start of the 2000's most laptop computers were equipped with small hard drives, and thus the user found it necessary to use external storage means such as disk-on-key and/or different types of discs. Memory cards such as those used on cameras, in media players, and/or in cellular phones are today smaller than a postage stamp, and their price has dropped to a few dollars.

The source of the problem is the accessibility of the storage media and their small dimensions, which enables them to be concealed in a pocket or in location, so that only a very careful examination of the computer or the cellular phone can discover whether one of these components was ever connected to the device.

I would further note that software development companies take pains to create software of a relatively small volume, so that all of a company's financial records, client records and the research and development program can be concealed on a storage component with a volume of just two gigabytes. For comparison .on storage medium of this volume it is possible to store 100,000 low resolution photographs and upload them to the Internet. A search for such a storage medium can be compared to searching for a 'needle in a haystack': all the wrongdoer needs to do is to destroy the memory card after he has uploaded the data, and thus the evidence has disappeared.

On this topic there are a number of schools of thought. The first states that it is necessary to conduct tests to validate the connection of external storage hardware on the website under investigation. Such an action will prevent the suspect from causing the evidence to disappear when computer investigators leave the scene. Another school of thought states that it is necessary to track the suspect and conduct the examination only in the laboratory, so as to minimize any damage that may be caused to digital evidence found in the hardware due to the lack of appropriate tools.

In my opinion, both approaches are correct. The chief field

investigator must examine the all the evidence and make an intelligent decision regarding the quality and quantity of the evidence and the likelihood that the suspect is carrying a small memory component. In addition, this person must document the reasons for their decision to act in a certain way.

Components can be divided into two parts: those connecting to the computer and drawing power from an external source and those taking power from the computer to which they are connected. If the external memory component draws power from a source other than the computer, then it is necessary to seize all the hardware components, including transformers.

Most of these media types function in a fashion similar to a hard drive. As a result, it is often possible to reconstruct the data contained in them. Therefore, it is important that all of the suspect's computer components that include data relevant to the incident or to the case, be seized and imaged appropriately.

Legal Issues

The main legal issue in a corporate investigation that does not include law enforcement elements, is that the components may be the suspect's (employee's) private property and it is possible that there is no legal basis for the confiscation of the component.

Global Positioning Systems (GPS) Components

In the past GPS, systems were characterized by maps that contained limited details. Their technological development was complex, their cost was high, and therefore most public and private sectors did not use them. In the middle of the first decade of the millennium, prices dropped dramatically, specifications broadened, and hardware components developed significantly. As a result, the components became so widespread that by 2007 the United Kingdom's National Bureau of Statistics included components of satellite navigation systems in the 'basket' of products and services that it used to measure inflation.

Today the use of these systems and their components is widespread. In addition, different types of high volume storage are also widely available. Together they enable the computer to include a large number of maps and points of interest, essential services, and other aids. The storage cards can be found in specialized navigational devices and in navigational devices built-in a car. They are also found in laptop computers, handheld computers, and smart phones.

In light of technological improvements and improvement of maps and reception ability, the possibilities for finding digital evidence in the devices, as part of the process of legal examination, has also increased. By their nature and because of their technological complexity, satellite navigation components are more expensive than computer components and, for our purposes, primarily the cost of hard drives. Therefore, in order to reduce costs, simple devices and removable memory cards are used.

The difficulties facing the legal digital evidence examiner when searching for and examining digital evidence are similar to those encountered in the case of handheld computers and cellular phones. On this matter, I would note that there are a number of shared global standards, for instance the communications standard that links different naval digital devices, including receptors (NMEA)[107]. This communication protocol is used to transmit data to and from the satellite.

The manufacturers of satellite navigation systems developed unique hardware components for the device's internal design, and these are constantly developing and changing as new models are released. TomTom is one of the most widespread GPS devices in the world, especially in the private sector. Some of the components of the device use Linux technology. Other manufacturers have assimilated Microsoft's Windows Mobile operating system in their devices the out of financial considerations.

Regardless of the device's operating system and/or hardware

---

[107] See the chapter of terms and definitions, components of global positioning systems.

components, all devices are, for the most part, programmed to document the destinations that the device travelled to, including saved destinations, 'points of interest', historical routes, and pre-programmed user definitions . Most GPS devices keep records, and sometimes it is possible to reconstruct data that was erased from certain hardware components.

GPS devices can be connected to personal computers for purposes of backup, updates, planning, and software system definitions. The manufacturer provides the updates, as well as the synchronization software, as with handheld computers and cellular phones.

One of the initial actions that legal computer investigators must do is to examine whether there is synchronization with the computer and whether the navigation device contains any useful information. In addition, there are GPS devices that can connect to cellular phones using Bluetooth, and under these circumstances it is often possible to retrieve telephone books, conversation lists, and even text messages.

Legal Issues

When executing a seizure warrant and/or the authorized authority makes a decision to seize a navigation component, the legal computer investigator must understand the contribution that the GPS device may have on the investigation's overall goals. If there exists a suspicion that a vehicle was misused or stolen, then the GPS can be connected to a cellular phone that can collect data from it.

The primary legal issue in the investigation that does not connect to law enforcement is if the component is the suspect's private and personal property. If this is the case, a warrant for seizure is required. Even if the employer provided the suspect with the device, the right to confiscate it may be limited, unless there is prior written agreement ahead as part of the employment contract and/or within the framework of any agreement signed at a later date and which constitutes part of the employment contract.

Data and Telecommunication Contents (Soundtrack)

There are few technical obstacles standing in the way of data collection and telecommunication content , especially when there are companies with advanced, smart technology as well as servers for information collection of and a range of technologies and methods for Voice over the Internet (VoIP) transmission[108].

The main goal of the telephony system is to facilitate telephone conversations through varying types of switchboards. In addition, the systems provide data regarding numbers dialed and on the time and duration of the call. These aids are intended to help manage costs, monitor conversations, and use additional smart functions to examine the quality of hardware components and the quality voice transmission/reception.

Consequently, output and data produced from the system have considerable value in the investigation process. To capture the content of conversations, a recording hardware component, usually a small hard drive with a large storage volume is installed on the −being monitored and/or on the main, secure server. Many businesses routinely record telephone conversations, as a means of verifying and executing transactions and/or to examine the workers' interaction with callers in order to identify areas for improvement in service.

On this matter, I would note that digital evidence experts face an immediate and important issue, namely, the ability to prove and show that the logs and/or recordings constitute original evidence. In other words, the digital evidence investigator must have the knowledge and the ability to manage and work with the telephony system on the capture site, including the ability to provide an explanation in all issues pertaining to the manner in which the data were collected and to the issue of the safety procedures that were adopted, including documentation of all decisions made and the methods of data preservation used.

---

[108] See VoIP (Voice Over Internet Protocol) in the chapter of definitions and terms.

After collection of the digital file, it is necessary to preserve it in its totality and then to take a 'digital fingerprint' using MD5[109], in order to protect the data from change following its seizure.

On the matter of voice monitoring, it is necessary to have the employee's declaration that he knew that conversations within the organization were being monitored. If the decision is to execute a partial capture of the soundtrack, then the digital evidence experts should use all means of caution. In addition, they must be able to provide an appropriate explanation for the decisions they made, including detailing the methods used for capturing a portion of the soundtrack, an explanation of technical terms, and verification and adjustment of time periods.

After all these steps have been completed, it is necessary to submit the logs in their entirety for the purpose of examination, in order to prevent data editing after seizure. Like the process required in the case of evidence from computerization systems, it is necessary to save and document processes; here too a neutral evidence expert needs to be able to repeat the processes of the retrieval of the evidence in the same manner and reach the same conclusion.

Legal Issues Regarding Employer-Employee Relations

The main difficulty in this area is the legal issue. Take, for instance, the monitoring and supervision of data and contents that derive from intra-organizational communication. Every action of the employer must meet the test of 'necessity', or 'least degree of harm', and the 'process' test.

In British law, within the framework of legal policy for every type of supervision, a number of principles were determined on the matter of 'least degree of harm'. As with Israeli law expressed in the National Labor Court's ruling on the matter of Tal Isakov - the Ministry of Industry[110].

---

[109] On the matter of MD5, see the chapter of explanations and terms, terms and definitions on the matter of telephony systems.

[110] http://www.moital.gov.il/NR/rdonlyres/689B0383-5FA7-4AC8-B964-11D974DD1AD2/0/isakov.pdf

The employer must examine alternative means for surveillance including technologies designed to block inappropriate use made of the computer by employees. Preference should be given to the use of surveillance technology that can constitute an appropriate substitute for accessing the contents and data of personal correspondence and reading digital email content.

The basic authority in British law for all issues pertaining to private telecommunication services is found in section 1 (6) of RIPA[111], which states that:

The circumstances under which a person delays communication during the submission of their information through a private telecommunication system are such that removes his behavior from the area of criminal responsibility, according to sub-section (2):

(A)   This is a person with the right to control the operation or use of the system or to supervise it or

(B)   This is a person who has received explicit or implicit agreement on the part of such a person to execute a delay of this type.

Detailed legislation that is related to legal delays are found primarily in the Telecommunication Laws 2000 (Legal Business Practice) (delay of communication means)[112]. To be included in the regulations, it is necessary to meet a closed list from which the data is derived, namely, the goals for which the information relevant to the business and/or private person was collected and that the use of the telecommunication systems is under the business's ownership.

---

[111] http://www.legislation.gov.uk/ukpga/2000/23/section/1
[112] http://www.legislation.gov.uk/uksi/2000/2699/contents/made

The following list presents the circumstances under which British law permits the monitoring and collection of information from the Internet:

- To establish the existence of facts.
- To ensure protocol adherence.
- To ensure the fulfillment of regulations, including quality control and training.
- To preserve national security. On this matter only certain public office holders are entitled to authorize monitoring.
- To prevent a crime or to reveal suspicions of a crime.
- To investigate or to discover illegal use of telecommunication systems.
- To ensure effective operation of the organizational system.
- In the event of anonymous telephone calls to emergency lines.

In Britain, similar to the collective agreement in force in Israel, there is a clear guideline on the issue of employer - employee relations. The guideline regulates procedures for the employment of workers within the technological context and defines the employers' obligations[113]. The guideline determines principles for the protection of data, forbids making decisions solely on the basis of processed data, requires employers to inform the workers regarding supervision policy, and sets limitations on the degree of supervision.

In addition, the guideline obligates the clear and explicit agreement of the employee before the collection of medical data or medical information. The guideline's third section addresses the means with which firms are legally entitled to track the email messages of their employees.

The employer has the right to track and monitor employees email messages, providing that the employer informs the employees, beforehand and explaining to the reasons for tracking and monitoring

---

[113]http://www.ico.org.uk/upload/documents/library/data_protection/practical_applicatio
n/ico_emppraccode.pdf

email. . The guideline for the protection of data covers a broad variety of supervisory and surveillance activities, including opening email messages, listening to voice mail messages on cellular telephones, examination of Internet use and closed circuit television recording.

On this matter I would note that companies are cautioned against clandestine and unreasonable surveillance of employees. This action is permitted only with the permission of law enforcement agencies and subject to their request. Companies and private individuals are entitled to receive, from telephonic service providers and/or cellular telephone services copies of personal telephone accounts and detailed records of incoming and outgoing calls. The permission derives from the fact that these are personal data owned by the company or user.

In practical terms, there is an inner contradiction in the European Parliament's telecommunications standard (Standard EC/66/97)[114] that negates the possibility of saving personal data for a longer period of time than necessary for business goals. In other words, records of conversations from earlier periods may not be available.

According to the nature of organizations, monitoring is both intra and extra-organizational. Data is transferred and collected by the main server and then filtered according to a variety of predefined criteria. Devices that collect data from the organization's network are generally found in regular use, so as to supervise the quality of the data and data movement loads through the communication network and to perform a variety of technical diagnoses.

When suspicion arises regarding any type of offense, the system shifts to a supervision mode and begins collection of data governed by a precise list of procedures that should be defined beforehand, to assure the quality and reliability of the information collected in an emergency situation. From a legal perspective, it is necessary to examine a number of technical issues related to the order of actions and to produce documentation and reports. The documentation needs to include a precise technical definition of the structure of the communication

---

[114] http://eur-lex.europa.eu/LexUriServ/LexUriServ.do?uri=CELEX:31997L0066:EN:HTML

network under supervision, it must include all computer systems and technical devices, and documentation of the hardware and software used for monitoring.

In addition, the organization must provide a detailed explanation of the processes and the means used to preserve the data and it must document what was seized and produce from it clear and structured presentations.

With regard to Israeli law the processes detailed must meet the test of 'admissibility of an institutional record', section 36 of the Evidence Ordinance. This matter will be addressed further in the chapter "Computerized Output and Institutional Evidence".

General Legal Issues

Subject to the awarding of appropriate authority and search warrants, law enforcement authorities and the governmental agencies in the United States, Britain, and Israel have access to Internet data and to contents that belong to private individuals and businesses in the field of telecommunications. This is also true in the issue of public companies, communication companies, cellular telephone companies and Internet providers.

In Britain a central law is the Regulation of Investigatory Powers Act 2000 (RIPA 2000)[115], from which it is possible to learn that it is illegal to block or prevent any type of communication during transmission with the consent of only one of the parties to the conversation or without legal authorization.

In Israel the situation is similar. The body authorized to approve wiretapping is the Minister of Defense, and this reasons of state security. The Police, with the permission of the President of the District Court or his deputy, are also authorized to implement a wiretap in order to prevent offenses and/or identify criminals. However, this is only possible after a judge has considered the extent and the possibility of an infringement of privacy as opposed to the severity of the case

---

[115] http://www.legislation.gov.uk/ukpga/2000/23/contents

being investigated in order to create a balance between the sides. In special and urgent cases, the Chief of Police is also authorized to approve a wiretap as detailed in the 1979 Wiretapping Law, section 7[116].

In Britain, as in Israel, in extreme cases permission may be granted for a wiretap without a court order. Such authorization may come from an authorized person such as a police officer in order to prevent offenses and/or identify. This is possible when the conversation will be held in a public place where it can reasonably be expected that the conversation will be overheard, without the suspects consent. This includes locations such as bars, coffee shops, in an elevator, on the street and so on. Conversations may also be listened to and recorded when held where a prisoner is being held – an interview room, a cell or in jail.

The law in Britain differentiates between disturbances in communication devices and/or the transfer of, including who called whom, when, and for how long, and between the examination of content and related issues. Transfer data also includes positional data, such as the place where the cellular telephone company keeps records of a specific base station at which a given cellular telephone was recorded in the past.

In British Law some of the data that Internet and cellular providers hold and collect are classified as 'communication resources data'. The Minister of the Interior can issue search warrants to examine content, subject to a variety of criteria that include 'national security interests', 'for the purpose of prevention and/or discovery of serious crimes' and 'for the purpose of protecting the economic wellbeing of Britain'.

The Minister of the Interior must be convinced that the process involved in the seizure of content is essential in the context of the circumstances and the severity of the issue. Section 17 of the Interception of Evidence Act[117] allows the law enforcement and

---

[116] http://www.nevo.co.il/law_html/law01/077_001.htm#Seif9
[117] http://www.official-documents.gov.uk/document/cm73/7324/7324.pdf

intelligence authorities to intercept communications data, including digital mail.

The authority of a warrant issued by the Secretary of State: The warrant is given for each of three goals – in the interests of national security, for the prevention and/or discovery of a serious crime, and for the preservation of the economic wellbeing of the countries of the kingdom.

Sections 21-25 describe the circumstances under which permits and memoranda are issued for the collection, discovery, and exposure of communication data and by whom. It is possible to issue permits and memoranda of this type for national security, in order to prevent or identify or the prevention of public disorder, for the economic welfare of Britain, and for public security, and also for civil goals in the broader sense, such as protection of public health, tax evaluation or imposition, debt, levy or another enforcement procedure and contribution to or payment to the government. It is possible to issue permits, also in cases of emergency, to prevent death, or prevent or ease harm or any other damage to an individual's physical or mental health or easing of harm or damage to the person's physical or mental health and for any other purpose contained in the order issued by the Secretary of State.

There is a defined list of 'authorized persons', who are permitted to issue official permits, providing the permit and its scope is essential and proportional to the circumstances.

Assuming that the data were dealt with appropriately, it is necessary to view them as digital evidence that is admissible in the legal process. It is possible to use this evidence not only to prove that the conversation occurred at a certain time but also to show and to prove patterns of relationships that may themselves hint at relations between the parties involved.

In Britain, as in Israel, within the framework that requires the disclosure of evidence to all parties involved, there is a mutual commitment by all sides to reveal all documents or evidence that could influence the result of the dispute.

With regard to third parties, namely, the Internet and cellular providers, the civil process for litigants seeking to obtain information from a company and/or a person who is not a p[arty to the litigation includes the necessity of obtaining a court order according to CPR 31.17. In the event that information is required before the commencement of the legal process, such as an *ex parte* application for the disclosure of the identity of an anonymous offender, according to CPR 31.17, 31.18, the action is facilitated through a court order for the disclosure of documents[118].

A court order is issued only in cases where the documents for which full disclosure is requested support the petitioner's request to the Court in a real manner and/or may significantly influence the case and/or the legal process as a whole. The judge will expect to be provided evidence and proof to support these claims.

Norwich Pharamacal[119] or the Antonin Filler order created a list of checks that the Court will conduct before granting the order. This process is intended to ascertain that:

- The evidence to be obtained to ensure that justice prevails.
- The evidence is essential to the success of the proposed legal claim, whether to identify the defendants or to obtain essential information.
- The timing is right.
- The third party, namely the person against who the order is issued, is involved in the said offense, even if in good faith, does not serve as a witness, and is not a party to the suit.
- The petitioner to the Court provided consistent data with which it was possible to assess the petitioner's full and honest disclosure.

In orders of this type, use is made of the legal processes framework adopted to act against copyright violators who are suspected

---

[118] http://www.justice.gov.uk/courts/procedure-rules/civil/rules/part31#IDARPTBB
[119] http://www.bailii.org/uk/cases/UKHL/1973/6.html

of stealing video games, computer programs, and films. The stolen, pirated material is, for the most part, converted through file sharing websites.

As a part of the order, the Court will request the disclosure the suspected IP address, which is affiliated with the website, the server, or subscribers connected to the computers suspected of copyright violations. Later the relevant internet service provider, to provide all information pertaining to the subscriber using the specific IP address at the time in question.

I would stress and point out that the only bodies that know the identity of the individual with the specific IP address and/or geographic location are the Internet and cellular providers. This brings us back to the issue of the time required by the providers to save and document browsing data, including documentation of the precise position of the IP address.

In light of the fact that wrongs may often be discovered years later and also that the wheels of justice often turn slowly, I would recommend that Internet and cellular providers be obligated to save data of this type for at least seven years.

In the physical world there is a clear technical differentiation between content and means of communication. The means of communication, such as digital mail, Internet browsing, cellular telephones, fixed line telephony and protocols for the digital transmission of voice over the Internet (VoIP) are the technical aspect. The transmitted text, the words written in emails, the content of websites, including pictures and video clips, as well as what is said over the internet (VoIP) - all this is the content.

Often the distinction is not clear and it is possible that there is room for clarification of legislation on the part of the Court and/or legislature. This distinction has significance in serious issues, for instance when will an email message be considered a message that has reached its destination and when it is considered a message in transit, in which instance its interception will be considered wiretapping.

In the ruling of Israel's Supreme Court of Criminal Appeal 10343/01 Mondir Badir v. State of Israel, with President Barak, Retired, and the Judges Dorner and Hayot presiding, it was determined that:

> Wiretapping is considered only if it is performed online. Therefore, listening to voice mail when entering an email and retrieval of information stored on the computer, both digital mail and voice messages, is not wiretapping – and thus a search warrant is enough and it is not necessary to obtain a Court order or to act in accordance with the Protection of Privacy Law[120].

In the matter of Binyamin Eliyahua against Tiberius municipality, Judge Ohad said:

> "I myself see no point in the distinction and separation between a message that arrived at its destination and was read and a message that is found en route to its destination, since the legislative purpose of wiretapping is intended to prevent a third person from listening to the content of conversations between two when neither of them agrees to the conversation being listened to".

I will now examine the matter in-depth, beginning with email messages. Today there are a number of different types of email services. The most common include email services that are offered 'free' by different content suppliers, for instance, Google provides Gmail, Yahoo has its email service, and there are many others. There are also private email services which provide private accounts and/or email servers for organizations, such as Microsoft's Outlook or its email server Outlook Exchange.

In the case of email accounts provided of content providers such as Google, email messages will never reach the final destination. Rather

---

[120] http://www.psakdin.co.il/fileprint.asp?filename=/plili/public/art_ccid.htm

the reverse is true; the user accesses the email server to view messages intended for them. Thus, the question is asked: does the seizure of material in an email account such as that of a content provider like Google require approval according to the Wiretapping Law rather than the Privacy Protection Law? Moreover, it is necessary to differentiate between Internet providers and content providers. Email accounts of this type (like Gmail) are from content providers and not Internet providers.

In this same issue, but from a different point of view, Microsoft's email software also raises some interesting questions. As opposed to a company that defines its email server as an independent service divorced from an Internet provider, in the case of Microsoft, for instance, the private user uses the services of the Internet provider via the POP3 protocol (See the chapter on terms and protocols). The basic email account is defined by the Internet provider, and when the user opens the email program on his personal computer, he connects to the Internet provider's email server and retrieves all email messages. Put simply, the mail box on the Internet provider server is temporary storage, and when the email account is opened on the user's computer all data is transferred to the local computer. Hence, the question arises, are the messages on the Internet provider's email server, like the Google email account of, considered messages that have reached their destination or are they still in transit?

In my opinion, the answer is clear. Given the fact that the email accounts are, in both cases, designated, for the user alone, and that the user assumes that other people will not have access to or be able to read their messages, it is necessary to view such messages as messages that have reached their final destination, namely these are not to be considered messages in transit. This is also true regarding the short message service (SMS) should the cellular phone be turned off for any reason.

As mentioned, over the years technology develops and the legislature and the Courts create legal precedents and thus the way of dealing in certain cases is determined. The voice over Internet (VoIP) technology is difficult to interpret legally: the finished product is similar to that produced by 'traditional' telephone systems but the technical system is different in both cases.

In the United States, Congress has deliberated the matter of a change to the Foreign Intelligence Surveillance Act, which determined procedures for the physical and digital surveillance and collection of information relating to both American citizens and permanent residents who are suspected of espionage and violation of United States law or those of a territory under U.S. control[121].

In principle, the United States National Security Agency is not permitted, by law, to listen to the conversations of United States citizens without proper authorization. However, since the development of VoIP technology, it is significantly more difficult to determine the actual location of the recipient.

Hence, the perception that it is easy to monitor an IP address by the path it takes through communications routers is mistaken. Because of their complexity, technology and the tools designed to combat criminal forensics blur the router's location and that of the IP address and provide a false picture. Thus, there is a very real difficulty involved in the identification of the precise location of the parties in a conversation.

The lack of knowledge creates fears in the intelligence community because of the argument that terrorists can use VoIP technology to transmit information and to organize attacks against the United States and its allies. According to the legislature, lacking a clear identification of the conversation's source, it will be very difficult to receive approval to monitor information. It is my opinion that, as a result of the global network's structure and technological progress as these reflect on Internet accessibility, browsing speed and the amount of information that is transmitted across the Internet, the United States and its allies will be forced, as part of a global defense constellation, to allow the legal authorities and intelligence organizations to monitor internet audio

---

[121] 50 USC Chapter 36 – Foreign Intelligence Surveillance

as well as all the information transmitted on the Internet.

According to legislatures in the United States, Britain, and Israel, the goal of the law is to protect the allied states from foreign threats, namely, this is a supreme value that allows for damage to the rights of the individual. On the matter of the harm the rights of the individual, the predominant approach is that there exists a duty to use monitoring technology that searches for malicious definitions and expressions. This the doctrine of the 'least possible harm' – since a technology as utilized by a machine is devoid of emotions and searches for the definitions solely according to its definitions and instructions.

The source of the problem lays in the ability of the criminal and terrorist organizations to easily trick the search mechanisms. The following is a basic example: the word 'terror' is defined in the system as a malicious word and information about its use should be monitored. When this word is written in the following manner, (1)t---(1)e---(1)r---(1)r---(1)o---(1)r" then the search engine will not necessarily identify it as a malicious word that necessitates examination.

This is a very basic example. In essence, there are an infinite number of variations including the reversal of words, the reversal of letters, encryption of parts of the word, and more. Therefore, for the security of the citizens of the allied nations and under the painstaking supervision of a number of independent agencies, it is necessary to allow the legal authorities and the intelligence organizations to listen, eavesdrop, and intercept information that is transmitted both online and on traditional telephony lines.

For this reason, it is important to differentiate between technology and content. It may become clear that some content is relevant to the issue of security offenses whilst different content will be defined as civilian and inadmissible in the legal process. On the matter of technology, it is necessary to allow the legal authorities to have unlimited access, although definitely controlled, in the fight against international and/or security offenses.

Today providers of voice over the Internet services are required to aid law enforcement authorities[122]. The communication providers and hardware manufacturers are required to make a change in the design of the equipment, so as to ensure that it will include the surveillance components that allow federal agencies to supervise, in real-time, all telephones, equipment, and/or Internet hardware and the voice transmission over the Internet. The goal is to improve the ability of the law enforcement and global intelligence agencies to conduct digital surveillance over the Internet.

IP Address

An IP address is a combination of numbers in a definite order that identifies the location of a specific computer and other internet connected devices attached to it.. The IP address can be seen as a temporary or fixed identity card for a computer, a cellular phone, or any other device connected to the Internet wherever in the world and at a certain point in time. The IP address may be recorded automatically in a variety of log files and in the computer's configuration. IP addresses will appear, for instance, in logs produced by Internet servers, in THE meta-data labels of digital mail, and in other documentation areas.

In light of the existence of system's that act to prevent digital identification, caution is necessary regarding the reliability and degree of identify of separate IP addresses. As a result, the data must be supported with additional facts and evidence.

In principle, communication networks connect computers and other devices such as printers, cameras, navigation systems and more. The devices can transmit data amongst them– there is no need for every device to include a two-way connection to every other device. To make this connection to the network possible a network card and a number of definitions are required. For example, every computer or device must be identified separately by its own, unique IP network address. The component must be connected with a network cable and/or other connection that connects, at least at one point, to every computerized device and to devices such as routers that allow

---

[122] http://www.fcc.gov/encyclopedia/communications-assistance-law-enforcement-act

communications between computers.

Network definitions, known as 'protocols' or 'network standards', connect to hardware connections. There exist a number of proprietary commercial communication networks, but the most widespread communication network is the TCP/IP communications network, which includes open source code and which is supported by a large number of software programs and network components. TCP/IP constitutes the basis for the Internet.

The TCP/IP protocol is constantly being developed and improved. The present network is IP version 4. The new network, currently being deployed, is IP version 6 (IPv6). The main reason for this new version is a global lack of IP addresses and the attempt to improve the ability to identify surfers on the Internet.

The problem is very similar to that of dialing codes in the world of telephony: computerized systems that include software and hardware components change and improve every few years, since growth predictions lower and not commensurate with reality.

With IP version 4, addresses are indicated using a decimal point that separates groups of, at the most, three digit numbers. Addresses are sent under a program implemented by the IANA (Internet Assigned Numbers Authority)[123] and by the Regional Internet Registry (RIR). Every RIR has, in a publicly available and searchable library records indicating the identity of the 'owners' of every address. The library known as the Who. A number of user friendly Internet websites enable an IP address to be inputted and information on the identity of the IP address's user and/or domain name to be obtained, for instance: http://who.godaddy.com.

In practice there are two methods to track IP addresses, and investigators must understand the principles behind them. One way involves translating the network addresses, while the second is a communication protocol that dynamically allocates IP addresses to

---

[123] http://www.iana.org

computers in a local network (dynamic addressing). This is achieved through a configuration protocol for the dynamic host configuration protocol (DHCP).

When translating a network address, corporate communication networks are used extensively. Every device, computer component, handheld computer, laptop computer and printer includes an IP address on the internal communications network. In many cases, the address is in the range of 192.168.0.0 and above. For internal communication only, the components can communicate among themselves directly. If they are required to communicate with the outside world, they do this through a 'router', in collaboration with the telecommunication service.

To differentiate from internal IP addresses, the router is linked to the Internet with an external Internet address. There are a number of ways to identify the external address. A convenient method is through a websites (Who Is), which will read and display the address. Many of these websites also provide reports on Internet service providers and attempts to provide an approximate geographic position.

The role of the router is to track requests from internal computers and other devices and transmit them, via its external IP address to the world. Hence, it is possible that it will appear to the outside world that there is only one computer or device, while the internal communications network may include dozens or perhaps hundreds of computers, including additional hardware components such as cellular phones, handheld computers, and so on.

The dynamic IP address is a means employed by the Internet services provider to make the use of publicly available addresses more efficient. Internet services providers have a database of IP addresses, which in general contains fewer IP addresses than the number of their clients. The system is based on the premise that the majority of internet users do not require a permanent connection to the Internet. Therefore, the user can use dynamic IP address for a short period of time and as necessary and will not necessarily need to purchase acquire a permanent, regular address.

The Internet connection will be defined automatically by software installed in a modem or router. This transmits to the Internet supplier that it wants to use the dynamic hosting configuration protocol (DHCP), which fundamentally constitutes a request to the Internet provider: please approve the external IP address.

It is necessary to take into consideration that the IP address of single or separate subscribers is not saved after disconnection. In other words, each time the user connects to the Internet provider they receive a new IP address from a database of available addresses. Consequently, the IP address itself is not sufficiently unique for the identification of the user of a specific computer. Additional information is required.

The Internet provider's computer systems there is equipment that allocates dynamic IP addresses to clients. The most frequent allocation method is the RADIUS protocol (Remote Authentication Dial-In User Service). This protocol verifies the data, provides a permit, and generates a report. A RADIUS log is produced and saved on the Internet supplier's servers. If the investigator encounters the IP address that matches the time or date stamp that he is examining, then, regardless of what is required in the legal process, he must complete the following stages.

- Locate the Internet service provider (ISP) using the Who Is website.

- In a civil case, obtain the proper legal permit, without which the Internet supplier is forbidden to reveal information and data on a specific IP address at a specific point in time.
- If of the issue involves a number of computers connected through one account but no records exist as to which computer was active at a specific time, then it is necessary to seize all computer and hardware components that can connect to the Internet.

- Every computer may have more than one authorized user, and therefore it is necessary to clarify the chronology of computer activity in order to ascertain who used it at specific times.

- It is necessary to take into account that the data will not always produce completely reliable results. For instance, if the account's communication network is am unsecured wireless network it is possible that an unknown third party, connecting from as far away as 400 meters from the wireless router is situated, is responsible for the activity.

To resolve such issues it is necessary, for the most part, to conduct a legal examination of all the computers and hardware equipment connected to the Internet that were also connected to the suspected equipment, in order to determine if activities took place that can be linked to events that lead to the original IP address records .

In the newer, advanced version of the addresses protocol, IPv6, the number of available IP addresses will be far greater. IPv6 addresses are in eight groups of four digits separated by decimal points, using base 16. Operating systems such as Microsoft's Windows 7 and above are already prepared to use IPv6 technology.

In Israel, like the rest of the world, the volume of connections to the new technology is still significantly low. It is my opinion that IPv6 technology will solve majority of anonymous issues on the Internet, if not all of them.

Definite identification of individuals solely through the IP address will not be completely possible, since it is likely, for instance, in public places like universities and cafés for example, that will be more than one person using a specific computer. Thus, this is an issue that has still to be addressed and resolved. It is also possible that the computer was attacked by a Trojan horse virus and was under remote control.

Data from the Internet Service Providers (ISP)

Internet providers in practice provide a package of services for a client. Typically, these include an Internet connection and digital mail services, which include receiving and sending messages via the Internet. Digital mail addressed to to clients are supposed to be received through the Internet supplier and then saved on its servers until the client uses the mail program to read the messages, whether by connecting and moving the messages to his personal computer or whether by opening the inbox through a browser.

The primary services Internet companies provide include hosting of websites that may include considerable information. These websites include digital commerce websites which accept transactions from surfers, from credit card companies and which create records about the company processes, including financial data of various types.

After the collapse of the Twin Towers and following the perceptual change regarding the importance of saving and backing-up organizational data, Internet providers began providing and marketing a new service, known commercially as 'the cloud'. This is a designated computer or server, connected to the Internet, onto which it is possible to store a variety of expert services. In legal terms, the Internet provider acts, for some of these functions, as a 'public conduit' or main channel that can be used by the general public, similar to services of communications and cellular companies that specialize in vocal communication systems.

Naturally, the operational mechanisms of Internet providers create a variety of logs essential for business, for maintaining the quality of service or setting prices, including for backup and security services. From the perspective of the digital evidence expert and/or law enforcement authorities, the volume of information stored on the Internet provider servers is vast and begins with the verification of the user service's remote dial-in log (RADIUS).

Legal Issues

As a rule, Internet providers, everywhere in the world, can immediately provide client details, including personal data and patterns of usage on the Internet server. However, the Internet providers cannot provide all data regarding third parties that connect to the Internet from a public place, for example cafés. I would state that the difficulty can be overcome by the verification and identification of users connecting to the Internet from a public place, even if this is a free service available to all.

Internet websites are hosted on an Internet provider's servers, with each being associated with a collection of servers known as a "farm". The provider can save Internet logs documenting traffic to and from the server. It is important to emphasize that these logs are not meant to be available to those without authorization or those with investigative authority (RIPA 2000)[124] or a court order.

Email messages are held temporarily on the Internet provider's digital email server computers of, before the user downloads them to their personal computer.

According to British law, while still on the server computers, digital email is considered to be a message found in the public domain for the purposes of investigation. According to Israeli law, such email messages are considered to have reached their final destination, namely, they are subject to the Privacy Protection Law and not to the Wiretapping Law.

On the basis of British law, to obtain information regarding the movement of data, appropriate permission, according to chapter 2 of RIPA 2000, is required. This evidence will be admissible, and the use of this evidence will be permitted to show that communication existed between specific people at a given time. However, at this stage, publication of the content. Furthermore, in British law, to obtain the content, it is mandatory to obtain a court order signed by the Ministry of Justice and the findings may only be used for the purpose of

---

[124] http://www.legislation.gov.uk/ukpga/2000/23/contents

obtaining intelligence information.

In the civil cases, litigants who search for information regarding an individual who is not a party to the legal process are required to have a court order according to CPR 31.17. This order provides legal coverage during implementation. Information can be obtained beforehand according to CPR 31.18 and more specifically through Norwich Pharmacal Decree. On this matter, in Israel, the Antonin Filler Order, drawn from British ruling, is more accepted, and hence the source of the similarity.

Digital Evidence from the Internet

It is possible that information contained in digital mail and/or on the website will be necessary as digital evidence. This can be messages of different types, for instance, an offer to purchase something, harmful text, harassment, misuse of property or any confidential information.

This raises the question as to how this type of data should be saved in order to ensure its admissibility in the legal process or to provide it to law enforcement agencies.

The first and simplest possibility, is to print the webpage. In most cases, everything shown on the browser's screen will be printed this includes the lower heading with details of the URL address (Internet website and specific page), alongside the time and date stamp. Since this is not an institutional record and is subject to undocumented changes, the printout may be disqualified within the framework of the admissibility of digital evidence,. Sadly, this argument is also valid regarding saving on an external drive, a CD and/or disk-on-key.

The Microsoft Internet Explorer and the Mozilla browser offer the possibility of saving the web page on a local computer (web page complete) in the basic Internet format (HTML). However, in this case as well, change of content before the capture is simple and easy.

Today there are a number of software programs that can save an entire website or part of it, including the structure of the website's libraries, and which can save such documentation on external hardware, such as a disk-on-key, for examination at a later stage. The software programs start the documentation process from the website's 'top' page or the homepage, and then identifies and follows all links and, in the process, capturing their content. This is known as "spidering". In addition, the software can supervise changes executed in the website after copying has been completed and document data that may help during the investigation.

There are two types of software programs for the capture of Internet websites. One type enables viewing of the entire website off-line, through the user's personal computer. In order for all the links to work, it is possible that website pages may need to be altered internally for viewing convenience, but with a loss of legal accuracy. In addition, website capture software is required that downloads copies of the original pages. In practice, it is sometimes necessary to combine both approaches.

These methods are subject to a number of limitations that should be taken into consideration. The first is that what is viewed on the screen is not necessarily what is found at a specific moment on the website. This is because the Internet server presents available pages in order to increase the effectively of available server memory (caches). In addition, it is possible that what is viewed on the screen consisted of information and content from a number of sources, page layers from different sources, thus the viewed data is not necessarily from the same server.

The can be the result of criminal motives or from innocent considerations, for instance, when the website designer uses 'frames' or 'Cascading Style Sheets (CSS)'. Older website capture programs will not always succeed in 'obtaining' all the information. This means that the website capture needs to be accompanied with the testimony and affidavit of person performing the capture process, namely, the authorized digital evidence investigator. This must be done with extreme caution, in order to deal with and address criticism. .

The second limitation is that the 'spider' acts only when the

Internet pages include regular content, or in other words, when the files indeed exist on the server or on a specific website. However, on many websites the content is dynamic; in other words, it changes according to the definition of the surfer's requirements while referring to the local database and/or through use of WE technology. Examples are 'results' pages produced by search engines such as Google or the 'Welcome' page on the Amazon.com website, where, as a response to data taken from the local computer alongside the specific user's surfing history, a page personally adjusted to the surfer is built, including a list of recommendations uniquely adapted on the basis of previous acquisitions, different searches, geographic position, currency adjustments, and so on.

Under these circumstances, it is possible that the sole evidence that can be documented is a controlled printout of the harmful messages during the documentation process. It is necessary to document what is done and to preserve the documenting computer as evidence faithful to the original. Without this type of documentation, it will be difficult to convince the Court of the admissibility of the evidence.

Internet activities leave information available on the computer's components. When we review and analyze the data, we may obtain supporting documentation regarding possible wrongdoing. Despite that said previously, not all commercial web pages are saved in the accessible computer components (cache), due to fears that information will be presented incorrectly to the user, a situation that may be especially sensitive with regard to financial data, such as credit card charges.

When there is a suspicion of wrongdoing and it becomes clear that this is a website that obtains its data from different sources and that it does not enable saving of accessible memory for the reasons I noted before, it is possible to place a camera opposite the screen and to document the screen's display. It is also possible to install internal software, which takes a photograph (screenshot) from the computer at predefined periods of time.

Evidence from a Remote Server Accessible through the Internet

Conversely, sometimes an organization or website owner saves traffic data, including data on surfers' behavioral patterns, in order to publish the data to satisfy other website users and/or for other commercial goals. A simple example is the 'likes' function of the Facebook social network. Another example is the collection of statistical data on surfers using the website, so as to present the data to advertisers.

These logs generally are saved in a shared log format in which the information is collected. From a legal perspective, these logs are no different from other types of computer logs; if it becomes clear that they are faithful to the original, namely no manipulation occurred during or following duplication in favor of commercial use and/or for any other reasons, then it is likely that it will be possible to use them as evidence in legal proceedings.

From remote server logs, accessible through the Internet, it is possible to obtain the following data, which may help convince the Court with regard to the offenses, as part of the totality of digital evidence:

- Description of the websites defined on the server, including a description of the computer system's overall functions and the role of the Internet server on it.

- Explanation and description regarding the length of time in which the system was implemented in its present configuration.

- The place and identity of the external factors that operate the Internet server.

- Existing security characteristics and handling modes.

- Information on the existence of similar systems, and ownership and history data.

- Description of the tools used to preserve evidence so that it will be possible to consider the evidence as being admissible, namely its believability is not harmed. For this purpose, it is necessary to perform computer imaging faithful to the original rather than copying selected files to other digital media, even if this is one-time writable media. In addition, it is necessary to produce documentation that proves the integrity of the copying process, namely the 'digital fingerprint' of the server or computer.

- Explanation regarding manipulation or analysis undertaken to make the data simple and easy to understand. This is a completely legal process; however, it is necessary to present original material so that the defense team can examine the manner of data analysis and repeat and achieve the same outcome using both the same tools and different tools.

In business organizations, the admissibility of digital evidence will be determined on the basis of the fact that the material is a 'business record' as defined in section 117 of British Criminal Law of 2003, similar to an 'institutional record' in Israeli law.

In civil issues, many documents will be included in the category of 'documents that may be accepted as evidence without further proof' under section 9 of the Civil Evidence Law 1995 and others may be accepted subject to the conditions of 'evidence by hearsay of the Civil Hearings Law 33. The topic of Israeli law will be addressed in the framework of the discussion of computer output and institutional evidence.

Closed Circuit Television (CCTV)

In the past, closed circuit television was composed of one, low resolution camera, connected by a cable to a screen. To record an activity, use was made of a recording device – generally a VCR device that worked slowly and necessitated frequent changes of tapes.

Today recording is based on a hard drive, and this has many advantages. The recorded material is less susceptible to deterioration than a tape, the capacity of the hard drive enables long periods of recording time, and it is even possible to define that a recording device will automatically erase the old recording and record again at the same location on the hard drive. In addition, time data are simple and easy to use, there is a wide variety of compression levels, accessibility is according to the desired quality of the recorded material, and it is possible to record from many sources and from a number of different cameras onto a single recording device.

Modern cameras are also capable of using communication network protocols and cables instead of the coaxial cable of the old camera systems. They can also use wireless communication, through the Internet, thus enabling a wider dispersion of cameras alongside a considerable reduction in the cost of installing the system. In addition, since these are films in digital format, it is possible to more easily use the software to analysis recorded activity.

In light of the advanced abilities of modern closed circuit television systems, I chose to include and provide an explanation of this important topic. I would note, from the start, that there are few established standards for the recording of CCTV video on a hard drive. I would also point out that hardware manufacturers also created the software programs, and it is sometimes difficult to extract video materials and still photographs without assistance from the manufacturer.

It is almost always possible to remove the hard drives from CCTV receivers and subject them to legal imaging. However, sometimes the legal digital evidence analyst will not be able to view the video, without a specific software program in the CCTV recording device, a software program that is installed on a small chip as part of the recording system's operating system which must be correspond to the method used to record the clip on the hard drive.

One of the main problems facing the law enforcement division and digital evidence examiners is that, in a complex investigation, when monitoring the activities of individuals, it is necessary to examine the output recorded from a large number of different photographic systems using a variety of different formats. In addition, to ensure the evidential value of the material, the CCTV system must meet requirements for photographic quality alongside the need to use. Following are the requirements:

- During the system's installation, it is necessary to know what the system is intended for and how this will be achieved (for instance, identify the face of the person walking in the corridor or read the license number of a car).

- It is necessary to define improvement characteristics. For instance, when monitoring (distress) buttons are used, the camera will 'zoom-in' and provide additional details.

- It is necessary to examine and ensure the effectiveness of the system through repeated trial runs and examinations.

- It is necessary to examine the picture quality obtained from the different cameras, including examination of print quality of the.

- It is necessary to ascertain that the system time and date are correct and match real time. It is necessary to repeat this examination once a month, out of the fear of change as a result of a fault and/or temporary electric outage.

- There should be no compromise on the quality of the picture in favor of a greater number of pictures compressed into the hard drive.

- It is necessary to maintain the camera regularly, for example, clean the lenses, examine that it meets water standards, etc.

Examination of Storage Media for Films/Photographs

- The approach to the system and to the recorded materials must be supervised, to prevent any illegal viewing of or alteration to the materials.

- It is necessary to document all those who had access to the system and when they did so and to use physical storage methods such as locked rooms to protect the equipment from harm and/or suspicion that data might be compromised and thus disqualified for admission as evidence.

- I recommend that all such records and materials be saved for a period of at least seven years.

Examination the Ease of Exporting Materials from the System

- The CCTV system must include a user guide to assist the investigator view the material and export it.

- Export of a moderate or large volume of data can take considerable time. The operator must know the time period saved by the system and estimated time required for the export of different volumes of data.

- If the software required for the viewing of the material is not included in the exported materials, the Police may find it difficult to view the pictures and films. Export of the system's event log of, including details of actions taken, inspection, and documentation will help establish the completeness of the pictures and the films.

- The system must be capable of exporting small or large amounts of video films rapidly and without harming quality. If the system has a 'plug and play' component for the export of materials to the hard drive, such as a USB connection, then this is an ideal solution for the download of a moderate to large volume of data.

- The system must have the ability to export the photographs/film in a manner that will not harm the exported material and/or the continuation of the recording.

Viewing the Recording

- The playback software must enable the investigator to search for the material effectively and to see all the information included in the picture/film and attached to it.

- There needs to be the option for the immediate playback of exported files without needing to verify the file again.

Legal Issues

The use of CCTV cameras is included in the British legal framework of procedures of the employment of workers, like the collective agreement in Israel and subject to rulings pertaining to extensive issues of workers' rights and the employer's ability to supervise his workers. If security cameras are directed at people who are not employees and/or document innocent civilians, then it is necessary to ascertain that the privacy of all passersby is maintained within the framework of the protection of human rights and the protection of data.

On this matter, I would note that the organization is obligated to provide a satisfactory explanation for the installation of cameras at a certain angle and to ascertain that the way in which the system is installed and operated does not lead to an invasion of privacy of any type, other than the essential invasion required for the achievement of the system's goals.

It should be remembered that procedures for the employment of workers in the United Kingdom cover a variety of activities, including monitoring and tracking of employees by opening digital email and voice mail, the examination of Internet use and CCTV camera recordings. However, this code also cautions businesses that clandestine employee surveillance workers and is even considered unreasonable unless it is done in response to a request made by law enforcement agencies. In other words, a if the business installs a camera to supervise its employees, this will not be considered an installation in a business's public area and thus the Court will reject any argument on the part of the person recorded that their privacy was violated.

The goals typical to the installation of this type of system include reducing cases of theft and the preservation of public safety. However, it is necessary to respect people's privacy. For instance, cameras should not be directed to areas where people are entitled, logically, to privacy and when there are no specific explanations suggesting that it is possible to identify an offense, unlike other places. Supervision using cameras in places where privacy is expected will need to meet the tests of necessity alongside the examination of alternatives that constitute less harm to the privacy.

In the context of storage of materials that were collected with CCTV systems, including digital files, in which employees and passersby are filmed – the devices used must meet a series of criteria established to protect the data as the recorded materials will be considered personal data. The data need to be precise, processed fairly and legally, and for limited goals – and in no case contrary to the goals, namely adequate, relevant, and not extreme.

In addition, the material should not be saved for a longer period of time than is necessary, and it must be protected so as not to harm the rights of the individual. The material should not be given to countries and/or organizations that cannot provide sufficiently good protection.

Institutional Output and Large and Medium Sized Computer Systems

As an introduction to this chapter, I will present an example of a company that meets global standards regarding information security requirements, including the use of communication protocols for the encryption of information in transit and the establishment of clear procedures for control and recovery. In the company's printed documents it is possible to see the relevant 'institutional record' on each and every matter. However, the company must prove that it meets these rules.

On this matter, one of the technological questions arising is whether the organization needs to perform legal copying of the hard drives, similar to the copying of a single hard drive in the organization or of a private person, so that defense electronic evidence experts can examine them or should the output be accepted as obvious. In a physical analogy, I would ask whether the organization needs to make a legal copy of the organization's entire system faithful to the original, including the complete communication network, including any subsidiaries it owns, such a bank. Such a copy will be justified, for example in a case were a bank's branch manager is accused of fraud, of collusion with clients in credit agreements, and who, in his interrogation, argues that the computer does not precisely reflect all of the company's business protocols and transaction queries.

It is unreasonable to make a copy faithful to the original of every computer system, and therefore it will be necessary to perform a localized 'analysis' of the facts, alongside specific examinations and choices. The following presents the main points.

The organization must prove to and convince the court that the computer output presented before it indeed reflects the facts indisputably. On this matter, it is necessary to prove that the data were compared to data retrieved from the organization's backup systems, including comparative data from the field and other computer data to which the accused does not have access. In addition, it is necessary to verify the data against a system of statistics and probability that proves a correlation between the data presented in the output and statistical data on this matter.

The organization must prove that the printed evidence is whole, namely, the production process was performed correctly and that it is unflawed. In other words, the evidence must be admissible.

Documents describing in full and in detail the functions of the organizations computer system, including details of the definition of configuration active when the crime was committed must be attached. On this matter, I would note that, from such a report, it is possible to learn clearly the approach the accused had with regard to in-depth data and to learn the extent to which they were able to change and distort the data. The report should be written so that a layperson can read it and gain from it an understanding of the computer arrangement. Put simply, a report written in a highly technical report on the structure of the organizations computer system should not be approved.

It is necessary to examine which external factors can reliably authenticate the credibility of the output. Take, for example, calculation systems pertaining to transactions that were executed with other companies and banks. Incompatible data, and calculation errors in the organizations computer systems will quickly lead to complaints from the banks and companies, which are a party to the agreement. In such a case, third party computer output may constitute a source for the credible authentication of data.

It is necessary to examine the existing security measures and how they are managed. This is in order to anticipate and prevent a combination of incriminating material against the accused with the evidential materials in materials presented to the Court.

It is necessary to add a detailed explanation of the material presented to the court. For example, the source of the output is it a copy of a report produced by a computer in an orderly manner and as a part of its regular functions, such as regular auditing or a routine log file.

In addition, it is necessary to examine whether the output is produced from a backup and/or orderly regular backup. If so, is this a complete backup or only a relative part of the backup? Is the output a product of a follow-up analysis or a professional analysis that is intended to examine initial suspicions and how the follow-up is determined?

It is necessary to document the processes used to collect and save the evidence in order to ascertain its admissibility and to determine that it has not been tampered with. The documentation will be prepared using technological methods, such as legal copying using legally acceptable technological instruments that were examined and found to be reliable, beyond any shadow of doubt.

It is also possible to copy selected files to write only media, such as a CD or a DVD and/or to create a digital stamp for the saved files. In this case, it is necessary to present the original material, in order to allow the defense team to examine whether there has been any technological manipulation of the files during the process of creating the digital stamp.

The organization must fully and completely cooperate with the defense team as part of the process of full disclosure. This will enable the defense team to examine and determine the reliability of the evidence and maintain the accused's right to defend themselves against the accusations, as part of the legal proceedings. The court must be convinced that the prosecution provided all required materials and that it cooperated fully with the defense team. If the facts do not indicate this, then the Court, subject to the issue it is facing, must reduce the degree of the evidence's credibility.

From a legal perspective, the admissibility of institutional evidence when presented in the form of output (printed, hard disk, digital media) is generally based on the fact that the material is part of the process of business recording. However, the same evidence may be disqualified if it was obtained unfairly and/or as a result of an infringement to required data protection procedures and/or resulting from harm to rights of privacy and/or of the individual.

In civil issues, a company is not always able to produce what is required to prove the admissibility of evidence from its private computer systems. This is because such companies are small organizations and businesses, which, although they use computer systems, they are not large enough to meet all the standards required of a large organization regarding information security. In such situations, it is necessary to make a copy, faithful to the original, of all the computer hard drives within the organization. This applies to handheld computers and tablets, cellular phones, backup systems, and others. The legal copy should be transferred to an agreed-upon electronic evidence expert, to be used to address the questions formulated by the parties.

If the issue involves a dispute that took place a number of years ago and in the event that a copy of computer systems, faithful to the original, existing at that time of the was not made then and/or close to that time, it will be necessary to back-up data found in documents from parallel organizations, which can verify the originality of the data. An example of such data can be obtained from the tax authorities and/or parallel business with which a transaction was closed.

In every situation, the Court must examine in minute detail any legal copying performed a number of years in the past. The court must be convinced that this is not a technological manipulation and/or a new copy being presented as an older one.

The digital evidence expert acting on behalf of the Court will provide scientific answers to these questions and others. If the answers are not satisfactory, and subject to the depth of the issue, the Court must reduce the evidence's weight – and even disqualify it.

Corporate Communication Networks

As mentioned previously, sometimes it is unreasonable or impossible to make a legal copy of the all of the organization's communication networks due to the vast amount of data involved. Often it will be necessary to disconnect and/or turn off the entire communication system during the copy process which may result in financial damage to the organization. In addition, since all other computers will continue to operate until the moment copying is performed, a situation will exist in which the data is unsynchronized. In other words, the data will not authenticate the state of affairs for the specific moment it time.

In such cases, since the proposed method cannot be implemented, it is necessary to choose an alternative method, which will enable the the organization's continued activity and will ensure the evidence's integrity. The organization's duty is to prove that the evidence obtained meets the legal definitions and requirements for original evidence and/or is faithful to the original, in order to prove the evidence's admissibility.

The organization is also required to prove the overall reliability of the communications network and the workstations examined, including the servers from which the evidence was taken.

The central points that may help convince the Court on the matter of originality and admissibility of the evidence presented before it are:

- The organization or company must present an overall description of the communication network, including the topography of the communication network, the number of servers in the organization, the number and types of routers, the manner of communication, configuration definitions for the computers connected to the Internet, information security systems, the way in which the communication network is managed, and so on.
- It is necessary to detail separately security characteristics, namely, the type of hardware and operating systems and their management. This data is important in order to discover, to understand, and to observe whether incriminating material was infiltrated into the organization's computer systems resulting in unexamined evidence being placed before the court.

- It is necessary to learn and to understand and to present to the Court data regarding the period of time that the communication network operated in its current configuration and which examinations were held before the accused assumed their job function and which checks were held over time.

- It is necessary to examine which outside factors can reliably authenticate the credibility of the output. For instance, calculation systems pertaining to transactions that were executed with other companies and banks. Incompatible data, and calculation errors in the organization's computer systems will quickly lead to complaints from the banks and companies which are a party to the agreement. In such a case, third party computer output may constitute a source for the credible authentication of data. It is necessary to examine the reliability of communication network components, on the level of operating systems, software and hardware. Objective outside criticism will provide a good answer to issues of this type.

- On the issue of the communication network, it is important to present the output's source, namely, whether this is a copy of a report produced by the computer as a part of its normal functions, such as a regular monitoring or a routine log file.

- It is necessary to examine whether the backup is methodical and complete or whether this is output presented as a part of unexamined backup.

- It is necessary to examine whether the material presented is the result of professional surveillance over time or only initial suspicions. On this matter I would note that evidence collected methodically over time indicate relatively believable surveillance. However, I would also note that it is important to examine the method of implementation before surveillance actually takes place as it is mandatory to know with certainty that the surveillance method is reliable.

- It is necessary to authenticate that this is a legally acceptable copy of the computer and the server. It is necessary to explain how the evidence was chosen and why it is possible to see it as evidence that indicates its originality beyond any shadow of doubt, in terms of the issues under discussion.

- It is necessary to prove that the evidence is considered believable to the extent that it will be possible to negate other potential sources of evidence. It is especially important to examine the servers' location, access to them, and the methods of information security as well as the methods used to collect the evidence presented before the Court.

  This should be facilitated through technological means such as legally acceptable copying using legal technological tools, which were examined and found to be believable beyond any shadow of a doubt.

  It is also possible to copy selected files to write only media, such as a CD or a DVD and/or to create a digital stamp for the saved files. In this case, it is necessary to present the original material, in order to allow the defense team to examine whether there has been any technological manipulation of the files during the process of creating the digital stamp.

- The organization must fully and completely cooperate with the defense team as part of the process of full disclosure. This will enable the defense team to examine and determine the reliability of the evidence and maintain the accused's right to defend themselves against the accusations, as part of the legal proceedings. The court must be convinced that the prosecution provided all required materials and that it cooperated fully with the defense team. If the facts do not indicate this, then the Court, subject to the issue it is facing, must reduce the degree of the evidence's credibility.

In recent years, commercial companies have developed products that enable remote supervision of workstations via the corporate communications network and even from outside of it. These products often require the installation of software on the workstation to be monitored after which the software transmits all data originating from the workstation. Communications between the monitoring work station and the workstation being monitored is through the shared communications network. Data transmitted through the network are encrypted, so that they may only be read by the monitoring workstation..

In relation to this matter, I would note that companies and organizations now requires that their employees sign, as part of the organization's overall security considerations, , a declaration that they are aware that their workstation, cars and cellular phones provided them by the organization as part of their job role, will include surveillance and documentation software . These programs transmit all the data to one main server, the role of which is to process the data and report actions defined as illegal in relation to the organization.

Returning to the issue at hand, as part of the encryption process, on the monitored work station's hard drive, in parallel to the extraction and transmission of data to the monitoring work station, the data are saved in a separate, write protected partition, , exactly as in the course of a routine examination. Thus, data integrity is assured and any suspicions of tampering on the part of the examiner can be dispelled and it is possible to prove the data's reliability beyond any reasonable doubt.

Despite my previous statement which indicate that this is promising approach, nevertheless there is still a very real need to examine it fully within the framework of the Courts. It is entirely possible that practical problems will be raised, entailing, for example, time taken by legal copying, the agents that managed the examination, the duration of the examination, the amount of evidence collected, and so on.

Every organization needs to consider the distribution of intra-organizational surveillance means and/or performance of remote surveillance, according to its size and economic resilience. These steps entail installation and software licensing costs of in addition to the implementation of relevant procedures and the development of appropriate processes.

If this wasn't sufficient, then it is also necessary to implement examination procedures for the collected materials, based on the understanding that every process to be implemented will be subject to criticism on the part of defense's digital evidence experts. The expert may examine the process, and if the process does not meet required standards, the defense can ask the Court to disqualify the evidence or reduce its weight to some extent.

Digital evidence experts must trace all the processes that led to the result presented before the Court, and it is the obligation of the company or organization to cooperate fully with the entire process.

From a legal perspective, the admissibility of the evidence is similar to that of material obtained from large computer systems, namely, the admissibility of institutional evidence, in the form of printed or digital output is based generally on the fact that the material is a part of the business recording process. However, the evidence may be disqualified if it was obtained unfairly and/or through a violation of required data protection processes as and/or an invasion of privacy and/or infringements of human rights. In civil issues, a business cannot always produce what is required to prove the admissibility of the evidence from its private computer systems.

CHAPTER 4: COLLECTION AND PRESERVATION OF DIGITAL STORAGE MEDIA

Computers are considered independent digital components that receive and transmit data, process data, store data, and produce results from data, namely, digital output. In many cases, other equipment is connected to computers, directly or via the Internet. Such equipment can include routers, disk-on-keys, printers, scanners, Internet cameras, MP3 players, GPS systems, RFID components, and more.

The data that digital components collect are stored on digital storage media of which there are many different types which differ one from the other in storage methods and memory size. The most well-known storage media are mobile external hard drives, mobile memory devices, CDs, DVDs, magnetic film, and different types of memory cards.

As a part of the digital evidence collection process, the authorized computer investigators must collect all the digital storage media found that may contain potential digital evidence. In addition, it is necessary to ascertain that a supposedly 'independent' component was not connected to the local communication network and/or the Internet. If there is a suspicion that such components were recently connected to the communication network or conversely disconnected from it, then it is necessary to consider it as a component that documents information in a manner different from the rest of the identified storage media. The reason for this is its ability to connect through the Internet, and thus there exists reasonable suspicion that it can collect and document data, a fact that can definitely assist the investigators.

In addition, when a digital component includes an interface to the communications network but does not have an obvious connection, it is necessary to conduct a number of examinations to identify other components, which were possibly connected to it. The digital computer experts must perform the following actions in the following order:

Status *Freezing*. It is necessary to preserve the status of the computers and the peripheral devices without change. If the computers or the peripheral devices are turned off, they must not be turned on. If they are turned on, then they must not be turned off, since these actions could lead to the destruction of potential digital evidence. If the computers are turned on, then the digital evidence examiners must photograph what appears on the monitors. I wish to stress that, in this matter, a written document or affidavit is not sufficient.

Documentation. It is necessary to document the types of digital components and the trademarks stamped or attached to the device. It is important to identify all computers and all peripheral equipment components that may be acquired during the initial stage of investigation. The components must be mapped to the computer they are connected, to and complete written records must be kept. Serial numbers, license numbers, and other identifying marks must be documented, including photographs and any signs of physical damage must also be documented.

Charging. If the digital component includes batteries that may empty, it is necessary to charge them to prevent loss of information. Cables, batteries and battery chargers that may be required at a later stage must also be seized.

Scan. It is necessary to examine the network to track additional digital components connected to it. It is necessary to take into account the possibility that the digital component is connected via the Internet and its geographic position is far from the place of seizure.

Investigators of digital computerization must be aware that network components located at the scene and outside of it may be able to identify the presence of testing components and evidence tracking devices and may, as a result, 'self-destruction' to destroy or render unusable, potential digital evidence.

During my research for this book, I looked, at depth, into the various directives relating to the behavior of organizations investigating the scene of a seizure. In the majority of cases, I observed that with certain judicial authorities and under these or other circumstances, it is possible to power up digital components found at the scene in order to determine their relevance to the case in hand.

On this issue, my recommendation is unequivocal: never turn on digital components that are turned off at the scene of the incident or the seizure. If the organizations are sophisticated crime organizations that are aided by sources of financing, it is likely that there are anti-forensic systems installed, as well as systems that identify attempts to enter incorrect boot passwords and that will react by formatting the hard drive and/or even completely destroy the hardware.

To a constant electrical current to the digital component, it is necessary to determine priorities and take these into consideration. If this is a critical component for the investigation, then it is mandatory to make a 'hot copy'[125] on site, without interrupting the flow of electricity. In addition, it is necessary to make every effort to not disconnect the component from its power source in an effort to maintain it in a powered up state whilst transporting the device to an authorized laboratory.

---

[125] 'Hot copy' is a technology that enables the user to copy the computer or the server and its partitions without the need to boot the operating system and/or stop the computer action, which may interfere with some of the other processes in the computer.

The Collection of Powered-up Digital Components

There are a number of guidelines which digital evidence investigators are required follow during the collection of powered-up digital components. Some constitute 'basic actions 'which must be adhered to and performed under all circumstances and at all incident scenes. Others are only relevant under certain circumstances and according to the type of component being investigated.

Please note that since it is possible that these are network components found in more than one geographic location, all required actions, including basic actions, and any additional actions, must be performed according to the laws and regulations applicable in the local jurisdiction. In addition, the duty of the digital evidence investigators is to have an in-depth knowledge and understanding of the technology they face and they must make every effort to fill all the handling directives and requirements for the storage media.

If the investigator is required to perform the basic actions that involve potential digital evidence and decides to seize the powered-up digital component, then consideration must be given to the possibility that powering down the component may erase the evidence. Therefore, it is necessary to maintain the device in the state in which it was found and to attempt to extract the evidence and transfer it to an external hard drive in real time.

In addition, it is necessary to be aware that active memory or inactive memory that has not yet been erased may contain encoding or data encryption systems. When there is suspicion of the existence of such a system, possible alternatives to collecting the digital evidence should be considered. It is important to remember that a functioning operating system may be unreliable, and thus it is recommended that the use of other reliable and valid tools be considered.

I would note that if a powered-up digital component is disconnected from its power source, then all potential coded digital evidence stored on the hard drive and/or in the volatile memory, will be inaccessible and/or in an unreadable format unless the decryption and encryption key is obtained.

'Live data', such as data shown in real time on the monitor or found in the background of operating system and that has potential value, may disappear if the component is disconnected from the electrical source. This may often lead damage suites and even to loss of life, for instance, in a case in which digital components control medical equipment. Digital evidence investigators must ascertain such issues before removing the electric cable from the power socket.

These actions are 'additional actions', and thus they are only required in cases in which they are relevant to the circumstances and according to the configuration of the seized digital component. When the seized digital component is a laptop, then it is necessary to ascertain that the 'accessible'[126] data are collected into a 'safe haven' before the battery is removed.

After the evidence is collected from the powered-up laptop, digital evidence investigators must remove the power supply's battery and to refrain from pressing the laptop's power button. Pressing the digital component's power button may alter or erase information from the system before it is powered down and may alert connected systems to the occurrence of an unexpected event that may erase data of evidentiary value before it is identified.

Digital evidence investigators must collect digital evidence at the same time as the collection of non-digital evidence, according to procedures, so as to ensure that all the evidence will remain admissible for the continuation of the legal process.

---

[126] The definition includes data presented in real time and/or to operating systems. There is a fear that following the disconnection of the electricity data will be lost.

Seizing of Powered Down Digital Components

As in the process of the seizing powered-up digital components, here too there are a number of guidelines which digital evidence investigators must adhere to. Some constitute 'fundamental actions', in other words, it is necessary to act according to them under all circumstances and in all scenarios, while others are relevant only under certain circumstances and according to the type of component.

In most cases, the storage medium must not be removed from the digital component until characterization and documentation has been completed as their removal increases the chances of causing harm or an error between them and other storage media. It is necessary to develop local procedures in all issues pertaining to the removal of digital storage media and they should be adhered to.

If the seized component is a laptop computer, then it is necessary to ascertain that it is indeed turned off, since some laptop computers may be in 'sleep' mode and may turn on when the screen is opened. In addition, it is necessary to remove the main power supply's battery from the laptop.

If field conditions necessitate the removal of the hard drive, then the digital evidence investigators must be certain to disconnect the digital component from the power source, so as to prevent damage that may be caused to the drive by static electricity. It is necessary to label the hard drive as a suspicious hard drive and to document all the details, namely, its manufacturer and model, the serial number, the storage capacity and physical size, and so on.

The Collection Process

As mentioned previously, there are three scenarios in which digital evidence may need to be collected from different hardware components. These scenarios are: when the digital components are turned on, when the digital components are turned off, and when the components are turned on but it is impossible to turn them off for reasons related to hardware complexity, fear of data loss, fear of encoding and/or encryption systems and/or systems designed to thwart digital identification processes by self-destruction.

In all these scenarios, digital evidence investigators must create a precise copy of the digital evidence and all storage media, including the digital components suspected of holding potential digital evidence. If it is impossible to create a copy that is faithful to the original, it is recommended to collect exact copies of the files suspected as including potential digital evidence. In addition, it is recommended that a principal verified copy be made and additional copies faithful to the original.

No further use will be made of the original and of the principal copy, unless it is necessary to validate the contents or to make an alternative copy if a copy being examined is damaged. The examiner must be aware that a functioning system may automatically lock or may activate a screen saver. Such situations are avoidable, but most of the actions required will the affect the system's status and are therefore, not recommended.

When there is fear that potential digital evidence will be erased in the event that the component is turned off, digital evidence investigators must examine the possibility of collecting 'volatile' data from components that are still turned on and to consider performing a 'hot copy' of the component. The collection of evidence in 'real time' or a 'hot copy' is essential to immediately obtain data from the components that are still turned on. The extraction of volatile data stored in the random access memory (RAM[127]) in 'real time' may

---

[127] See the chapter of terms and definitions.

preserve information with value such as the status of the communication network, decrypted applications and passwords. 'Real time' collection can be performed on the control panel or remotely, using the communications network.

The imaging process or that of making a copy faithful to the original must be saved onto a hard drive, through an imaging tool that has been evaluated to insure its reliability. The digital copy must be documented, stored and secured on a storage resource that maintains the original's reliability and protects the copy from physical harm.

When there is the suspicion encoding or encryption, then it is necessary to examine the possibility of collecting data from volatile memory. First, it is necessary to examine with a tool or equipment for the detection of encoding systems if such a system is indeed installed. It is necessary to remember that the operating system installed on the digital component may be under the 'influence' of the encoding system and/or an anti-digital identification system, and therefore it should be viewed with suspicion and may be unreliable.

In addition, it is necessary to use a reliable time source and to document the difference between time data taken from the digital component and real time data. Digital evidence experts required to execute this documentation process through the use of digital signatures, biometrics, and photography.

There is no dispute that it is easier and simpler to handle a component that is turned off than a component that is turned on. The reason lies in the fact that, first and foremost, no questions arise regarding data stored on volatile memory and, secondly, a turned off device does not need a supply of electricity nor require neutralization of network access. However, a number of actions must be strictly adhered to as a part of the process for the acquisition of the turned off digital component.

First, it is necessary to ensure that the component is indeed turned off, and if so, it is necessary to extract the storage component, namely, the hard drive, from it. Afterwards, it is necessary to perform the imaging process (creation of a copy faithful to the original), using an imaging tool that has been tested for its reliability and its ability to create a faithful copy of the suspect's hard drive.

Due to constraints in certain situations, a partial collection of digital evidence may be performed – but this is not recommended. The reason can include a hardware failure, limitations imposed by the scene being investigated such as when shutting down a server will cause substantial harm and damage or the using of systems and tools that anti-forensic applications will identify, causing them to react by destroying data or even self-destructing. There may also exist legal limitations such as a search warrant that limits the scope of the seizure, subject to local law.

Lack of sufficient storage volume is not a reason for partial collection of evidence even if the server or data base is large or when the system cannot be shut down. As mentioned previously, it is possible to make a 'hot copy'.

If, despite this, a decision is made to perform a partial collection of digital evidence, it is necessary to include in the documentation all actions taken regarding the identification and documentation of the folders to be collected, including documentation of the user or owner name. This data will allow the forensic investigator to link files to specific users.

In most cases, at the scene of the incident it is possible to find a wide variety of media and digital storage media. For the most part, this media will include stable, non-volatile data which will have a low priority in the evidence collection process. However, the importance of the storage media is considerable and often external digital storage media will include evidence for which data analysts are looking. Therefore, digital evidence experts must examine and document the independence of all types of external hard drives of every type, and all digital storage media found on the scene. All such devices must be seized as part of the data collection process.

I would note that digital storage devices are able to store different volumes of data. Digital evidence investigators must be aware of the time defined by the device's manufacturer to save and document data. Digital evidence investigators must also be aware of the maximum period of time allowed by judicial authorities that a digital component may be held before it is returned to its owners. On this matter, I would further note that if this is an issue of state security, then the legal authorities can 'confiscate' the component permanently.

Data Preservation

After completion of the collection process, digital evidence investigators must lock and save the evidence using verification functions and/or digital signatures. This process preserves the originality of the copies and ensures the admissibility of the evidence in the legal process.

If the investigation involves security issues that require specific monitoring and control procedures and tools, then it is necessary to implement principles pertaining to the preservation of secrecy, to ensure the integrity and accessibility of potential digital evidence, and to protect the evidence from corruption.

Environmental aspects should be assessed using the appropriate indices. I would note that digital evidence experts must take pains to use appropriate verification functions to ascertain that copied files are of equivalent worth to the original files. Sometimes it is necessary to facilitate this through the use of digital signatures and biometric tools.

All digital components that were seized must be preserved and maintained. It is necessary to take into consideration that different types of digital components may require different data saving methods. Potential digital evidence should be saved throughout its entire life period, a period whose length may vary from one legal jurisdiction to another and according to progress of the legal proceedings.

Collection of Components Connected to the Local Network and to the Internet

Computers and/or other digital components connected to a communications network, whether wired or wireless, are defined as network components. This includes mainframe computers, servers, desktop computers, entry controllers, power supplies, routers, mobile components, handheld computers, mobile phones, Bluetooth components, closed circuit television systems, and so on. It should be noted that during the first stages of an investigation it may be difficult to know with any degree of certainty where to search for potential digital evidence, since the data may be found anywhere on the communication network or even on a remote digital component.

After the identification of all network components, and before the process of the data collection and seizure of digital components begins, it is necessary to visually document the network's structure, using photography, graphic sketching on video, or a sketch of the area as it appears when entering. In addition, it is necessary to document details of all digital components found in use, including their type, trademark, model, and serial number, and to identify all additional digital components that it may be necessary to access or seize during the initial stage.

It is necessary to document the serial numbers of all mobile components and accessories found at the scene, such as memory cards, SIM cards, chargers etc., as well as all identifiable devices and to seize them as needed. If the component is connected to the local network and/or to the Internet, then digital evidence investigators must identify the services provided by the components in order to understand the network's entire structure, including relative dependence between the components. Furthermore, the investigators take steps to guarantee that it will be possible to inspect all of the components connected to the network prior to a specific component being disconnected from the network

This is a preliminary stage in cases where the components operate task control functions or other process that do not allow imaging when turned off and/or imaging may cause corruption of potential digital evidence, continuation of the process must be carefully considered before disconnection from the network.

Nevertheless, if there is a real threat to digital components, which may harm the quality of potential digital evidence, then it is possible that digital evidence investigators will need to disconnect the component from the communications network in order to protect the data. In such situations, it is necessary to consider whether to disconnect the component itself from the network or to disconnect the network from external connections, namely to disconnect it from the Internet. There is the constant concern regarding possible anti-forensics systems, and unfortunately there is no one unequivocal and correct answer on the topic.

If the networked component is a closed circuit television system, then the digital evidence experts must note the number of cameras connected to the system and which cameras are operating. In addition, it is necessary to document the components' manufacturers, models, and basic system definitions, such as display settings, present recording definitions and storage site, so that if it is necessary to make changes to facilitate the process of collection and acquisition, it will be possible to return the system to its original state.

In addition, it is necessary to use a wireless transmission detector to discover and identify the wireless frequencies of concealed digital components. This is a very serious issue necessary to identify the entire network. It is possible that the encryption key and/or file is contained in one or more concealed components and after the components are turned off and disconnected from the network/Internet they will no longer work, and if an attempt is made to turn them on and/or crack the code, then the devices will erase the data contained on them (format the hard drive).

The collection and saving process is performed in stages. The digital evidence investigators must decide whether to collect the components or to extract potential digital evidence from them on site.

The decision must take into account the circumstances, cost, time, available sources, and priorities.

When it is impossible to disconnect components from the communications network because they are critical to the use or the organization's activity, or because there is a fear of corruption of potential digital evidence, , digital evidence examiners must make a real time 'hot copy' , when the component is connected to the communication network.

The processes involved in the collection and documentation of potential digital evidence from networked mobile components are, by their very nature, complex. The components may be found in a number of countries and in different states of interaction, such as Bluetooth, radio frequencies, touch screens, and infrared. In addition, mobile component producers, as mentioned, use different types of operating systems, which necessitate different methods and processes for the preservation of potential digital evidence. Additionally, there are a wide variety of memory cards used in mobile components, and the removal of these memory cards from powered mobile components may interfere with the components processes.

Powered down mobile components, such as handheld computers and mobile phones must not be turned on in an attempt to collect any potential digital evidence. This could result in a change to their operating environment such as a change of global clock settings, change of ISP or cell phone provider when moving between countries, reception of transmissions of different types, and so on.

In addition, care must be taken to properly mark copies in order to avoid confusion. Two copies of the same digital device, mobile and/or handheld computer with network connection capability, may fail verification of originality tests which include the working status of the component, verification of originality, namely, the test of the working order of the component, and its cryptographic compilation, or in professional terms, hashing.

In addition, Wi-Fi or Bluetooth components should not be

brought to the scene of the incident. These components may unintentionally interact with on-scene components and could change information and disrupt digital evidence. In extreme cases, the introduction of cellular devices with Wi-Fi or Bluetooth capabilities at the scene of the incident may reduce the evidence's degree of reliability and its weight. Sometimes it is necessary to leave networked components connected, so that it will be possible to track their activity and document what is done. If this is not essential, then it is necessary to seize the components.

Before the disconnection of communication networks, it is necessary to track connections to digital components and to clearly identify and mark them, so that in the future it will be possible to reconstruct the communication network in the same configuration as found at the time and scene of the incident. A component can include more than one method of communication. For instance, a computer can include two or more network cards, including a wireless modem and a mobile telephone card. Handheld computers can also connect to the communication network via Wi-Fi or Bluetooth connections or through mobile telephone connections. It is necessary to identify all communication methods and to adopt suitable actions to protect the components against possible corruption of potential digital evidence.

Digital evidence examiners must be aware of the fact that disconnection of components that are connected to the network from their power source may cause the loss of volatile data, such as processes occurring in the component or in routers that connect between the various hardware components. Loss of data is typical primarily of home routers, when their disconnection from the power source immediately erases all documentation regarding transmissions.

As noted, sometimes the components are connected to more than one physical and/or virtual communication network. For example, a component connected to a network using a visible physical connection may also operate a virtual private network (VPN) and a virtual device[128]

---

[128] On the matter of VPN and virtual servers, see the explanation in the chapter of terms and definitions.

with more than one IP address.

In the case of network components defined as those whose activities should not be stopped and/or which should not be disconnected from the network, it is necessary to prevent the component from connecting to a wireless radio network and/or satellite transmission (GPS). The digital evidence investigators must isolate any such radio sources using methods permitted by local law. However, it is necessary to be cautious and to ensure that the component has an appropriate source of power, since isolation methods may cause it to increase satellite reception transmission signals and thus use more power.

On the same topic, it is necessary to take into account that the use of a component which disrupts frequencies can block transmission through the creation of strong interference, especially when the component transmits signals in a range of frequencies used by mobile components, including Wi-Fi or Bluetooth frequencies. Disruptors may detrimentally influence the behavior of digital components, such as medical devices. Therefore, it is necessary to carefully examine legal directives and to decide whether the use of disrupting components may violate legal requirements in some judicial authorities.

Collection and Preservation of Films and Pictures from Closed Circuit Television Cameras

The extraction of video clips from computer-based closed circuit television cameras is different from the conventional extraction of digital evidence from the computer. Before the start of the video clips removal process o, digital evidence experts must clarify whether the system documented the relevant video sequence. Afterwards, it is necessary to examine the time framework of the specific video clip, to compare the time noted in the system and real-time, in order to determine if there is a difference between the two. In addition, it is necessary to examine which cameras are to be accessed and whether it is possible to obtain from them every clip separately. It is important to note the manufacturer's name and the system model. It is possible that this information will be required to enable replay of any collected films.

To prove continuity as part of the evidences admissibility in a legal proceeding, it is necessary to preserve all the film material recorded on the relevant cameras during the defined period of time. The digital evidence investigators must document all the cameras connected to the closed circuit television system and examine whether they record continuously or only when motion sensors are activated.

Digital evidence investigators have a number of ways to obtain potential evidence from closed circuit television systems. These include recording onto (burning) a CD, DVD, or Blu-ray disc, and other methods. It should be noted that changing the file format to reduce its size, for instance to Mpeg or AVI format, is not considered a change of version and/or distortion and/or change regarding the originality of the evidence, namely video material in an alternative format is considered faithful to the original providing it was copied and converted using legally acceptable methods..

Despite said that said regarding conversion of digital formats, it is always preferable to use the original format, without compression and/or change. This is because compression may cause a change to the original picture data, similar to a change in format between digital mail software programs. Therefore, investigators should not rely 100% on compressed data, as long as the original data exist and is available for analysis.

When it is impossible to obtain a direct copy of the files from the recording component, digital evidence investigators must attempt to obtain an analog copy from output found on the original recording component, by using an appropriate analog recording component.

After the process of evidence collection has been completed, it is necessary to examine the file obtained in order to confirm that this is indeed the correct file, that it is complete and that it is in working order. It is necessary to examine the file using a software video player by opening the file and viewing the films or pictures so as to examine and confirm that the file is viewable from start to its finish.

As I have already noted, it is impossible to view the majority of files produced from closed circuit television systems in other viewing systems. The appropriate software for replaying may be available for downloading and installation from the closed circuit television system's installation package and/or from the manufacturer's website.

It is necessary to view the digital storage medium with the collected file as a copy faithful to the original digital evidence. If the file is downloaded to a laptop computer, memory card, or USB component and installed there, then it is necessary to produce from them a principal copy as soon as possible

When it is not practical to deal with the files at the scene of the incident, it is possible that digital evidence investigators will need to collect all of the digital storage media. Another method to rapidly collect potential digital evidence involves the seizure of the closed circuit television system's hard drives, replacing it with an empty hard drive. The use of this method necessitates attention to detail and caution. For example, the digital evidence investigator must make certain that the new hard drive is compatible with the system and that the sized hard drive is compatible with other systems for examination.

If it is impossible to use any one of these methods, then it is necessary to remove the closed circuit television system entirely from the scene of the incident and to perform the digital evidence extraction process in the legally approved laboratory. This is the digital evidence investigator's last resort, assuming that this is possible in physical terms, since some parts of the closed circuit television systems are may be extremely large and complex. Before the entire system is removed, it is necessary to assess the risks and the legal implications that removal entails, including providing a response to insurance issues.

Because of the nature of the digital components and potential digital evidence, the guidelines for preserving closed circuit television systems are similar those for preserving computers.

CHAPTER 5: DIGITAL EVIDENCE AND MOBILE DEVICES (CELLULAR PHONES)

In recent years, mobile devices such as cellular phones have become an inseparable part of everyday life in Israel and around the world. In addition to their regular and conventional uses, these devices are also used to facilitate and promote different types of criminal activity and constitute a basis for the committing of crimes.

Only recently the FBI published a warning, which stated that cases were found in which global crime organizations, using the services of computer experts and the Internet, had succeeded in developing a new type of spy program (Trojan horse), which is capable of encrypting computer files and any type of document. Owners of computers that are 'infected' by this spyware will not be provided the encryption key until they pay a ransom. This crime can be ascribed to a protection racket and/or blackmail and threats as all demand that the victim pay a ransom to avoid potential harm. After the computer owner has paid the ransom, they will be provided the 'key', which enables encrypted documents to be unlocked. Past experience shows that international crime organizations planted malicious software in gambling websites of legitimate casinos and demanded the website owners to pay monthly sums.

In this case, the method of encryption used by the criminal organization was rather simple, and fairly easy to circumvent (crack). As a rule, encryption methods use the principals of cryptography[129], which enable control over the encryption process and/or decoding of the information using a symmetrical or asymmetrical algorithm.

HA hostile attack on a target computer usually takes the form of the insertion of malicious software that infects the computer in a variety ways. The insertion process is usually disguised as a seemingly innocuous process such as surfing a website or opening an "innocent"

---

[129] Regarding the encryption keys, see the chapter on symmetrical and asymmetrical encryption key (cryptography).

email message. The software exploits a security crack (sometimes referred to as a "back door") and installs a file on the computer. From here the encryption of the files and their unavailability to their owner is but a short step away. In today's cellular world, because of the vastly improved capabilities of the cellular phone, which as a computer in every way, and because of the ease with which the vast majority of cellular phones connect to the Internet, a new window has opened for the world of crime. If previously most crime was restricted to a local environment, today it has become global with criminals in one location being able to extend their wed across the world using modern communications technologies.

One of the main differences between computers, including laptop computers, and servers and other hardware components is that the servers for the most part are intended for many users, while mobile components (phone and tablets) are generally intended for use by an individual person.

Keep in mind that these components are used to surf the Internet, to connect to social networks, to send pictures, blogs, audio and video recordings, diagrams, and more. Therefore, despite their small physical dimensions, these mobile components can contain a considerable amount of personal and business information, including call history, text messages, email messages, digital photographs, GPS history, video clips, calendar items, memos, address books, passwords, credit card numbers, and so on. As technology develops, data transfer speed increases and enables the transmission of a larger amount of information, so that the volume of data that can be found on the mobile device is constantly increasing.

By their very nature and because of their relatively small dimensions, these devices fit into the pocket and are frequently carried everywhere the user goes. This fact enables the location of the user to be pinpointed at any given moment thanks to the devices GPS system and/or cellular relays.

It should be remembered that different technological developments create opportunities for the commission of a crime, but also open new opportunities for law enforcement agencies. To put it simply, mobile computerization systems in general, as well as wireless and cellular communication technology, enable the commission of crimes but conversely also aid in the capture of the criminals. As I noted, the information stored in the mobile device can help provide an answer to critical questions during an investigation and reveal information about relationships, information transmitted from the device, and where they were during the communication.

In recent years, we have seen an increase in use of mobile devices by sex offenders in order to create an initial contact with the victims, to exchange pictures and/or video clips, and to cultivate a future relationship of dependence. Conversely, the same systems enable the digital investigators to track and follow the cellular components' path and document events.

As mentioned, the camera is one of the many hardware components available in the vast majority of cellular telephones. Pedophiles or other sex offenders will often use the photographic and video capabilities of their mobile device when committing an offence against a minor or unwilling partner to document their acts. Using these recorded materials, the pedophile may threaten to expose their victim and thus force themselves on the victim, transforming the victim into a sex slave as the majority of victims of such crime do not wish to have their experience revealed to their families and the world.

The camera installed on the mobile device has a place of prominence among young people as well. Recently I encountered an event in Israel in which two youths in their late teens had sexual relations with a girl in her early teens, documented the entire event using the mobile phone, and then uploaded short clips to the WhatsApp application and the YouTube website. If this were not enough, the movies were sold to all comers at affordable prices.

Without entering into issues of age differences and legality and without addressing the question of consent, the simple viral manner in which concrete documentation of this type becomes the province of all through the Internet, cause intense mental trauma and distress to the victim and family members and may even lead to cases of suicide or murder.

Cellular devices also "star" in the area of murder. Ronald Earl Williams murdered his wife Mariyama, supposedly in a fit of rage after he realized that she had had an affair. Williams knew that his cellular phone had dialed his wife's cellular phone during the murder and that the conversation reached her phone's voicemail. In the recording, saved on his wife's voicemail, threats that he is going to murder his wife were documented, and then the screams of the woman and their couple's daughter, pleading for him to stop, were also heard[130].

Because of the availability of the Internet, and the negligible dimensions of cellular telephones and their ability to act independently, namely, without dependence on a regular source of electricity and/or physical connection to a local network, these telephones have become a tool in the hands of criminal and terrorist organizations. They are used for the purposes of surveying and coordination, as well as smuggling of equipment and materials over national borders, and are often smuggled into prisons.

Today criminal organizations and groups use mobile devices to coordinate actions and share information, even when one of the parties may be serving a prison sentence. Digital evidence investigators can learn about the behavior of these groups through information retrieved from the mobile device.

Over the years and as a result of the development of computer technology and the reduction of the cellular phone's physical size and the multiplicity of functions that the modern phone includes, these devices are, as stated earlier, often used by criminal organizations. Take, for example, the use of money transfer applications such as Bitcoin[131], scanning of credit cards for anonymous bank accounts around the world, changing electrical voltage as part of a planned crime, temperature, and ballistics. These applications enable flexibility that

---

[130] http://tinyurl.com/q4783so
[131] See chapter of terms and definitions.

goes beyond the manufacturer's original intentions.

Dealing with Mobile Devices as Sources of Evidence

In this chapter I will show how mobile components serve as effective and diverse sources of digital evidence. In addition, I will address the basic operation of mobile components and present some of the tools and techniques in use by digital investigators for the examination and collection of potential digital evidence from these devices.

Mobile components are dynamic systems that present, from a legal perspective, many challenges. In addition, new and advanced cellular phone models s appear on an almost daily basis and around the world. From the available data in we learn that every week approximately five or more new cellular devices are released.

The steadily increasing number and variety of mobile devices make it difficult to develop a single process or single tool that can cope with the technological and legal issues that digital evidence investigators face. In addition to the steadily increasing variety of smartphones, user interfaces (operating systems) also change frequently.

In recent years manufacturers of software and hardware have identified the innate potential of mobile devices, and the result is a wide variety of operating systems, such as Android, Blackberry, Apple's iPhone, Windows Mobile, and others. It is necessary to add to these the unique operating systems used by the manufacturers of cheaper, generic phones, which use OSS (Open Source Software) systems. It is a rather ironic situation for a proprietary version.

There are many considerations for keeping mobile devices as a source of evidence. The vast majority of mobile devices are networked components, which send and receive data through telecommunication systems, wireless network points (Wi-Fi and Bluetooth).

The fact that these devices are connected to the cellular network and to the Internet and that data is rewritten, exchanged, and substituted for new data as a result of the device's routine activity or which are erased through a remote malicious command, lead to the fact that it is possible to easily lose potential digital evidence that may be transmitted through the previously mentioned communications networks.

In addition, to extract information from the device, it is essential to create an interaction between the device and the examination systems and frequently it is necessary to change the devices operational status. The interaction with the mobile device, just as with interaction with computers, may damage existing evidence and/or distort it. It is necessary to maintain regular work procedures that are designed to prevent loss and/or disruption of digital evidence and thus to ensure the legal admissibility of the evidence.

Mobile devices also constitute a challenge from the perspective of the retrieval and analysis of the data they contain. The multiplicity of functions they perform and databases stored on them and integration with hardware components indicates that they are, in all respects, computers, with the ability to store data and to effectively integrate diverse media types.

From a legal perspective, the advantage of mobile devices is their ability to include information that was erased, namely, which is not visible and which the user is convinced cannot be restored. The reason for the existence of the supposedly erased data on the mobile devices lies in the use of flash memory for data storage. Flash memory is physically durable and can withstand damage, high temperature, and pressure, which makes destroying it a very difficult task.

In addition, from the user's perspective, the flash memory card has a structure that can be divided into partitions. Specific partitions, can be erased without effecting data on other partitions on the same card. The fact that other information found on the card is not erased creates, from the investigator's perspective, a significant advantage for the search of justice.

In addition, mobile devices use unifying calculation methods so as to 'distribute' writing and erasing across flash memory areas. This fact causes erased data to remain in the memory for some time. New data are written to other parts of the memory leaving the "erased" data intact. To obtain access to the data and to reconstruct older or erased version, it is vital to obtain a full copy of the physical memory. This matter will be addressed later on.

From a legal perspective, a mobile device personal data that link the device owner and digital evidence. Despite that said, it is necessary to take into account that a third party can access and use the cellular device without the device owner knowing that his property is suspected of or a partner in the commission of an offense.

In general, I would note that the data extracted from mobile devices and then analyzed constitute an excellent source of digital evidence and can provide insights and information that cannot be obtained from other components. This fact is also true given that cellular devices backup their data on a remote computer, in the same way as a handheld computer.

Technological Elements of Mobile Devices

As previously stated, mobile devices constitute computers in all respects. A mobile device has a CPU (Central Processing Unit)[132], memory, and batteries, input interfaces such as a keyboard and microphone, and output interfaces such as a screen or ear buds. The data held in the device's memory generally are the focus of the legal examination. However, considerable understanding is required regarding input and output components so as to enable access to them.

In certain cases, it is possible that it is enough to operate a component manually and to read the information from the screen. However, to reconstruct data that was erased or to conduct an advanced examination, approved tools are needed, which can bridge between the different components. In most cases, it is possible to

---

[132] Hardware components of the type of processor, which performs on the computer the orders stored in the memory.

extract the required information from the mobile device through a direct connection to the data interface. However, in other circumstances it is necessary to connect directly to the electric circuit, namely, the device's motherboard, so as to obtain the required information.

With regard to the operation and storage of data in mobile devices, considerable knowledge is required. Sometimes, in order to extract digital evidence from mobile devices without altering the data, it may be necessary to use conversion/translation technologies, since the materials in their raw form are not readable, in much the same way as a foreign language. Connecting a digital component to the computer with the goal of obtaining information from the digital component may cause the component to synchronize with software installed on the computer and with the resulting risk that evidence on the mobile device may be totally eradicated.

Mobile devices by their nature use radio waves to communicate with communication networks using a variety of frequencies and protocols. One of the most commonly employed protocols is GSM (Global System for Mobile Communications), this is the most common network in most European countries and the system used in Israel by the major mobile networks - Partner (Orange), Cellcom, and Pelephone.

Another network is CDMA (Code Division Multiple Access), which uses a method for the sharing of transmission capabilities between stations according to prior coordination. Another common technology used in the United States and in a number of other countries is IDEN technology (Integrated Digital Enhanced Network), a technology for wireless mobile communication that was developed by Motorola and which enables integration of properties between a walkie-talkie and a cellular phone.

GSM device components each have a unique 'International Mobile Equipment Identified (IMEI) number[133]. On CDMA telephones, such

---

[133] See the chapter of terms and definitions, cellular devices.

as iPhones and others, an eleven digit number is used, where the first three digits indicate the manufacturer and the rest of are unique to the specific device. This is known professionally as ESN. The ESN is substituted for MEID, which is the CDMA equivalent of the IMEI.

On this matter, I would note that there are many software programs and online databases, which can be used to decode a large portion of the number printed on the device[134]. In addition, manufacturers of mobile devices tend to print unique serial numbers for the mobile devices they manufacture. Bluetooth components also have a unique number printed on the hardware. The numbers constitutes documentation regarding the source of the component and definitely facilitates the process of tracking the source of hardware or the documentation for the linking supplier.

Additionally, in the United States, Europe, and Israel, as in many additional countries around the world, there is an identification component of the United States Federal Communications Commission Identification (FCC-ID), through which it is possible to identify the company that manufactured the component and the name under which it was documented. On the basis of commercial labeling, it is possible to search for details that pertain to the component on the United States Federal Communications Commission web site[135] and obtain different data, including user guide and photographs.

SIM Cards

A SIM (Subscriber Identity Module) card is a printed circuit on a small plastic card. This device is intended to create one-to-one identification between the cellular network and the land line network and the entire world. The identification is accomplished through the data contained on the SIM card, which is found in the device that initiates communication. The card can be transferred from device to device, while maintaining the user identity.

GSM devices use SIM cards to perform authentication of identity

---

[134] For instance: www.numberingplans.com
[135] http://transition.fcc.gov

with the communication network and to store a variety of types of information, including certain activities executed by the user. SIM cards meet standards that determine what information is stored and where it is stored on the card.

There are different types of SIM cards of different size and made from different materials. Despite the physical difference between them, their functions are identical and all SIM cards include information. The cards consist of a micro-processor and different sizes of hardware memory components. In addition, the card includes a "smart" unique identification number, a serial number for the SIM or ICC-ID as it is known professionally.

The ICC-ID includes a mobile country code and a mobile communication network code, as well as the card's serial number. The goal of these smart cards is to authenticate the identity of users of the GSM and other communication networks. The SIM card includes information about the communication network, including required validation information, which enables connection to virtual space. The subscriber's personal identification number is the key to the limited use of the SIM card and/or to the audit required by management of the users.

As mentioned, the SIM card contains an international mobile subscriber identity (IMSI) component that is affiliated uniquely to the subscriber and consists of the country code, the mobile communication network code, and the subscriber's identity number. The SIM card may also contain identification of a temporary mobile subscriber, including identification of regional position.

I would note on this topic that not all information stored on the SIM card is accessible and that it is necessary to painstakingly examine the nature of the data. I would further note that it is necessary to differentiate between the mobile device and the SIM card, since the SIM card can easily be transferred to another mobile device. I would emphasize that mobile devices operating in previously mentioned technology cannot operate without a SIM card and, if no SIM card is installed when the device is turned on, a message that the user must insert a SIM card appears.

It is completely forbidden to insert a SIM card into the device being examined, since the device may execute a transfer action or an erasure of historical data. For instance, devices with the Windows Mobile operating system automatically import the contents from the SIM card when they are connected. Thus, if you insert your personal SIM card into the device, then the device will be identified through your personal data from the SIM card.

It is important to keep in mind that as a part of the process for the seizure of the mobile device itself, it is important to search for concomitant items that may include data or will help extract data from the device. Mobile memory cards or SIM cards can include more data than the device itself, and it is possible that there will be the need for communication coordinators so as to connect the device to an evidence collection system.

It is mandatory to document the types of hardware and their serial numbers, and it is also required to photograph each item and maintain accurate written records.. If the device is in an operational state, then it should be kept that way (if possible), since turning it off may activate a password locking mechanism, which will make the process of removing the data from the device at a later stage significantly more difficult. It is further required to document all the visible information, including information viewed on the device screen, such as date and system date and time.

Types of Evidence in Mobile Devices

The legal benefit that can exist in mobile devices within the framework of an investigation changes according to the type of offense, the nature of the actions being investigated, the capacity of the mobile device, and the manner of its use. Digital evidence can be found in three main locations in mobile devices: fixed memory, mobile memory connected to the device, and the SIM card.

I would also note on this issue that not all the components

mentioned previously will be available and/or essential to all investigations. Conversely, I would note that it is possible that some of the devices there may be used by people with a number of different SIM cards, a number of removable storage devices, and there may be more than one mobile device. These facts make the process of examination and data retrieval more difficult.

Criminal organizations are aware of the risks entailed in the use of mobile devices. To prevent criminal identification or any possibility of identifying members of the organization, it is generally assumed that such organizations/users will utilize a number of SIM cards lacking user identification– and these SIM cards will be used in pre-purchased mobile devices. In most cases, it is difficult to track these devices, since they are not linked directly to the identity of a certain person or organization.

Another method through which criminal organizations operate is the use of previous generations of cellular devices, which are limited to receiving and sending messages and calls. Alongside the fact that these are negligible abilities in comparison to the abilities of more advanced devices, it is very difficult, even impossible, to track and collect data from these devices

After the SIM card or the mobile device has been in use for a pre-determined period of time or after a crime has been committed using the device or the organization understands that sufficient time has passed to blur all connection between the device and the event, the users may attempt to destroy the device in order, to prevent the reconstruction of data.

On this matter I would note that damaged and/or broken SIM cards can benefit an investigation, since sometimes it is possible to reconstruct information from them. Members of criminal organizations are not indifferent to technological developments and they may often carry with them prestigious personal mobile devices that can provide digital evidence investigators with insights into their everyday conduct.

In light of the wide range of possibilities innate in a device that is part of an examination/investigation within the framework of a forensic technological examination, it is recommended to examine all of the device's abilities and functions to gain an understanding of the type of digital evidence that may be found on the device. The manufacturer name, the model, and the production year can provide this information, and therefore it is important to document them.

Short text messages (SMS) are fully documented by the cellular provider for a predetermined period of time and subject to the laws of the country. Unlike records of phone conversations, date and time signatures of messages received are generally accurate, since they are documented on the network services provider's systems rather than locally on the mobile device itself.

Conversely, short messages have considerable drawbacks. For example: a system that documents the first time that the message was read and/or whether the message reached its target does not exist. Sometimes messages are not transmitted in full to the recipient, due to technological failures between the communication networks or differences deriving from different types of hardware or telephone systems.

I would note that some of the methods that obtain data may reconstruct erased messages. However, it depends on the data's extraction method, and this will be discussed later on in this chapter. On the same topic: since it is likely that the message did not reach its target completely and/or was not read, then the question arises regarding the message's legal status of a that reached its target, such as an email message.

Pictures and audio-visual files can provide convincing digital evidence in legal proceedings. For example, there was a case in the United Kingdom in which a fifteen year old girl was found guilty of being an accessory to a crime and of encouraging murder, after she recorded a beating that led to the death of another person. As I already explained in previous chapters, frequently partners to the offense use mobile devices to record a crime, either for future criminal usage such as blackmail and threats or for reasons of their own.

The more advanced generations of Smartphones not only have internet capability but, in fact, compete with the abilities of personal computers. An advanced smartphone will store Internet browsing history, unique internet storage regions , Internet addresses, messages and picture messages (MMS – Multimedia Message Service), electronic mail, pictures, video clips, and applications. In addition, the device can transmit information and computer files easily and rapidly.

The mail and Internet browser history provide many legal insights. Moreover, in cellular devices third-party applications are installed that hold considerable information about the user, for instance, WhatsApp, Facebook, Twitter, online games, and so on. Internet application interfaces were first seen not long ago, but today they play a central role in the user's experience and greatly increase the ability of the mobile phone to provide considerable information about its owner at a specific point in time.

For example, if a mobile device user is documented as using an application for a certain period of time and at the same time a crime was committed, then it is difficult to assume that he was at the scene. This statement is correct subject to identifying the device's position at the time relevant to the event and/or the time that a message and/or email message was sent or received and examination of the user identification in the applications installed in the device. The digital evidence experts must adjust for this issue.

Information about the Position of the Mobile Device

The ability to determine the position of the mobile device at a specific point in time or the period before or after has considerable meaning within the framework of the investigation. Some of mobile devices document their position in relation to the cellular transmitters with which they were in contact, and the cellular provider can extract historical records about user positions during the given period of time.

GPS receivers constitute an inseparable part of the cellular device, and they may include remnants of maps and records of positions from the past, which can be used for the purpose of the investigation. In addition, data regarding the history of the digital pictures taken with the mobile device will contain information about the times and places they were taken. I would also note that the date and time at which the picture was taken, including the type of device used to take the picture, constitute additional data for cross-checking with GPS location data and the position where the picture was taken.

Malicious Code on Mobile Devices

At the beginning of this chapter, I noted that as greater use is made of mobile devices for managing bank accounts, purchase of goods, and so on, the devices increasingly become targets for computer criminals, who seek to steal funds or valuable information.

Kaspersky, which specializes in information assurance and development of anti-viruses applications, reported that the number of threats to the Android operating system has jumped by 700% a year. According to a report published by Kaspersky which summarized threats to mobile device platforms, in January 2012 there were fewer than 6,000 malicious code signatures against the Android operating system in the company's database, and at the end of the year there were more than 43,000. The report further indicates that more than 99% of the new threats focused on smart mobile devices and on handheld computers based on Google's Android operating system and less than 1% were directed at devices that use Symbian operating systems or Blackberry.

A fake bank application for Android devices was distributed among innocent users which sent information to a third party without their consent. Sophisticated computer viruses enable criminals to delay online banking transactions and thus withdraw money directly from the victim's bank account.

This is how the malicious Trojan program Zeus worked. It was intended to take over user activity on the computer or cellular device and to steal bank information from the devices. The program was first identified in July 2007, when it was used to steal information from the United States Department of Transport. A variation of the program was installed in user computers in a number of states and caused them to provide information regarding bank and credit card accounts.

Another action that caused harm to users was when the software delayed online banking communications in the attempt to track and capture authentication and confirmation numbers of banking transactions and to alter the fund's transfer path to the perpetrators account.

Additional malicious software programs enable activities on mobile devices to be taken over, including Windows Mobile, Blackberry, and iPhone devices. These programs, also known as spyware, enable effective surveillance of the device's user. In addition, they enable the collection of messages and text files, the documentation of conversations, browsing history, and online surfing on the Internet, and GPS positions. The data are recorded and the intruder can view the data through the Internet. These programs leave traces on the mobile devices, which can be identified through a legal check.

As mentioned, as modern society relies more and more on mobile devices, computer criminals will dedicate greater effort in an attempt to exploit these devices and thus to defraud innocent users and break into corporate communication networks .

Mobile devices, like any component that can connect to the Internet and cellular network, can serve as a platform for the launching of an attack against other computerized systems. Consequently, a number of information security mechanisms for computers and networks have been especially adjusted for cellular devices. Interface scanners, wireless communication network security analysts, and systems to examine of the scale of computer and network penetration— all have been adapted and/or developed for the Apple iPhone, for Android devices, and so on.

The duty of digital systems investigators is to keep in mind that mobile devices have the ability to connect to a variety of communication networks using cellular antennae and Wi-Fi and Bluetooth access points. From a legal perspective, I would note that the nature of mobile devices is to create opportunities and a developing environment, but conversely risks are also created and we must be aware of them.

Generally, communication networks include considerable information that can help in investigations that are linked to mobile devices. Conversely, the connection to the Internet allows criminals to implement remote destruction mechanisms in an attempt to blur and destroy incriminating evidence.

On this matter, I would note that device manufacturers develop these systems as part of the service that they provide to all users. Apple, for example, provides a network-based service that allows remote erasing of a variety of data found in an iPhone that was lost or stolen. Organizations that centrally manage Blackberry devices can erase, from a distance, the operating system of a stolen or lost device and thus destroy the device entirely.

In a different analogy, criminal organizations, with the assistance of experienced hackers, are aware of these inherent abilities which are an inseparable part of the device. Thus, if the device is seized by law enforcement agencies, the destruction system may be implemented, leading to the total erase of the device and the information it contains.

Communication network service providers can provide considerable information about the use of the cellular device, which can be cross-checked with data obtained from the process involved in the reconstruction of the mobile device. Communication network service providers save many subscriber account records. Clients with a new mobile contract will receive a detailed account that shows calls, messages, and data activities associated with the mobile device in their possession.

Like Internet providers, cellular providers can provide historical information about conversations and messages that were not directly reconstructed from the mobile device. The types of information that can be reconstructed are various, for instance, different bills, connection indications to cellular antenna, messages, Internet browsing data, location data, and so on.

Regarding the issue of tracking the device's location using the identification of antennae to which the mobile device connected, I would note that this is an imprecise method for determining the device's physical location at any specific time. The reason for this lies in the fact that newer mobile devices can be operated in various modes, such as flight mode, the device can transfer to a different type of network, and so on. These possibilities give the user the ability to conceal their exact location – and even to create a false location report.

Further on this matter, I would note that if the user chose to do this, then it is difficult to impossible to reconstruct the data from the mobile device itself. The duty of the digital evidence investigators is to be aware of the fact that using these tools it is also possible to hide telephone numbers dialed from the device, a fact that makes the device superfluous with regard to possible relationships between the victim and the owner of the seized device.

From a different angle, I would note that this is a circumstantial relationship and not direct evidence and that in most cases it is possible to obtain this data from the cellular company. As mentioned, if there are many conversations from the mobile device to the same number, then it is possible to conclude that there a relationship indeed existed between the parties. In other cases, it could be argued that if the conversation were not held, then this is information in transition or it can be argued for technological interpretation, for example, the dial button was pressed inadvertently pressed whilst the device was in the user's pocket.

Conversely, communication network service suppliers, as mentioned, generally save records of call details. Namely, they can provide specific information about each and every call and message sent or received by the mobile device. On this matter, I would note that it is necessary to examine local law on the matter of the obligation of the cellular company to save and document the data and on the matter of the required period of time.

In my opinion, it is necessary to establish a uniform law for the cellular network, similar to my proposal on the matter of the Internet, and I will explain my statements. The fact that the mobile device, registered originally in one country, can move without interference to any other company and connect to a cellular network requires uniformity on this issue as well.

Frequently it is possible to find data from cellular devices on laptop or desk top computers that were synchronized with the same cellular component. It is possible that items that were erased from the cellular device will still be found on the desktop of the home computer or office work station. The information can include email messages, personal data, and text files in different formats, including picture, video and audio files.

The data can be collected into a proprietary format, or in other words, as a separate unit. However, it is likely that there will be a need for a designated or unique software program to convert the files into a readable format. In addition, in an in-depth examination of the seized device, digital evidence investigators can obtain information pertaining to online accounts to which the device connected, for instance, cloud-based services[136]. This data can be found in the mobile device 'keychain' databases and they can include bank account details, user details for different websites, information about email accounts, and so on.

I would also note that cellular devices can transfer documents and multimedia files created by the device to remote storage services, namely, 'cloud' based services, for long-term storage. Mobile devices with Internet browsing capabilities can connect to these data services from any place and at any time.

On the same topic, I would emphasize and note that Google's Android operating system automatically synchronizes between the cellular device's pictures and file folders and the Google's cloud environment as part of the free backup service provided for the

---

[136] On the matter of cloud technology, see the chapter of concepts and definitions.

device's owner.

In addition, cellular devices can connect to online social communication networks such as Facebook. This fact enables digital evidence investigators to retrieve additional material regarding patterns of behavior, social relations, statements, and hints between two or more friends on the social network.

During the first years of the Facebook social network, the US government used the information uploaded to the site. Young people from Israel who shared information such as "I got a visa to the United States, I am going to work in a sales cart" (when the visa was a tourist visa) with their friends were denied entrance into the US and were forced to return to Israel. Hence, digital evidence investigators can retrieve valuable data from this environment, information that may possibly be erased by the user from the mobile device for his own reasons.

Within the framework of my work in Israel, I was required to address a rape case that came before the Court. The complainant argued that following the original rape case she has been suffering, for many years, from deep depression. As a part of my examinations, I looked through the complainant's user profile on Facebook t and lo and behold: I saw pictures from parties and excursions from the period during which she had said she had suffered from extreme depressed. Moreover, the text that accompanied the photographs indicated that depression was not the state she was actually in.

As mentioned previously, digital evidence investigators can retrieve information from mobile devices and thus learn about the user's behavior patterns on social networks. I would note that the cellular device, even a basic model, can provide considerable information about the user's activities on social networks.

When we examine the term 'social network', the picture revealed is of Facebook or similar online social network. However, 'social network' is a much broader term. When examining the relationships between the user and those around him in virtual space, we must understand that in certain communities the term 'social network' has another meaning. Hence, even earlier generation telephones, with limited Internet ability, include address books that may provide a measure of the user's 'social communication network', including details about his work, family, and so on.

The ability to reconstruct data from 'social communication networks' is especially useful in the investigation of criminal organizations, including drug dealers, gangs, pimps, and terrorists. As previously mentioned, drug dealers and organized crime organizations often use cheap mobile devices that cannot be identified with a specific service provider or user, in order to conduct criminal actions. Nevertheless, and despite the fact that this is a device lacking an officially attributable identity, digital evidence investigators can retrieve information from these devices, such as call history, pictures, and so on, which provide an insight as to the relationship between the suspect and the device, including the suspect's identity and connection to the activity/crime under investigation.

In general, cellular devices indicate the owner's patterns of behavior including habits and acquaintances. However, these devices have additional advantages that can help during the various investigations. In cases in which a number of cellular devices are involved, analysis of overlapping communication networks can provide hints about shared friends and acquaintances and about ways of communication among seemingly unrelated groups. Moreover, analysis of recordings of conversations will provide further insight into the strength of the relationships amongst the device owners, including data about communication time lines.

Priorities in Emergency Situations

In light of the dynamic nature and accelerated technological development of cellular devices, digital evidence experts are often required to capture data during transmission and in real time. These are extreme situations, such as military operations, threats of explosive devices, fear of potential loss of life, and so on.

In such situations, the time dimension is a critical variable, and hence the obligation of digital evidence investigators is to act immediately to extract the information from the device. I would note that the emphasis is on the speed of action and that every delay may allow the implementation of a security locking system or may provide a window of opportunity for the remote erasing of data.

Effective and efficient instruments and correct processes for the determination of priorities at the scene of the event may preserve digital evidence that, in another case, may have been destroyed. As part of the process for protecting data on the device, digital evidence experts must ensure that no harm was caused to the device and/or no suspicious changes were made. In most cases, a visual, external examination of the device will be possible; however when we are dealing with a criminal or an experienced criminal organization, possessed of technological knowledge, it is necessary to use high resolution microscopic devices to identify physical harm or changes to the device.

More modern mobile devices include a standard component that allows for the easy insertion of a memory card that considerably improves the device's data storage capability. Sometimes digital evidence investigators ignore these storage components, and sometimes it is difficult to find the slot used for the insertion of the storage components. If, during the capture and/or examination of the device, it is found that the device supports a mobile storage card, then it is necessary to search for the proper type of memory card. If a mobile storage component is found in the device, then it is necessary to remove it, and thus to preserve the information found in it.

Further on this issue, I would note that it is necessary to address the data found in this type of storage medium in a way that is identical to the handling of other storage media. It is obligatory to document the memory component's serial number of the, to determine if damage was caused to the storage component, to use devices and protocols that prevent the memory card from being written to and any data altered, , and then to make a legally acceptable and admissible copy, using approved tools, that is faithful to the original. The legal examination should be conducted only on the legal copy. This can be done through the use of recognized legal software, while evaluating the possibility and feasibility of reconstructing of erased files.

Legal Preservation of Cellular Devices

On the matter of acceptable means to preserve mobile devices, I would note that the same legal principles that apply to other devices apply also to cellular devices. The aim is to enable other professionals to validate digital evidence submitted to them. Keep in mind that the goal of the legally established process is to document the evidence and authenticate its admissibility and that it was not changed or replaced from the moment of seizure.

Examiners involved in the examination of mobile devices must document their names in all documentation relating to their examination in order to ensure transparency and repeatability, while providing the possibility for a third party to evaluate and repeat their work process. In addition, it is necessary to evaluate and document the data thereby enabling other professionals to ascertain that nothing was changed from the moment that the original data was obtained. On this matter I would note that it is necessary to document the steps taken to protect and preserve the device throughout. Hence, it is necessary to document every transfer of the device to another person, as part of the process dealing with, retrieving and examining data.

It should be remembered that cellular devices, by their nature receive and transmit data using wireless communication networks and/or a GPS transmitter and/or a Bluetooth component. Hence, there is a fear that data could be rewritten or erased. Taking into account the circumstances of the event, the investigator must make an intelligent decision – whether to prevent or enable the device from obtaining new data through wireless communication networks.

Removal of the battery from the mobile device will prevent its connection to the 'world' but could also implement security measures such as locking codes and encoding, which may prevent further access to the data found on the device. If it is necessary to activate the device as part of the examination process, then it is necessary to prevent the component's ability to transmit to the outside world, for instance, by placing it in a sealed room or placing it in flight mode. It is necessary to take into account that in a situation in which the device is placed in a sealed room it will strengthen its attempt to transmit to the world, similar to when the rate of transmission is increased when a cellular device is placed in an elevator. Therefore, it is necessary to ascertain that the mobile device is connected to a source of electricity and thus to maintain its regular operation.

Isolating the device from the communication network ensures that the telephone's contents will reflect the time at which it was seized and thus will 'freeze' any possible change in the device after its seizure. These are devices for which it is possible to define a configuration to prevent communication with the outside world, such as flight mode. If the device does not have such capability, then it is possible, for example, to isolate it from radio waves by placing it in an evidence container armored against radio frequencies, which blocks network communication.

Frequency-distortion systems are another means of preventing communication between cellular devices and the outside world. However, this type of equipment is illegal in certain countries, because of fear of the disruption of legitimate frequencies, and the fear to human life. It is necessary to be sure to adopt conservative work procedures on this matter. It is possible to isolate the device for the purpose of examination and legal analysis through the use of sealed examination rooms that block transmission frequencies or through the removal of storage components from the devices.

In light of the wide variety of cellular devices available today, it is not surprising that there is no one, single, definitive and correct method of obtaining access to all the devices so as to remove from them data while using software or hardware components. This is one of the primary obstacles faced by laboratory workers and digital evidence examiners.

I would note that it is clear that not all means for the extraction of data from cellular devices are always available, and it is possible that the solution will not necessarily supply the required results. Therefore, in such a situation the digital evidence investigators have only one possibility: manual examination.

As a result of obtaining of data from cellular devices, we see a wide variety of methods through which it is possible to learn details of the incident and the legal case. It is possible that a single examination device will not provide an appropriate solution for constellational the cellular devices that are being examined, and in addition it is possible that it will become clear that the device for the identification of evidence in one device may have limited application when examining another cellular device. Generally it is recommended and desirable to extract data from a cellular device while using two or more of methods, making it possible to compare the results and verify that the information upon which the work is based is correct and accurate.

Sometimes, a manual examination is enough if all that is required from the device is a specific 'piece of information'. It is necessary to verify that the investigator has the knowledge required to operate the device, namely, he has attempted the action on an identical device before the performance of the manual examination. For this reason, and to enable the manual examination of the device and to develop effective examination tools and techniques, laboratories for the identification and handling of legal digital evidence that specialize in this type of examinations have a wide variety of mobile devices.

During the manual examination, it is mandatory to record and film all actions taken, using a camera and/or video recorder, so as to enable other professionals to evaluate the quality of the examination and that all rules and procedures are adhered to.

In light of the complexity of mobile telephones, during a manual examination of the mobile device, it is easily possible to mistakenly 'skip' areas of digital evidence because they are new, innovative, or invisible, namely, not familiar and/or do not arouse suspicion.

During my work, I was often required to address cellular issues and as a part of the examination I conducted I was surprised to discover that different areas in the cellular device were not examined at all, apparently for the reasons I noted previously. If this is a device that has considerable value for a specific investigation and since it is possible that it is a manual examination, it is recommended that every screen and every application be examined methodically and to painstakingly document the results. In addition, it is recommended to bring the mobile device for another examination, by another team, without providing any information about previous examinations. In this way it will be possible to cross check the examination findings and to ascertain that everything that needed to be done was done.

The most frequent mechanical method to access to devices is the use of a data cable followed by wireless methods such as Bluetooth. When access to the device is obtained, the primary obstacle is to determine the most effective means for the removal of data from the device.

Most cellular devices support standard access through basic commands. However, method provides access to a limited selection of data. Many mobile devices include unique proprietary protocols of the device owner and necessitate a manufacturer's tool, such as a key, to execute the task. In certain cases, the information that can be obtained through a physical connection to the device differs from the information that can be obtained through a wireless or Bluetooth connection. Therefore, it is possible that obtaining of data from the device may require a number of methods to ensure that all available data is obtained.

Within the framework of the legal process and since the Bluetooth component and/or receiving components installed on the mobile device may erode the technological stability of the device, communication disruptions and/or suspicions of disruption of evidence may arise, which may, in turn, lead to the partial disqualification of evidence and/or a reduction of its credibility and/or weight in the eyes of the judicial authority.

On this matter, my recommendation is that when it is possible to perform a physical connection to the mobile device, then this should be the preferred procedure. As mentioned, the primary advantage in obtaining the device's physical memory is that there is a more complete capture of the data, including items that were erased. In addition, methods of physically obtaining data can also be implemented on faulty mobile devices. This generally involves fewer changes to the original device when obtaining the data.

There are a number of approaches to obtaining a legal admissible physical copy of mobile devices. Today digital evidence investigators have at their disposal different and diverse legal instruments, which enable control of a number of hardware layers and the software system of the mobile device. Despite said that said, it is important to emphasize that the removal of the physical memory component may disrupt and severe the logical structure of the file system, which necessitates the removal of undecipherable or unknown data or the deciphering of raw information from file system.

Naturally, manual and logical methods for obtaining data necessitate reduced interaction with the examined device. Frequently, for logistical or technical reasons, it is not practical to obtain a precise copy that is 100% faithful to the original mobile device. Therefore, sometimes to the investigator has no choice but to trust the cellular device's operating systems and hope that this will not cause a change to the memory structure while performing read operations. If, during the examination, the data analyst reaches the conclusion that a certain technique for obtaining data resulted in a change in device's structure, then it is necessary to document this.

I would further note that in laboratory conditions it is possible to obtain the full contents of the mobile device's physical memory. This provides access to data that were erased, including SMS data, call logs and identity data obtained from SIM cards that were previously inserted into the mobile device.

If the user activated a personally adjusted locking code mechanism on the mobile device, then it is possible to obtain complete information regarding the entire memory store, and then to use it to enter the device logically. These are unique instruments, which require considerable knowledge alongside high technological abilities and they are not part of the skill set of every legal digital evidence investigator.

In some of the devices, it is possible to obtain the unlocking code and/or bypass it while using legal tools that obtain logical data from the mobile devices. The advantage in the obtaining of data logically is that this provides digital evidence investigators with another possibility of documenting data. I would, however, note that for certain devices these instruments are not effective and all that is possible is the removal of limited information using the manufacturer's backup program.

On the password protection, as mentioned, mobile devices by nature enable users to define a password that will restrict access to the device, similar to passwords for computers and/or handheld computers. In some cases, it is possible to bypass this protection, by reconstructing the password.

I would emphasize that it is completely forbidden to attempt to guess the locking code or password, since certain mobile devices will erase their contents after a defined number of failed attempts. Such an attempt by a digital evidence examiner is negligence and may invalidate the admissibility of the evidence produced from this cellular device.

As a part of technological development, software companies work on the development of legal technological instruments that will provide an effective means of obtaining data from a variety of mobile devices. Most devices and software programs to examine cellular devices, as already mentioned, operate through a physical connection, or in other words, a cable and/or infrared device and/or Bluetooth/wireless device. These instruments operate in a similar manner: they send orders to the cellular device and record responses that include information stored in the device's memory. The volume of the information that can be retrieved through the use of these methods depends on the connection mechanism and the device model.

One of the basic ways of obtaining data is the creation of an interaction with the telephone's operating system, similar to the method used by cellular telephone manufacturer's synchronization systems. Naturally, this is a very limited way of retrieving information and the reason lies in the inability of the system to retrieve data from invisible layers. Using this method is not possible to retrieve information from the deeper layers of the device, for instance, from data that was erased and overwritten. As mentioned, mobile phones by nature include basic data, for instance address books, logs of calls, messages, and photographs; however additional information is not secure.

The activation of the mobile phone may endanger the trustworthiness of the digital evidence, since, as already stated, it is possible that the telephone will make changes in its memory areas. I would note that it is not possible to verify the hypothesis that the cellular device indeed will make these changes without the original code and the cellular device's hardware electrical circuit diagrams Which are rarely, if ever, available to the general public.

System developers operate in different ways in order to obtain a commercial advantage over their competitors. Certain legal instruments act by inserting and implementing a file into the mobile device. This action, known as a 'software agent', is comparable to spyware (Trojan horse) that is inserted into the mobile device with the aim of obtaining data from it.

From a legal perspective the use of a software agent has advantages since it is trustworthy and provides a detailed process audit report. Conversely, if the software agent communicates with a legal instrument that cannot operate on the examined device, then data will not be obtained. It is necessary to take into account that in a situation in which specific files in the mobile device are not inaccessible via the operating system (for example, files that were erased or files that are in a different format obtained from another device) then certain and important information will not be obtained.

One of the main problems in this matter is the fact that the implementation of a software agent on the device will necessarily change the device and may even lead to the rewriting of data. Conversely, it is necessarily to take into consideration that in certain cases the sole available possibility of obtaining data from the mobile device will be with the activation of a software agent.

The duty of digital evidence investigators is to examine and evaluate these issues against the advantages to be gained from obtaining specific information from the device. In addition, it is essential to explain why the digital evidence obtained in this way is trustworthy, despite the technological difficulties faced, and to provide answers to questions that arise following the use of the software agent on the device.

The New JTAG Standard IEEE1149.7

The new JTAG standard IEEE1149.7 is a relatively new standard that the International IEEE Institute[137] defined, in 2009. The standard addresses the test of mathematical logic in combined electric circuits, which provides easy access allowing the examination of the relationships between the combined circuits when they are connected to the printed circuit board and the examination of the combined circuit itself or any change of activity in a circuit during the component's regular operation.

This standard has a rather long title: "IEEE Standard for Reduced-Pin and Enhanced-Functionality Test Access Port and Boundary-Scan Architecture". It is not intended to take the place of the old standard, 1149.1, but rather uses it as a foundation to improve the performance of the existing standard and to extend its use. It should be noted that the 'traditional' standard, IEEE 1149.1, has successfully used these checks for more than twenty years, it is 'alive and well', effective and efficient, and will continue to be so in most of the leading technological instruments for examinations now, and in my opinion in the foreseeable future.

In the matter under discussion, the standard is, as mentioned, an interface for the examination of combined electric circuits, reciprocal connection between elements, and a means for the observation of the electrical circuit during the implementation of the components and for changes in its activity. This is the standard characterization found in many mobile phones, since it provides interface manufacturers with a deep layer, independent of the operating system.

Naturally, manufacturers of mobile phones do not provide data required regarding JTAG specifications to all comers. The JTAG interests legal investigators and legal data analysts, since it can provide direct access to the mobile phone's memory, without fear of change or harm to the reliability and credibility of the digital evidence. However, for this purpose considerable time and knowledge are necessary, which

---

[137] http://ieeexplore.ieee.org/xpl/mostRecentIssue.jsp?punumber=5412864

necessitate not only an understanding of the standard as it relates to every device model but also the ability to reconstruct binary data from the mobile device's memory components.

Despite the existing limits to the use of JTAG as a legal mechanism for obtaining data, this is the most common and reliable method for the physical extraction of data. The reason lies in the fact that there is a uniform and effective standard, shared for the most part by all manufacturers of mobile devices. This uniformity allows the development of effective legal instruments for access to the information bases of the mobile device, without fear of harming the operating system and/or the activation of the self-destruct system.

In digital components found in everyday use there is a chip that is used to turn the device off. The removal and direct reading of memory chips from the device is the most exhausting method of data extraction. However, it has the advantage of allowing the most direct access to the data. Removal of the chip and the physical extraction of data is the most comprehensive data extraction method available. From a legal perspective, data read directly from the memory chip is considered the 'cleanest', namely, there is no fear of harm and/or distortion of the digital evidence. The reason is that the data is not based on a communication system and/or operating system that mediates between the device and the examination component. Reading the chip directly studies the memory structures and enables direct analysis of the data.

This method 'suffers' from the same problems as the JTAG extraction. This is the most complex method for the extraction of data and the rate of failure is considerable. It is considered unpractical in many situations in which there was no need to present evidence in the legal proceeding, namely, in cases when the accusation is not established or where there is no trial process.

In light of the complexity involved in reconstructing data that was erased from the flash memory of mobile devices, it is generally recommended to provide further validity to the examination results. For this purpose, there are a variety of approaches to such as manual examination and comparison of the data through use of logical/physical systems.

Many smart mobile telephones use SQLite databases to store information. If items were erased from the mobile phone, then the contents may still be found in the database. All that has been erased is the entry record (index table) which causes the data to be hidden. However, Through the use of a database browser, it is still possible to reconstruct the data.

I would also note that some of mobile devices use proprietary file parameters to store information, and these may include erased data as described in the section on databases. For instance, mobile devices using the Windows operating system store communications data in the database in a folder which is affiliated with Microsoft's operating system and can preserve items that were erased.

Examination and Legal Analysis of Mobile Devices

As previously mentioned, the goal of the legal examination is to find and extract information related to the investigation, including data that was erased, communication and data transmission methods, whether through the Internet or the cellular network, including transmission and reception of GPS signals. At the end of the process, there is the burden of proof regarding the reliability of the digital evidence and the possibility of following up the examiners actions as a part of the process for the extraction of evidence from the mobile device.

To differentiate from PCs and/or laptop computers, with cellular devices there is concern of harming the extracted data's credibility and admissibility,   whether logically or physically, because of the complexity and variety of devices, and as a result of constant new technological innovations that that results in a lack of up to date knowledge amongst digital evidence examiners.

The problem of constant technological innovation and development makes it increasingly difficult for digital forensic experts to provide adequate solutions. This results in the courts and presiding judges lacking the tools required to cope with the serious question regarding the admissibility of evidence.

In light of the pace of technological innovation, we can learn that there is no similarity between the world of technology and the physical world, which, in academic frameworks and in the Courts, we analyze day and night. In other words, even if there are articles, research studies, and Court rulings from the past which address the in-depth issues regarding mobile devices, and painstakingly examine the nature of the evidence that is obtained as a part of the examination process, Court rulings are, for the most part, irrelevant unless they address the identical mobile device and the identical model.

Despite that mentioned previously, and since most of mobile

devices meet standard 1149.7, which constitutes the hardware basis for mobile phones systems, it is necessary to define and meet uniform standards regarding the examination processes. The following are general examination standards.

- Review the accessible components in order to recognize and understand the mobile device's main information sources. Only then should the data reconstruction process, which includes erased items including files, messages, call logs, and multimedia files, be started.

- Collect information about data from the active items and from the reconstructed items, such as date and time stamps and names of files. Next clarify whether the messages were read and whether the calls were incoming, outgoing, or unanswered calls.

- Perform a methodical and thorough search and examination of all the findings, including a search for key words for known specific items related to the investigation.

- Perform an analysis of available data and the information relationships were obtained from the memory, including the event time line and a relationship diagram. It is important that an additional examination using alternative tools is performed to validate results. This is because even when using legally approved and acceptable instruments that have been subjected to examination processes regarding their trustworthiness, the possibility of a failure (bug) is always an issue that must be addressed.

- When dealing with the mobile device's active data on the base line, it is necessary to examine all the messages that were obtained and the call log, calendar entries and other items that are stored on the device.

A review of the data obtained from the study of the mobile device's folders and the contents of files in the device can lead to effective and useful items and facilitate the development of a strategy for the 'analysis' of the mobile device. On this matter, I would emphasize that this process does not constitute a substitute for a methodical and thorough legal examination.

As a part of the legal examination process, alongside analysis and cross-checking, it is necessary to take into account what we know about the crime or action under investigation and the types of information we are searching for. For example, in a legal case in which a specific period of time is defined as noteworthy, an examination of all the actions performed with the mobile device and reconstruction of the time lime and events may be an effective strategy.

In a case in which digital photographs are relevant to the legal case, an effective strategy for finding the sought after pictures could be a combination of examining file systems and the reconstruction of pictures that were erased and/or sent to websites and to social networks such as Facebook, YouTube, WhatsApp, and so on, and a search for keywords and extraction of the relevant files.

Furthermore, on the issue of photographs that were found and/or reconstructed from the mobile device: it is necessary to examine and validate that the photographs were indeed taken with the examined device and not 'downloaded' from the Internet, thus creating a direct relationship to offense attributed to the owner of the mobile device.

In addition, on this issue I would also note that every series of mobile devices has its own format for system files. I will further note that system formats range from the simple to the exceedingly complex which constitute part of the folders that include the device's operating system core files o. For example, LG and Motorola devices use a component to receive wireless network with a BREW operating system (Binary Runtime Environment for Wireless), which was developed by Qualcomm and includes a private device file system stored in a separate folder.

In devices that use CDMA[138] transmission technologies, we can find BitPim[139] file systems. However, when using the BitPim system, it is possible that seeing the date and time stamps associated with the files or obtaining the whole file system for examination at a later stage through the use of other instruments may not be possible.

On this issue, I would note that it is possible to obtain information in the opposite manner, namely through the time stamp appearing on files that were obtained from other sources, such as email messages, Word files, photographs, Internet browsing data and data supplied or obtained from the cellular supplier that indicate the use of the device from a certain point of time and in a specific geographic location.

It should be noted that commercial legal instruments such as Cellebrite[140] are known to retrieve the complete file logic system from most of mobile devices, including information about data such as time stamps (date and hour). The software developed by the company was examined and found to be trustworthy on the issue of the admissibility of digital evidence in the cellular field.

As I have already noted, in certain cases it is not possible to retrieve a complete copy of the mobile device's physical memory. Although alternative methods will not necessarily lead to the retrieval of all the erased items, it might still be possible to obtain solid digital evidence pertaining to web browning history and additional data that are not presented automatically by the legal instruments.

In situations of this type, the legal examiners' duty is to identify the desired information in the file system and to interpret it. This is one

---

[138] Code Division Multiple Access of CDMA is one method of a variety of transmission methods between coordination stations and cellular devices. On this topic see the chapter of terms and definitions.

[139] A program that enables the presentation and operation of data on mobile telephones using CDMA technology from LG, Samsung, Sanyo, and other companies. On this topic see the chapter of terms and definitions.

[140] Cellebrite is a global company known for technological breakthroughs in the cellular field. The company was established in 1999 by a team of professionals from the field of communication and mobile telephones. http://www.cellebrite.com/company/about-cellebrite.html

of the main reasons for the importance of understanding the technology that is the foundation for the mobile device, and the investigator/examiner should not rely solely on automatic technological instruments.

As mentioned, more than once, as a part of the investigation process, investigators are required to perform a data reconstruction process from mobile devices. On this matter I would note that when use is made of common file systems, such as FAT or HFS, it is possible to reconstruct files that were erased by using reconstruction instruments that are part of the device's operating system. For instance, it is possible to reconstruct items such as MMS[141] messages, which were erased by the previously mentioned software programs.

In certain mobile devices, when a file is opened, a temporary file remains, a sort of background document created in the volatile memory, which is later erased. The reconstruction of this file type, if possible, is another example of the data reconstruction process for data that was erased and that may have considerable value in the legal proceeding. Reconstructed items of this type may contain considerable and vital information regarding access to the file, including time stamp documentation.

Hardware layers in conjunction with the erosion and loss of data in the device resulting from continuous use over time may make data reconstruction difficult with regard to flash memory components. Put simply, the greater the length of elapsed time since the event being investigates, so the harder it will be to find and reconstruct data from the mobile device (as with any other electronic component I have addressed in this book).

The Court must ascribe to this difficulty a factual value regarding evidence presented to it as part of the legal proceeding. In other words, if the digital components were seized near the time of the event, it is possible to attribute to the digital evidence retrieved from the mobile devices greater weight in the matter of the admissibility of

---

[141] See the chapter of terms and definitions.

the data. The longer the device's date of seizure of the device is from the date of the event, it is necessary to reduce the weight of the evidence's admissibility. Nevertheless, since methods for retrieving evidence along the time line are constantly developing, this issue will be examined subjectively in relation to the type of hardware and the nature of the findings submitted to the Court.

Mobile devices store data in a variety of formats. To decode data in mobile components and in order to validate, in-depth, important results, legal investigators must understand the various formats b. This requires that they take into account the types of operating systems installed on the mobile device. In addition, understanding hexadecimal[142] binary numbers is required; examiners must have in-depth understanding as to how these methods suit the ASCII (American Standard Code for Information Interchange[143]) keys.

In contrast to the form of storage commonly used in computers, cellular devices do not store SMS messages in ASCII but use a seven-bit alphabet. This demands considerable attention to ensure that the key word search is executed using seven bit coding as the message text will not be visible in a different bit environment.

Explanation

The terms 7, 16, 32, or 64 bits are related to the way in which the computer's processing unit (CPU) 'handles' the information. The 64 bit version of the Windows operating system, for example, can deal with large quantities of information in its random access memory (RAM) more effectively than a 32 bit system[144]. This fact, as with many others, indicates the radical difference between computer systems that we looked at previously and mobile phone systems, which operate in a totally different manner from desk top computers.

---

[142] Counting on a hexadecimal basis is counting by base 16, which today is used primarily in the field of computers, because of its suitability to the representation of the content of the computer memory.

[143] Code for representation of keys in the computer memory and in its files, like digits, letters, punctuation marks, and so on. See also the chapter of terms and definitions.

[144] On this matter, see the chapter of terms and definitions, even and odd bits.

I would also note that over the years in the pace of computer development is shown in the ever increasing calculating speed, the size and power of hardware systems and the ability of software to use hardware components. In mobile phones, in contrast, development has been characterized primarily by the introduction of innovative technologies, which replaced outdated and large hardware with hardware of minimal dimensions and with software with a reduced need for volatile memory.

As already mentioned, in addition to a variety of data types, mobile devices make use of data structures so as to represent call logs and other information. Digital evidence investigators and developers of technological tools conduct research in the field of data structures so as to assist the investigation in different ways, in the attempt to achieve a greater amount of data and in the attempt to correctly decipher the extracted information.

To summarize this topic, I would emphasize again that the Court must examine information regarding the date of the cellular device's seizure as well as the way in which the evidence extracted from it was handled. It is necessary to understand the profound difference between a home or a laptop computer and the cellular phone. Both meet the definition of computers, but on the matter of the legal examination test there is a radical difference, and hence our duty is to address these components differently.

Legal Analysis of Microsoft Windows 7 and 8 Operating Systems

I will begin this section with a brief history of the development of Microsoft operating systems. These systems have changed greatly over the years, changes that weigh strongly on the world of digital evidence extracted from mobile devices with innovative operating systems.

In 2003 Microsoft launched its first cellular phone operating system (WM). Thus system was known as Windows Mobile 2003, and was replaced by WM5, WM6, and so on. In 2010, after Apple and Microsoft upgraded their cellular phone operating systems Microsoft stock values dropped considerably in the smartphone operating system market. Consequently, in the same year, the company decided to completely change the structure of the operating system, including an image change and renaming the OS as Windows Phone.

The new Windows cellular telephones operating system was called Windows Phone 7 (WP7) and was launched on February 15, 2010 at the Global Congress for Mobile Devices. The new operating system replaced the older WM6 operating system. Microsoft's previous mobile operating systems were based on proceeding versions and included technological improvements and upgrades from previous versions of the operating system.

For instance, the WM6 system was based on WM5, which was based on WM 2003, and so on. In contrast, the WP7 operating system was built from scratch, namely, it replaced all the old hardware and software components and was developed differently from the older operating systems.

This fact brings us to the same problem I addressed previously, namely, the combination of technology and law, the trustworthiness of the evidence presented in Court, the method by which evidence is extracted alongside the information that can be learned from past rulings. In other words, this question is relevant primarily in light of the fact that contrary to 'traditional' offenses, which have barely changed for hundreds of years, in the case of offenses or digital evidence, in light of the pace of technological change, legal precedents from the past quickly become irrelevant, since they are not based on the same technology nor the same legal instruments that were used in the past to obtain digital evidence from older devices.

Moreover, legal instruments that were examined in the past and were found to be trustworthy with regard digital evidence presented with their aid need to undergo a far-reaching change of structure so that they can cope with new technologies. Therefore, the following question arises. Does the evidence presented to the Court reflect what is actually done and/or it is possible to rely on what is presented in an unshakable manner?

On December 27, 2012 the WP8 Windows operating system was launched, replacing the company's previous operating systems, WP7 and WP6. WP8 is different visually from its predecessors and includes a number of technological additions. However, there are no essential differences between it and WP7. Hence, I will focus on WP7, which brought into the world a different technological model and resulted in a turning point in the manner in which dealing with digital evidence and its extraction from cellular device's was approached.

As mentioned, it is possible to address the WP7 and WP8 operating systems as operating systems that are completely different from their predecessors. Microsoft designed the operating system completely from scratch, so that the system is not based on the old WM model and/or on previous versions. WP7 and WP8 will not work with older hardware, namely, on old mobile phones, and they will not operate any older generation software or application. As already stated, in the new systems there are many visual changes, in the matter under discussion, the significance is that following some of the changes, the techniques for the handling of digital evidence changed. From a different perspective, legal instruments that were able to extract data from the older generation devices will no longer operate in the new systems.

The operating system comes with a new user interface, which includes a touchscreen and virtual keyboard (on screen). Instead of symbols, the system uses a version called 'tiles'. This is a dynamic design that enables the user to shape the user interface as they see fit.

Standard operating system applications include, of course, an Internet browser, email software – including email programs accessed through the browser such as Hotmail, YahooMail, or Gmail, multimedia music , video, and photographs players, Office (or comparable) applications, and so on. As with smartphone platforms of competing companies, Microsoft's operating system enables the installation of third party applications, for instance, for the downloading and using music players, different types of navigation systems, video clips, and so on.

As mentioned, during an investigation which involves digital evidence in the WM operating system, use is made of tools and forensics techniques to extract data from the cellular device. In the first stage, device is imaged, namely, legally acceptable and admissible copy, faithful to the original is made. Then the data obtained are examined, so as to find data that is relevant to the investigation.

One of the accepted ways to extract data is to connect the device to a personal computer (PC) either with a USB connection or through direct physical access to the mobile device's memory. The WP7 operating system indeed connects to the personal computer using a USB connection, but the mechanism which facilitates communication between the telephone and the personal computer has changed. The change to the way in which the mobile device communicates with the personal computer may cause legal instruments recognized for the examination and collection of digital evidence not to work in the WP7 operating system.

On the matter of direct access to the device's memory, forensic instruments and techniques existing today in operating systems such as WM do not allow the extraction and/or analysis of data from a mobile device with a WP7 operating system. The significance of the operating system change is expressed by the way data is stored in memory. In other words, it may not be possible at all to analyze the data obtained using existing instruments and techniques.

There are instruments for the collection of digital evidence from WM systems that can obtain data from the device by installing software on the mobile device. Installation is performed through a USB connection to the personal computer, after which the software transfers the contents from the device's memory to the personal computer. I would note that the fact that the installation is performed on the device itself and not on a copy faithful to the original raises, as mentioned, doubt as to the reliability and credibility of the digital evidence as a whole.

In addition, I would also note that situations do exist where it is impossible to install software on the mobile device, for two reasons. First, the method of communication between the WP7 system and the personal computer is different from that used in the past, which increases the possibility that installation of the software on a mobile device using existing tools will not be possible. Second, as mentioned before, the WP7 operating system cannot implement older generation software, so that even if the software is installed on the mobile phone, it is likely that it will not run correctly, in at all in the WP7 environment.

I would further note that to date I have not seen any information that proves, beyond all reasonable doubt, that programs and applications installed on the mobile device do not harm digital evidence that may be found on the device. It is my opinion, that a gap still exists between instruments for the identification and collection of digital evidence from mobile devices in general and forensics tools for the WP7 operating system.

As mentioned previously, legal preservation of mobile devices in general and of digital evidence in particular necessitates considerable knowledge and experience regarding the device from which the data were extracted. A legal investigation that includes digital evidence from mobile devices and in particular from devices with the WP7 operating system is carried out using technological forensic tools intended to examine and analyze mobile phone devices.

The legal principles that apply to all computerized devices apply also to cellular devices. This enables additional professionals to authenticate the electronic evidence that was obtained by the original investigation team. It should be remembered that the goal of the legally-based process is to document the evidence and to validate its originality, or in other words, to show and proof that it was not changed or replaced since its identification and collection. These facts are the root of the problem with regard to new devices, for which experience, so far, has been minimal.

The investigators must document all their actions with regard to the mobile device and the data it contains. This is to ensure transparency and to support repeatability, while providing a third party the ability to evaluate the work process and repeat it. In addition, it is necessary to calculate and to document the data obtained, so as to allow other professionals to ascertain that that the original data has been unchanged since its original collection.

It was further required to document failures encountered by investigators during the examination and collection of the data, for example, failures deriving from the installation of previous generation software on a new device. In my experience, new operating system provide frequent error messages, and at the time of writing, it has still to be proven definitively that in such a case the device's contents was preserved in their entirety.

In general, advanced methods enable the physical collection of data from the mobile telephone. Indeed, physical access will yield a better result in terms of the information and data collected. However, the risk of causing harm to the device, including harm to any potential digital evidence, is also greater. Moreover, the physical method necessitates special professional equipment as well as an in-depth knowledge of all aspects of the mobile device. Despite this, the physical collection of data creates a precise, one-to-one copy of all the data stored in the mobile device, including data that was erased and data that was not allocated to a defined sector.

In light of the pace of technological development, and until it has been proven conclusively that legal examination software operating logically functions appropriately and that evidence extracted from the mobile device is whole, then, in most cases, the physical method is preferable. A process of legal digital investigation changes primarily according to the importance of the investigation, policy guidelines and the situation and individual circumstances related to the investigation. The process of investigation generally includes four main stages: collection, examination, analysis, and presentation of the data – and together they constitute the required digital evidence that will be the output and serve as the factual basis of legal suppositions. Correct performance of the process, including its full and accurate documentation, will lead to the admissibility of the evidence in the legal proceeding.

In many jurisdictions around the globe, there are guidelines and procedures for the investigation of mobile phones in general and specifically on the matter of the WM operating system. The implementation of these guidelines changes according to the organization, the goal of the investigation, and any special circumstances.

Over the years legal models have been developed to deal with Microsoft operating systems, but the short history of WM telephone devices in general alongside the differences between the operating systems of older models and the WP7 and WP8 operating systems has resulted in a situation where the reliability logical analysis procedures and processes cannot be verified. Following the main changes to WP7 and the fact that there is no compatibility between WP7 and all previous WM operating systems, techniques and instruments that are used in the legal investigation process today are not suited for the WP7 mobile telephone.

One of the main changes that may influence the digital investigation is the manner in which the WP7 operating system interfaces with the personal computer. WM type digital investigation devices approach data in both a logical and physical way, by using an ActiveSync/WMDC connection between the mobile phone device and the personal computer. The WP7 operating system, unlike older systems, uses Zune and not ActiveSync/WMDC. Existing evidence analysis devices are limited in the way they can interface with WP7 devices and there exists doubt that they will be able to extract all data from WP7 devices.

In older operating system versions it was possible to install an 'agent' program in the mobile device, which collected the data from the device's memory and transmitted it to an external examining device. With regard to this I would note that the WP7 operating system cannot implement previous WM applications   so that even if the 'agent' software is installed successfully, it is possible that it will not work and/or its abilities to transmit data from the examined device will be limited. Moreover, on the legal issue, it was not proven that the data extracted by the 'agent' was trustworthy and that it can be seen as reliable, original evidence.

In addition, in operating systems such as WP7 the mobile device's internal memory and SD card are used together to form one virtual storage region. I would note that there are a number of methods for the extraction of data physically one of which is the removal of the memory chip from the device. Since WP7 and similar operating systems make parallel use of the memory components, the fear is that the removal of the data physically will remove and/or distort important data.

To the best of my knowledge, it is difficult if not impossible to predict which files will be found in the mobile phone's memory and which on the SD card. Moreover, the SD card in the WP7 operating system is coded and cannot be deciphered using standard methods that were used with previous generations of the WM operating systems.

The WP7 operating system compression method is different from the file and compression system in WM operating systems. WP7 uses a TexFAT file system and XPH compression, while WM uses a TFAT file system and XPR compression method.

The new file system and compression methods implemented in

the WP7 operating system is not sufficiently recognized in the world of digital investigations, so that it is still not possible to determine explicitly whether the presented evidence is indeed sufficiently reliable within the framework of legal proceedings. Even if we use the physical method and obtain a full copy of the WP7 mobile, the existing techniques and devices will not necessarily identify the file system and/or will not be able open and decode their content.

As mentioned, WP7 and WP8 cellular phone operating systems s are completely new and have a different hardware structure, including exact guidelines regarding software and application development. These changes make the device unique in all issues pertaining to information security, speed and efficiency of use, alongside far-reaching innovations in the world of technology in general. In order to clarify the extent and significance of the change, I show the differences between new systems and previous generations of Microsoft operating systems.

As mentioned previously, the new operating system will not work with the previous generation of cellular devices. Unlike the new operating system, the previous generation of operating systems allowed the user to remove the storage media. Previous generation operating systems also supported external storage media.

This is not the case with new generation operating systems the system uses the device's internal memory and the memory card (SD) together. The new operating system addresses both memory components as one unit or as one file system, and therefore the physical separation of the two components, as was possible in older systems, is no longer an option.

If the SD memory card is removed from a new generation cellular device, then the information will be missing or unreadable since only a part of the information is found on the card with the rest being found on the device's internal memory. Moreover, the operating system will not work without the removable memory card. In cellular devices using a previous generation operating system user files are also stored on the external storage media, which can be retrieved and analyzed legally independent of the mobile phone device.

One of the actions commonly taken by almost all users is the transfer of data between the cellular device and the laptop or desktop computer to backup or synchronize data and applications between the devices. The types of data transferred in the synchronization process include email messages, contact details, music files, text files in different formats, and other personal data.

As a part of the synchronization process, the previous generation operating system presents the entirety of the cellular phone on the computer and enables free access to most of the internal files. The new operating system, in contrast, enables only the synchronization of user media files, such as text files, email messages, photographs, and so on; namely, it is not possible to see the operating files of the new operating system with the personal computer.

There is also an essential change in the device's hardware which improves the user experience. Despite that said, most of the hardware changes are not supposed to influence the investigation process, aside from certain changes performed in the random access memory and synchronization mechanisms, which we will discuss later on.

In cellular devices, as with computers, the temporary volatile memory (RAM, random access memory) and the regular memory are read-only memory (ROM). As long as the device is working, some data exists in the volatile memory and some in the permanent memory. After the device is turned off, only data in the regular, ROM, memory is preserved. This method enables greater access to available data and thus increases the device's speed and improves the user experience. In the new system, the volatile memory component may preserve data even after the device is turned off, and thus the component is more useful in digital legal investigations.

With regard to the new system's permanent (read only memory) memory, data is stored in the ROM memory and on the internal SD card. The WP7 system does not have user removable memory card. In other words, the user cannot remove the internal SD card and replace it with another SD card. The SD card is locked, and therefore it is impossible to use it in another mobile device. The insertion of a new

SD card into a WP7 device will lock the new SD card, and the operating system will revert to the manufacturer's default definitions (factory settings). This will erase all files, applications and data added by the user that could have been used as evidence in any legal proceedings.

The internal SD card, in combination with the ROM, creates one file system. From examinations I have conducted, from professional articles, and consultations with colleagues, I am not aware as to how the files are shared between the ROM memory and the internal SD card. Changes made to data stored in ROM memory may result in legally acceptable technological data retrieval tools being unable to perform their function.

The new operating system includes far-reaching changes in terms of its physical appearance, user experience, and response speed. The goal of Microsoft was to provide a different type of user experience, as rich as possible, which would compete with the competing products and thus restore Microsoft to its former glory. As I have noted, the new system is not compatible with previous versions of Microsoft mobile operating systems, or, in other words, it cannot work with telephone devices that were designed to work with the previous software generation.

This far-reaching change is characterized by the data compression method, in the format in which data is preserved, by the way in which storage partitions are divided, and in their location on the memory components. These, along with additional technological changes, created a situation in which legal technological tools intended to retrieve data from previous generation operating systems are now unable to perform their function in the newer generations of cellular devices.

These facts also create uncertainty regarding the reconstruction of erased files. In the past a 'physical' picture of the mobile device was taken. However, because of the technological changes in the new system and changes to the structure of the file system itself, including additional factors described previously, it is possible that the techniques used to reconstruct erased files from older systems will be ineffective in the new systems.

Most of the data required in the process of the digital legal investigation is found in the user's data, including as contact lists, messages, pictures, email messages, and Internet browser history. As mentioned, in the new system the structure changed, for instance, contact lists are stored in a database file in a format different from that of older versions. What is more, the new system enables the transfer of data immediately through the data transfer interface (IM), including synchronization of data with websites such as Yahoo, Facebook, and so on.

Alongside these changes and others, it is possible to see in reality, the method storing contact lists and email messages in the new system is different from that of the old system. Email messages in the old operating system include SMS messages, text messages, while in the new operating system they also include multimedia messages (MMS), which include text, photographs, and video files. The manner in which messages are displayed has also changed, and the change is expressed both in the hardware and in the operating system, as previously described. In this matter, the changes in the email message storage method influence the manner in which the data can be obtained.

Email messages in the new system: The system will present the entire list of contacts in one place, although it is possible that different contact's come from different sources. This is similar to a calendar application, which presents many meetings from many different sources in the system.

User documents and photographs: In the old system, the user's personal files, such as documents and photographs, were stored in the My Documents folder, as they are in the personal computer. In was possible to read the files directly on the personal computer, to copy them to the personal computer, and/or to synchronize them with it. In contrast, user files in the new system cannot be copied to the personal computer and/or viewed in the same way; the new system uses a different data synchronization technology known as Zune.

Some claim that the synchronization method, whether it is performed using method A or method B, is not important as long as the system synchronizes and the data exists both in the mobile device and in the home computer. I accept this statement, but I would emphasize that with regard to the new operating system the trustworthiness of the synchronized data, the background documentation relating to the files, and additional technological parameters that indicate the source of the files have not yet been proven, and thus there is doubt regarding the issue of the synchronized data's reliability.

In this chapter, I reviewed basic issues regarding uncertainty and concern as to the reliability of evidence extracted from WP7 type mobile phones. In many cases there are, as mentioned, essential differences between the systems, which may possibly harm the credibility of the digital evidence extracted from mobile telephones of the new type.

Moreover, the cellular systems technological 'arms race' creates a situation in which, when a technological solution is found for these difficulties, the manufacturers of cellular systems in particular and technology companies in general will develop new systems that will continue the cycle of uncertainty and will adversely affect the technological legal ability to deal with the progress in a complete and absolute manner.

With regard to legally admissible technological instruments in general, as of today it is important to be aware of the fact that even if this is a legally admissible technological instrument that passed all tests of reliability and credibility of digital evidence extracted from other devices, this does not guarantee the reliability and credibility of findings from new models with more advanced components. I would emphasize that the difference between devices often creates a difference in the in the way that the handling of digital evidence is approached. Therefore, I would recommend that digital evidence experts in the situation in which there is a lack of knowledge and/or lack of clarity regarding the appropriate way to handle digital evidence, should examine the device's deeper layers rather than that of the operating system.

In addition, it is mandatory to examine the technological instruments used to extract electronic and digital evidence from the mobile device and to examine whether the device has been examined previously and under what circumstances and whether the data extracted from it was proven to be trustworthy to the necessary degree. For these reasons and others, it is recommended to seize additional hardware and software components, such as laptop computers and PCs, with which it is possible that the cellular device performed synchronization.

From the legal perspective, I would note that if supporting evidence is not presented to reinforce the evidence obtained from the new cellular device, it is recommended the weight of the evidence retrieved from this device be reduced.

Legal Analysis of the Google Android Operating Systems

In 2005 Google purchased a small company that had developed an innovative operating system called Android (Android Company Ltd.). The fundamental purpose of the acquisition was to provide an answer to competitors, for example, Apple's iPhone operating system. The operating system is based on the Linux platform and operates on open code. The decision to use open code, a decision that definitely surprised many people, is a part of Google's strategy in the 'war' against its competitors.

As previously mentioned, the main characteristic of the Android devices is the availability of its open source code. This presents a significant improvement for the digital evidence examiners. Conversely, I would note that the fact that every hardware manufacturer develops its own unique version of the Android operating system, which is different from its competitors' systems, makes things difficult for digital evidence examiners.

In practice, digital evidence experts are forced to deal with completely new hardware systems, similar to Microsoft's (WP7). This is a game of 'cat and mouse': manufacturers of technological legal identification systems must examine, investigate, and learn every new model that is launched by the many mobile telephone manufacturers and suppliers, so as to enable adjustment and adaptation as a part of the digital evidence extraction process necessary for each device.

In other words, every new Android based model f and/or any other cellular device necessitates examination, learning, and re-planning, so as to develop appropriate techniques that will enable its examination, including the extraction of the data from it in an optimal manner, the data that, in the end, will be placed before the court in a legal procedure.

Identification and Extraction of Digital Evidence from Android Devices

I would note at the beginning of this section that due of the tremendous number of Android devices, Android digital identification methods are improving constantly. Android devices, like other cellular devices, can include a tremendous amount of information about users and their practices. Digital legal analysis of a mobile device can reveal considerable information about the user, which can have a significant contribution to the investigation.

Many cellular device users feel that they hold in their hands a personal device to which only they have access to its contents. Consequently, in many cases, considerable information about the device owner's behavior can be found on the devices.

One of the main dilemmas with which digital evidence investigators deal is the question as to which technique should be used to extract the maximum amount of data from the device, without losing or changing its content, in other words, to create a copy that is identical to the original. The accepted and recommended technique, because of the volatile nature of the device's memory, is to remove the data 'live' when the device is operating. Obtaining the data 'live' is recommended as the device's volatile memory can hold a variety of data that may be significant and valuable for the investigation.

The number of devices with an Android operating system in no way reduces the number and complexity of the challenges faced by digital evidence experts when they attempt to extract evidence from the system.

Data on the Android devices is stored in a number of places, for instance, on flash memory with a large storage volume, on an SD card, or on a remote server to which it is connected via the Internet. On the matter of flash memory cards (NAND), I would note that the large storage capacity of the card and its limited physical dimensions create a significant advantage over competitors in the field.

I would further note that flash memory is not volatile memory, and aside from system files it also stores significant the user data, such as text messages, contact lists, call logs, email messages, IMs, and chat conversations, GPS device landmarks, photographs, and so on. Flash memory has been available for many years; from the perspective of technological development, the innovative design presents a challenge to programmers and analysts of legal technological systems.

As with other cellular devices, there are many weak points regarding the ability of examining and extraction of real data from an Android device. The fact that Android devices are relatively new in the smartphone market and that new models and operating systems regularly enter the market, makes it difficult for digital evidence experts to identify the devices' weak points, because to lack of knowledge or lack of experience in the handling of devices of this type.

The weak points of Android devices' are main concerns for many organizations and corporations, since there is no proof regarding the device's level of security or the likelihood that it will be exploited.

Legal Techniques and Procedures for Dealing an Android Device

The process for dealing with an Android device is identical to that of a personal computer, laptop computer, or other cellular device. It includes the five basic stages for dealing with digital devices: identification, preservation, obtaining data, data analysis, and producing a report.

In every digital legal investigation, it is necessary to maintain the the chain of custody, regardless as to whether the investigation is held in a corporate environment or as a part of a criminal investigation. It is necessary to take into consideration that the investigation will lead, in the end, to a legal proceeding, and hence the obligation to adhere to rules and procedures.

Following is an abstract of the main actions that should be adopted as part of the investigation process. It is necessary to ascertain that the actions adopted by digital evidence investigators and/or law enforcement agencies do not change the data, which in the end will constitute evidence placed before the court, stored in the computer and/or external storage media,.

When circumstances exist in which digital evidence experts find that it is necessary to examine the original data stored in the computer and/or the original storage media, they must be capable of explaining why this was essential and justifying the means used.

It is necessary to audit and record all the processes performed in and/or on the electronic component, so that an independent third party will be able to examine the same processes and reach the same result.

Dealing with an Android device during an investigation as with all cellular phones, is different from the methods used when dealing with a personal computer. Cellular devices tend to lose data if the device is turned off. In addition, it is important to prevent the device from locking itself, from accessing a communications network, and from a loss of power (electricity).

One of the main dilemmas in dealing with cellular devices in general and with Android devices in particular is whether to keep the device in an 'on' or 'off' state. If the device is on, then my recommendation is, if possible, to keep it this way and to extract the data from when it is turned "on" and operating.

It is important to prevent any changes being made to the device, for instance, a change of the device's access code. In most Android devices it is possible to bypass the access locking code by increasing the time until the locking mechanism is implemented, so as to prevent or postpone the locking of the screen and the device.

It is necessary to maintain a constant source of electricity to the device as well as isolating it from communication networks. I would emphasize and note that isolating the device from a communications network is extremely important as, with Android devices, it is possible to remotely access to the device and t completely erase data. On this matter, I would recommend to digital evidence investigators to place the cellular device into flight mode and to negate the possibility of remote access. It is further necessary to turn off the Bluetooth component and the wireless network card.

Investigations Private Company Cellular Phones

The various law enforcement agencies are the primary actors in the field of mobile device security, since they have the authority to study crimes and secure sensitive information. In the civil area, the investigation of cellular devices is often related to personal interests such as divorce agreements, custody battles, property disputes, and so on.

Corporations also express considerable interest in cellular device information security so as to protect themselves against commercial espionage, financial theft, and intellectual property theft. Therefore, it is possible to benefit from the tracking of smart phone devices in investigations in both the civil and criminal fields, including intra-organizational investigations (private investigations).

This chapter focuses on internal investigations in organizations so as to instill proper behavior patterns and to prevent theft of intellectual property, copyright infringement, abuse of equipment, embezzlement, sabotage, espionage, and so on. Information security experts, working on behalf part of the organization will not be subordinate to the meticulous legal procedures regarding the acquisition and use of information that apply to investigations in the field of law enforcement. However, at the same time, they are required to adhere to techniques and legal rules in generally and especially laws regarding the protection of the individual's privacy.

To extract data from cellular devices during an intra-organizational investigations, physical access to the device is required. An exception to this issue is the EnCase Company, which as of October 2012 can conduct legal remote imaging of cellular devices with an Android operating system through the communication network.

Obtaining Data from the Device

As I have already noted, obtaining data from cellular device in general and from an Android device in particular is performed in a logical or a physical manner. The logical technique is based on the remote identification and removal of designated data from outside of the device. For this purpose, it is necessary to obtain direct access to the cellular device's file system. This way is the easier of the two, but it may harm the trustworthiness of the data obtained.

In situations in which there is no logical access to the device files (for whatever reason), data may be accessed and removed physically. The following are some means that may be used in order to obtain data physically.

JTAG is a technique in which access interfaces (TAPs) to printed electronic circuits are used for wiring and testing. Using the connections, access is possible to the Android device's central processing unit. This technique necessitates skills and considerable electronic knowledge, since one mistake may cause the loss of the data and the hardware. This method needs to be used as a last resort.

Chip-off is a technique for the removal of the chip from device. The technique is performed in stages the first of which is the physical removal of the memory chip from the device. The chip legs which physically connected the chip to the device's circuit board and which will have been damaged by the removal procedure, must be repaired. The final stage is the connection of the chip to a unique device that can read data from the chip memory. The high costs of equipment and the destructive nature of the method deter the digital evidence examiners from frequent use of this method.

AFPhysical is an in-depth process that requires direct connection and access to the target device. After the connection, it is necessary to identify the memory partition that is to be examined. One of the greatest advantages of this technique is that it also works in cases when the device is locked, namely, an access code is needed.

General Device Usage Trends

In general, I would note that data that is customarily sought for is similar in all cellular devices. The difference lays in the structure of the device, which leads to an essential difference in the memory structure and in the appropriate manner by which data extraction should be facilitated. To remove all doubt, I will refer again to come of the central details that should be sought in cellular devices in general and in Android devices in particular.

Searching for the 'unlock screen' function, an examination user actions along a time line indicate the active use of the phone. For instance, typing a lock code and opening the device. Using this data, it is possible to determine whether the device operated in the framework of time ascribed to the offense, to discover and identify unauthorized or users impersonating the device's user.

Through access to contact data and communication functions, it is possible to discover and to identify names of contact's or telephone numbers that constitute a risk to the organization. It is necessary to perform a search and examination of the content documented in the SMS and MMS messages, so as to identify suspicious activity and to examine messages sent to a large number of contacts. It is important to emphasize that the time documented in the SMS message does not rely on the clock of the cellular device itself.

Subject to the circumstances, when a picture is documented using the telephone's camera and is sent immediately as an MMS message, this may necessitate and justify further investigation. It is necessary to examine the precise position of the cellular device through identification of the GPS transmitter, since it is possible that the suspect has documented forbidden data from within the organization.

In addition, it is necessary to examine the last positions that were documented in the device, namely, the latitude, longitude, and picture capture time. On this matter, I would note that it is necessary to ascertain that the GPS system works by opening the Google Maps application opens to ascertain that the current position is displayed. If the GPS transmitter is turned off for any reason, then it is possible to get this data from the cellular provider. In addition, it is possible to crosscheck the data obtained with the event log documented in the calendar and that may help the investigation. Documentation of the user's meetings can help in the examination of any alibi provided and in the planning of any follow up actions.

Internet history is a record of the user's online history, including browsing and/or searches at the time of the event and the identification of the device. This is essential information from which it is possible to learn about the suspect's behavior, for instance, uploading intellectual property to external Internet websites. In addition, it is possible to analyze browser searches so as to learn about the user's possible intentions. I would emphasize that there are a number different Internet browsers and that it is necessary to examine all those installed on the device.

It is necessary to examine the possibility that the user took actions for the destruction or concealment of evidence and/or the use of anti-forensics software. In addition, it is necessary to examine the possibility that an attempt has been made to falsify evidence in the mobile device, for instance, the addition of forged data to a series of data with the goal of misleading investigators or avoiding an offense.

Examination and Legal Analysis of SIM Cards

As mentioned previously, most of the mobile devices that we use include a SIM card, which is associated with GSM technology. On this matter I would note that during the legal examination of the devices with this type of component, an in-depth examination of the contents associated with the SIM is required. I would add that in certain cases one person may use a number of SIM cards in different countries or for different purposes.

This issue is a global problem similar to the matter of cybernetic space. The fact that a specific cellular provider can be geographically located in a country that does not, for reasons of its own, meet the required standards and/or is not a signatory to international conventions constitutes a 'shelter' for Internet users who act for hostile purposes and/or as a part of criminal organizations. In this situation, legal authorities, law enforcement agencies and the courts have no appropriate response or solution..

To illustrate, imagine a person who uses a cellular phone with two SIM cards and/or two cellular phones, one of which includes a SIM card from one of the previously mentioned countries. The conversations he does not desire to reveal, for whatever reasons, will be conducted from the cell phone with the problematical SIM card. This results in a situation in which the only collectable information is that found on the device and the card. I would note that whilst it is possible to intercept information in transit, this action is one that lays in the law enforcement sector and I will not address this issue at this time.

As mentioned, the storage capacity and use of cards is steadily increasing and may include considerable amounts of relevant information. If the user erased information from the card, then it is possible that an attempt to reconstruct the erased data will reconstruct it in whole or in part. Different models of devices will contain 'remnants' of data erased from the card, for example, short messages.

The card's hierarchical storage structure is open, and the content is defined in the GSM technical specifications, which we addressed previously. The component includes one master file in refers to all the files found in the card. Without going into detail regarding the technological issues and since we have already learned about the BIT concept, I would note that every file is classified with a unique two bit value, the first bit notes whether this is a master file or another file in the tree of mutual relations.

As mentioned, the card may contain different types of information, such as the regional position identifier (LAI) and country identifier, communication network, and precise position. Every time the mobile device moves to a new region, information about the position is updated on the card.

On this matter, I would note that it is possible to block or to prevent the recording of this information on the card. Despite this, I would note that there still exists problem of the dual card and the problem of cards affiliated with a provider or country that does not meet global standards of accepted law.

Security codes can provide an obstacle to the extraction of data from the card, as in the mobile devices. Therefore, it is important to understand how it is possible to overcome this type of security protection. Users are entitled to set a personal identification number (PIN) which limits and restricts the access of outside agencies to their card. It is important to emphasize that there aggressive action to attack, circumvent or otherwise defeat the password should not be taken as the manufacturer's default in such a case could instigate an automatic card reset and data erasure after a set number of failed attempts.

It is customary to mistakenly think that the user's data is permanently stored on the SIM card. However, the card is produced by the manufacturer, and the cellular company coordinates between data permanently stored (burnt) on the card and the user and providing the user with the required communication package, including Internet access, use of a device in different countries, and so on. The fact that Internet browsing is made possible through the SIM card enables some mobile phones to eliminate the password barrier through Internet service providers. In other words, Internet providers can bypass the code and the password and thus achieve access to the locked card.

Therefore, in a case where digital evidence experts find that the SIM card is blocked or locked for any reason, it is possible, subject to local law, to turn to the Court asking it to instruct the cellular provider to reveal the password that will unlock the card.

CHAPTER 6: DIGITAL SIGNATURE (AS WRITTEN IN THE ELECTRONIC SIGNATURE LAW)

During my years of work and from my deep understanding of the secrets of technology and law, I have often wondered why the legal world in general, including legislatures around the globe, 'personify' the digital signature in different technological areas.

To the best of my understanding, a change in thinking alongside technological development, will enable a better understanding that in the virtual world, as opposed to the physical world, the actual 'signature' has lost all value and that the term "signature" today refers to the process of technological identification, such as verification of personal details, encryption of a one-to-one code or key that is transmitted to the 'signatory' who then confirms, identification using different technologies, including identification of IP address (in IPv6 technology), and so on.

To reinforce my statements and emphasize the difference between the material signature (as a means of confirmation/identification) and digital confirmation, I would note that at the end of the process a physical signature on a physical document is confirmation that the agreement was indeed signed (offer and acceptance). The situation is different in all issues pertaining to confirmation processes that use a digital format.. Email correspondence and/or a contract made over the Internet and/or digitally, save additional data that validates the parties expressed their willingness to enter into a contract. Hence, the actual physical 'signing' loses importance in light of technological developments, which create new norms of authentication, confirmation, and 'signature'.

We learn from these factors that documents transmitted via the Internet in formats that we will address later, when using strict information assurance procedures that meet legal standards for institutional evidence (which we shall also address later) are preferable to a physical signing.

For further clarification, I will address the issue of the validity of a contract made using electronic mail, which we discussed in the chapter "Issues on the Matter of Electronic Mail". This issue constitutes, to the best of my understanding, an important milestone in the understanding that the physical signature in "cyber space" has long lost its importance. In the middle of the 21st century's first decade, the Israeli Court officially validated the signing contracts via email and authorized the legal validity of this type of contract.

In Civil Case 29488/04[145] brought before the Tel Aviv Magistrate Court, Judge Noa Grossman determined that a series of email messages between parties creates a valid contract that obligates the parties. Thus, the Court, in essence, for the first time ascribed validity to a reality that had existed for a number of years, in which the signing of contracts and obligations through email messages is a part of our daily routine.

In an in-depth analysis, and beyond issues regarding the identification of the parties, it appears, as stated, that the physical signature has lost all value, namely, a physical contract is an agreement based on the process of offer and acceptance, as customary in both British and United States law. In the ruling, it was determined that since the world is a "global village", and since the Internet enables the immediate transmission of messages and the creation of contracts and obligations via the Internet, this method of creating contracts and documents of obligation is, according to the circumstances, valid, except in situations which obligate an actual, physical, written document.

---

[145] Civil Case (Tel Aviv – Yaffo) 29488/04 Computer Sky v. Prime Medical Company.

The Israeli Electronic Signature Law, 2001

As a part of the process for the regulation of technology in general and of the issues of the electronic signature in particular, the Israeli *Knesset* (Parliament) legislated the Electronic Signature Law in 2001. The explanation for the proposed law is as follows[146]:

> In the world of law, the concept of the 'signature' is a concept with significance from the field of contract law and evidence, which has been accorded different interpretations. In the developing technological era, it is possible to execute the signature in ways different from the past, and therefore the need to anchor the technological possibilities in legislation arises.
>
> The signing of the document was intended to achieve a number of goals, which should be ensured also when the signature is performed using electronic means. One goal is to provide an expression of the intention of the signatory and the finality of his opinion, and this through the objective discovery that he indeed intended to sign the discussed document and to approve its content. Another goal is the identification of the signatory himself, through the association of a certain signature to a certain person.
>
> The main goal of the proposed law is to increase certainty regarding actions performed electronically by ensuring the identity of the signatories through certain electronic means and recognition of the evidential status of these signatures. The lack of certainty arises especially in connections via the Internet, which is an open communication network, characterized by the absence of reciprocal

---

[146] http://www.knesset.gov.il/laws/heb/FileD.asp?Type=2&LawNum=2915&SubNum=2.

identification and absence of a direct relation between the sides connected in a transaction.

These statements were written in 2001. At that time, the legislature had not yet internalized the fact that identification was performed through a technological process rather than the act of physically signing. Conversely, I would note that the legislature had internalized the evidential status of the electronic identification process as a part of technological development in general.

In addition, the law differentiates between two types of electronic signatures, as shown in the statements explaining the law's proposals:

> The proposed law specifies two types of electronic signatures – secure electronic signature and secure electronic signature validated with an electronic certificate, which has a higher degree of trustworthiness, achieved by the fact that in the process of signing, an external factor is added – the approving factor. The proposed law determines a different significance for each of the signatures. Thus, for example, for the purpose of admissibility in the Court, it is enough to have a secure electronic signature, but for the purpose of the signature requirement according to law, validated and secure electronic signature is necessary.

> In the process for the approval of the validated and secure electronic signature, three factors are involved: the signatory, the approving factor, and the side relying upon the signature, which requires for the purpose of the contract that the signature be validated. To prevent, to the extent possible, misuse of the validated and secure signature, the law proposes that there is an obligation both on the signature owner (for example, to keep the means of the signature in his hands) and on the confirming factor (for example, to use hardware and software

systems that meet certain requirements).

The sections of the law and the explanations regarding the validity of the electronic signature show that there are three levels of electronic signature:

- The simple electronic signature, which is, in essence, the confirmed information that is transmitted via an email message and constitutes a basis for an offer and acceptance agreement, between two or more sides to said agreement, as a part of the commercial process. The 'simple' concept is intended to define the other ranking levels in the matter of the electronic signature as required, as stated in the explanation of the proposed law[147]:

  > The proposed law does not regulate the use of the 'simple' electronic signature (such as the signature at the end of an email letter). The validity of this signature will continue to be determined according to the laws and interpretations accepted today… the proposed law is not limited to a certain technology, but determines a general framework, into which it will be possible to integrate new technologies in the future. This enables maximal flexibility, and does not obligate adherence to a specific technology or method.

- The secure electronic signature, which is an electronic signature that meets the requirements set by law, namely, a signature produced through a secure system, which is validated using data unique to the user. According to the proposed law[148]:

  > The proposed law specifies two types of electronic signatures – secure electronic signature and secure electronic signature validated with an electronic certificate, which has a higher degree of trustworthiness, achieved since in the process of the signature an external factor is added – the approving

---

[147] http://www.knesset.gov.il/laws/heb/FileD.asp?Type=2&LawNum=2915&SubNum=2
[148] http://www.knesset.gov.il/laws/heb/FileD.asp?Type=2&LawNum=2915&SubNum=2

factor.

- The secure and approved electronic signature, namely, a signature that meets the requirements of information assurance, when the validating factor is an organization that meets signature identification and verification standards which will be addressed later

Before I assess the complexities of the electronic signature and analyze the practical significance, I would refer to p. 243 of the Ruling in the case of Bank HaPoalim Ltd. vs. Shaul Rachmim Ltd.[149], in which three situations in which it is possible to clearly identify a traditional signature on a document were defined : through the direct evidence of the signatory or a witness who was present at the time of the signature, through a graphological comparison of the signature under dispute to a signature given to an authorized party, and through the testimony of a person who knows the handwriting of the signatory whose signature is under dispute, who will testify to the validity of the signature.

> 6(1). When a sued party denies his signature on a document, the plaintiff must show that the signature on the document is the sued party's signature. This rule derives from the fact that the burden of proof regarding all elements of the claim is that of the plaintiff. (261 (d)).

> (2) There are three main ways in which it is possible to prove that any signature is the signature of a given person. First, through direct evidence, namely the evidence of the signatory or somebody who was a witness to the signing. Second, through comparison of the controversial signature to a signature known as true, while following points of similarity and difference between them. Third, through the evidence of a person who knows the

---

[149] Civil Appeal 5293/90 HaPolaim Bank ltd. vs. Shaul Rachamim Ltd. Court Ruling 47 (3) 240.

handwriting or signature under dispute and who can testify to the degree that the document under discussion matches the signature (1261-6-7).

(3) The common denominator of these proofs is the existence of evidential elements outside of the document under dispute, which shed light as to the rights of the party who prepared the document or the party signing it. The document itself is not sufficient to even *prima facie* evidence as to who is signed it, and the party who has the burden of proof must provide additional evidential elements which, together with the document, will be enough to provide proof as mentioned previously. (262a).

(4) When a prosecutor relies on a document and the defendant denies his signature, the prosecutor must prove the trustworthiness of the document, even if the defendant does not deny it when the document is submitted as evidence. (262b).

In the world of technology, there exists a method of advanced signature verification, and it is the most reliable. This involves authentication through digital/technological means, which the person cannot deny, and, as I already have explained, to differentiate from a person, the computer can only provide facts rather than an interpretation or supposition namely, whether something was or was not. Hence, there is a proven advantage to the use of technology with regard to the methods used in the court ruling in the case of Poalim Bank Ltd. v. Shaul Rachamim Ltd. We must not make the mistake, this is a different way of thinking, in which the physical signature loses its importance when faced with the process of technological identification of the signatory, whose role it is to approve beyond all shadow of a doubt that this is the same person.

Computerized Graphic Signature: Meeting the Instructions of the Circular on Graphic Signature

On April 3, 2012 the Ministry of Finance, the Department of Capital, Insurance, and Savings Market in Israel published a Circular for Agents and Consultants, entitled "Computerized Graphic Signature". This Circular replaced the previous circular that defined this issue. Section 1 of the Circular explains that the goal is to improve the efficiency of processes, but we will focus on the sentence "to improve the reliability of information and remove technological obstacles". In other words, the Israeli Ministry of Finance internalized the undisputed advantage of technology on the matter of reliability, as follows:

> The goal of this circular is to improve and to increase the efficiency of the manner by which documents fare transferred from the license holder to the institutional body, to shorten the time required for the transfer of the documents, and to improve customer service, and all without harming the customer's rights. This circular is a part of the general arrangement designed to increase the efficiency of work processes, to improve the reliability of the information, and to remove technological obstacles.[150]

In section 2, Definitions, the following definition is presented: "Computerized graphic signature – signature preserved in a computerized manner as a graphic file". Let us examine the definition of 'graphic file'.

A graphic file is originally a file in a format (such as a Word file or any other written format). As a part of the file (the document) creation system of the file's graphic layers are combined into one layer (a process known as flattening) and is locked as a picture file. Namely, it is converted to a picture file and/or undergoes a change in the file

---

[150] Ministry of Finance, Department of capital, Insurance, and Savings Market, Circular for Agents and Consultants.

structure, becoming a flat picture file.

The essential difference between different types of written files and a picture file lies in the fact that the picture file is composed of pixels (small dots on the screen that the human eye can identify as a picture), as opposed to a written file which includes text, software, design, and graphics. Further on the matter of the picture, I would note that as the number of pixels increases (there are more dots and they are denser (the picture/screen resolution is higher – and in the eye of the beholder the picture is sharper. The process of the picture's creation in certain formats (for instance, in gif or jpeg) uses flattening, namely, elimination of picture layers of that existed at the time of its creation,

Comment: I would note that if the picture in one of the previously mentioned formats is a part of the investigation process and if the base data of the picture was not mistakenly or intentionally destroyed by anti-forensics programs, then it is possible to return to examine the picture layers of the original and to extract data that can shed light as to what was photographed.

Further on this matter I would note that many today websites use anti-forensics software programs to prevent copyright infringement lawsuits against them and/or against the website's users. These websites include the message sharing system WhatsApp and the social network website Facebook, which declare the use of such resources in their 'data use policy' that can be viewed on the website. My checks show that the historical data of the pictures published on these social network websites are indeed erased.

Returning to our issue, a computerized graphic signature is a signature preserved in a computerized manner as a graphics file (like a photograph). The signature itself is made using a graphic board and/or a digital recording – this is a touchscreen of any kind, namely, a device through which it is possible to perform a recording, signature, or vote. The device enables input using a pen made of plastic and/or any other material defined in the circular as an 'electronic pen', through a mouse-like device or through the finger contact on the surface or screen. Touching the board or the screen is converted to a cursor position on the computer screen and when pressed the computer translates the position to a computerized graphic illustration.

The computerized illustration is a graphic marking, namely, the creation of pixels pressed on the touchscreen, and hence the source of the ruling that the digital signature on the touchscreen of laptop computers, cellular devices, iPads, or digital signature surfaces connected to a computer creates a graphic illustration equal in its definition to a computerized graphic signature.

I would emphasize and note that during the stage of the signature creation and after the flattening process , no action is performed that examines the identity of the graphic signature as opposed to signatures from the past and/or between the signatures themselves so that the same signatory can 'scribble' a different signature each time that in no way resembles their material, written signature and that this cannot be examined in any means beyond a physical, traditional examination, which compares signatures using the human eye.

Section 3 A (4) the Signing Process, states, "The license owner will not use any means, technological or other, to copy a graphical computerized signature of a client from one place in a document that requires his signature to another place". These address the question of whether it is possible to copy a signature using technological means and without leaving traces that indicate that the signature was copied.

Explanation:

Beyond the fact that the signature itself flattens the picture, for the most part the process implements an action of asymmetric decryption[151], in which a private key is used for signing and a public key is used to verify the signature. Lacking a key for the authentication of the signature, the encryption system identifies the process of signing and changes the indication for an unoriginal form or file, namely, there is a change that necessitates examination of originality.

---

[151] On the matter of encryption, see in the continuation "key (Cryptography)".

The reason for this is that there is one-to-one fit between the private key and the public key. The verifier can be convinced beyond all doubt that only the individual who holds the appropriate private key is the one who signed the document, and therefore attempts of change and forgery will result in a change to the value registered by the penetration verification function and the rejection of the signature.

Further with regard to asymmetric encryption and keys, this is a digital certificate produced and authenticated by a known and reliable authority and meeting the most stringent standards, such as Standard PKCS 12, the encryption standard in the public key that was formulated and published by RSA Security[152]. This standard is the most widespread today and is included in the framework of other standards, including the ANSI X.509 standard, the IEEE P1363 standard, the SSL systems known to the user as HTTPS[153] at the beginning of the secure website address, and WAP that is known as a cellular browsing technology. In other words, security against hacking and falsification is for cellular devices, tablets, and every other device with a touchscreen.

Further on the issue of information security, in the circular 'Background Document on the Electronic Signature – Secure Electronic Signature versus Confirmed Electronic Signature' of the Ministry of Justice of Israel it states[154]:

> One of the requirements for the recognition of a secure signature is for the signature to be produced 'using a signature medium that is exclusively controlled by the person with the signature medium'. In the context of 'exclusive control' the question was raised – under which circumstances is it possible to preserve the electronic signature not

---

[152] An American information security company, which provides security instruments for software and communication, including communication via the Internet. The company developed the asymmetric encryption algorithm RSA and the cryptography libraries RSA BSAFE for the authentication of data.

[153] See the chapter of terms and definitions.

[154] http://www.justice.gov.il/NR/rdonlyres/735E0187-8A1C-4E4D-A1DB-D7B25A136296/18655/chatima_electronit_Reka1.pdf

on a personal device that naturally is found under the physical control of the owner of the signature, such as a smart card – but on a designated secure server that is used to perform electronic signature actions in communication.

On this matter we note that the American information security standard FIPS 140-2 on level 3 and 4 recognizes the possibility of obtaining a certification label for a secure server that holds encryption keys, which can be also be used for the purpose of the signature. This so long as the server enables the one-to-one identification of the user and in addition prevents the access of the network manager or any other maintenance factors to the personal means of signature. In other words, storage on the server does not, necessarily, harm its exclusive control but it has considerable importance to the mechanism that ascertains the exclusive control.

However, since the means of signing are not found under the signatory's physical control, it is necessary to carefully examine that in relation to the type of server and selected use the exclusive control is maintained in another way. Accordingly, completion of the means of security for this purpose is necessary. On this matter it is possible to distinguish between the use of a secure server in the organization, when the signatures were created primarily in the organizational context and which obligate the organization along with the signatory and a case in which the secure server is found in the hands of a uninvolved or unknown third party to the authorized to sign for the organization. In the last case, the security threshold that should be achieved for the purpose of providing proof of exclusive control is higher.

In the organizational context, as the signature is kept in an organizational means, it is necessary to protect the status of the individual – the signatory, and in this sense that the organization will assume the responsibility for use and will not harm the user's rights.

The Circular teaches us about the information security required for the performance of the secure electronic signature, including the manner of control of the institution with equipment and emphasis on the global standards. In addition, I will refer to the circular written by the Israel Inspector of Banks, entitled *Management of Information Technologies: Proper Banking Management (1/11)[155]*, Chapter 4, "Information Security" and Chapter 5 "Backup and Recovery".

Section 3 B (3), which addresses the signing process, states: "The signing of the document with a secure electronic signature ...as per the meaning in the Electronic Signature Law, 2001 ... will be considered a reasonable means for locking the document and protecting it against changes."

On this matter I would note that the secure electronic signature must meet the required standards and is subject to strict laws of information security, including encryption, accessibility checks, issues of post-disaster recovery, and issues of inspection and work procedures. Assuming that it was examined and found that the signature meets the required standards and that it should be seen as meeting the Electronic Signature Law, 2001.

Section 3 (B) 7 of the Circular states, on the issue of the signing process: "Paying attention to technological changes or changes in the encryption methods used to preserve the document". On this matter, I would note that the license owner has the obligation to prove that at all times he adopted all the means and processes required to authenticate

---

[155] http://www.boi.org.il/deptdata/pikuah/nihul_takin/357.pdf

the signature. In this section and in relation to the document itself, it is necessary to examine whether it is possible to change the manner of encryption without documenting the change.

Further on the topic of required means and processes, the license holder must prove reliability of the information transmitted using Internet interfaces and information encryption protocol (SSL)[156]. The process of authenticating of the reliability and security of the information is very important, since the SSL protocol is used to transmit sensitive information.

This protocol is used by banks and Internet websites such as Amazon, Google, and PayPal, which transfer billions of dollars every day through their systems. These websites rely on the fact that the protocol secures the originality of the transmitted data and the originality of the data presented on their website.

In September 2009 in the EKOARTY exhibition for information security in Buenos Aires, Argentina the proof-of-concept called BEAST – Browser Exploit Against SSL/TLS – was presented. This is JavaScript code (a coding language) that is integrated in a Network Sniffer. It is a communications protocol that enables remote control of different types of computer systems. The goal is to decipher small identification files (known as cookies), which are installed on the computer at attacked websites.

The attack method is called plain test recovery attack, and it was attempted successfully on the SSH protocol as far back as in 2008. However, until now success against the SSL protocol had not been reported. I will emphasize that this is true for every type of hardware, namely a laptop with a touchscreen, such as an iPhone, iPod, tablet, and so on.

Further on the matter of information security, it is necessary to ascertain that an operating system is installed that meets the FIPS standard and UB 186-3 of the United States government as a federal

---

[156] On the issue of SSL, see the chapter of terms and definitions.

standard and as a part of the DSA (Digital Signature Algorithm) standard, which addresses a digital signature algorithm and provides protection for the private key.

Importing a Computerized Graphic Signature

The process begins with the input of the transaction data into a 'smart' form, which can, at a later stage, flatten the data and transform file into a picture format. The data is inputted manually into the computerized form.

After the data's input, when the sides are interested in signing the form, a technological transition to a 'signature acceptance process is implemented. I would emphasize, above all else, that the identification of signatory is an essential part in the process. At this stage it is recommended to add to the process additional identification technologies such as closed-circuit television (CCTV) and/or a photograph of the signatory at the stage of the signature. In addition, it is recommended to use voice technologies, which authenticate that the signatory is aware of his actions, and a check of his legal competence is required for the execution of the signing.

The issue of the legal competence and mental state of the signatory can be examined using a variety of questions that the signatory provided beforehand and/or the use of information databases attached to the CRM system[157]. Thus, it is possible to ascertain that the signatory is indeed in a state appropriate for signing.

The acceptance of the signature is accomplished by pressing a designated software button, after which the data is flattened and the form is locked. I would emphasize that without the locking action and the flattening of the form, it is not possible to execute the signature action. Once the form has been flattened , it is no longer possible to change the data inputted in the 'data input' stage without the color in the indicator box changing from green to red which indicates that the file has undergone a change and that it should not be seen as an original

---

[157] Client management system – see the chapter of terms and definitions.

file.

I would further note that the action of flattening can be compared to the process of transforming the file from one in which there are text elements, software, design, and graphics to a file in which each of these previously separate elements cease to exist as a unique and separate element, such as in the flattening of the picture file.

If there has been a mistake in any of the data inputt into the system and/or the user wishes to change data after the signature stage, then it is necessary to cancel the entire process and produce a new form.

Electronic Signature – Legal Background

On the legal issue, the first question I will examine is whether it is possible to implement an 'organizational electronic signature', or in other words, a signature that is not designated for a specific role-holder within the organization but rather one that can be used to represent the entire organization.

Current regulations do not allow the use of an electronic certificate for a corporation but require that a specific role holder in the corporation be authorized to execute the signature. To the best of my understanding, the goal of the legislature in its attempt to anchor the electronic signature in law was to provide this type of signature with the same validity as that of a regular, physical signature.

This means that it is not possible to accord the corporate signature the validity of a secure and confirmed electronic signature, since the corporation itself, as an abstract body, cannot sign a document physically but only through its authorized signatories.

Conversely, I would argue that there is no reason to create a physical electronic signature, when the element of identification and documentation in it has importance and not the authorized signatory whose only role is to ascertain that the client did indeed sign. In other words, as already explained, in light of the fact that it is possible to sign a digital signature using toothpick, a plastic stick, or any other hard object, including the person's fingernail, the importance of the signature is dwarfed by the importance of the identification and documentation of the signatory, through the use of all the technological means already mentioned.

The legislature must change its approach to the matter of the electronic signature in particular and electronic equipment in general and internalize that this is a fundamentally different environment from the environment they were accustomed to in the past.

I will refer later to the Bank HaPoalim Ltd. v. Shaul Rachamim Ltd. Court Ruling[158], in which the three situations where it is possible to clearly identify a traditional signature were defined. In the advanced technological world, the method of advanced signature verification is the most trustworthy. This is user authentication using a method which the person cannot deny or repudiate. Hence, we see the unequivocal advantage of technology over each of the methods presented in the Bank HaPoalim Ltd. v. Shaul Rachamim Ltd. Court Ruling and the lack of importance of the authorized signatory (the flesh and blood person) as a part of the technical process. However, I would note that this is an issue that has not yet been examined in court rulings.

In light of my approach to the matter of signature authentication even without the authorized signatory, I will examine whether an insurance agency and/or any other institutional organization, such as a bank, is permitted to sign with an electronic signature even without the authorized signatory.

The organization or agency must meet all legal requirements and directives regarding the unique signature, in other words, a signature that is a uniquely identifiable with the signing organization, produced through means of a signature under the exclusive control of the signature owner, namely, the institution. In addition, the organization must meet the most stringent standards used for electronic signatures and standards of information security that I have mentioned and must use systems that enable identification of changes made in the electronic document following implementation of the signature.

I would note that the creation of a unique signature is undertaken using a basic technical encryption process , which includes use of unique encryption keys and that from a technological perspective indeed it is possible to create a 'unique signature' for the signing body. I will discuss this matter further at a later stage

On the question of the exclusive control of the signature's owner, since this is an organization and not a human entity, it is necessary to 'neutralize' the ability of an individual within the organization to make any use of the electronic signature. It is possible

---

[158] Civil Appeal 5293/90 Bank HaPoalim Ltd v. Shaul Rachamim Ltd. Court Ruling 47 (3) 240.

to establish rules and procedures at the level of director and/or senior management regarding the individual's access to the information security system that holds the organization's electronic signature system. In other words, it is possible to overcome the technical obstacles regarding the institution's electronic signature.

Conversely, if the organization signs using a 'corporation signature', then the organization itself must take responsibility for the use of the electronic signature, as mentioned, and thus the question regarding the inconsistency of the individual in the organization, since the responsibility of the authorized signature does not fall on them, even if only partially. In addition, I argue that it is possible to see the authorized signatory's responsibility as a human filter for the intentionally inappropriate use and human errors.

Further on this topic, assuming that the electronic signature in the organization meets the detailed requirements of unique signature for the same organization (with unique identification and is produced using signature means found under the organization's exclusive control), then even if it is not recognized as 'a secure electronic signature', since this is intended for a flesh and blood person who can use their discretion regarding a specific event, to differentiate from a business organization which is an abstract entity, I maintain that with regards to maintaining and adhering to all legal directives and the directives of the Circular and issues relating to the production of the electronic signature. In other words, the circular does not obligate the use of a secure electronic signature but determines the proper means of use of this means.

The circular emphasizes the issue of information security, including the integrity of the technological means used for the creation and implementation of the electronic signature. If the organization meets information security requirements, then it is necessary to see the electronic signature as evidence faithful to the original and as institutional output, as detailed in section 35 of the Evidence Ordinance [New Version], which defines an institutional record as a "document, including output, prepared by the institution during the institution's regular activity".

I would further note that the entire system which produces a secure electronic signature and meets the conditions of the circular based on the electronic signature law should be seen as a confirmed system and that if the document is signed with the signature of the authorized signatories, then the signature will be considered an authorized electronic signature and the document and/or output will be considered an 'institutional record' in all respects. The company must prove that it indeed meets the rules of information security, including procedures of inspection and recovery.

Regarding the issue of the Circular's requirements, to ensure that the system meets all requirements, it should be determined that the system executes document locking, namely, the flattening of the file and its conversion into a picture format. As previously mentioned, this action does not allow the file characteristics to be changed, and with the help of the indicator box it is possible to identify all attempts to change and/or sabotage the file after it has been locked.

The circular mentions locking with 'reasonable means' so as to ensure all requirements are met. In my opinion, this can be interpreted negatively, since 'reasonable" is a subjective value, which changes from person to person. The issue of information security, including aspects of encryption, recovery systems, security systems, procedures, and technological protection means should be measured based on the nature of the data held by the organization and not on the basis of a generalized expression such as 'reasonable means'.

I would further note that in light of the dynamism of technological systems in general, it is necessary to conduct regular examinations, by an objective person, at least once a year on the matter of meeting requirements and procedures and on the matter of information security.

Symmetric and Asymmetric Encryption Keys (Cryptography)

Encryption keys or 'cryptography keys' as they are known professionally, are part of the process for the secure transfer of data via the Internet. The encryption key is a 'piece' of information that enables full control of the encryption process and/or the decoding process.

In an abstract manner, encryption is a process for the concealment of the readable message through functions (software), which transform the message into a sequence of numbers and signs —code. The code, subject to the file complexity, is not readable by a person who does not have the suitable encryption key that will allow for the reconstruction of the data to its original, unencrypted status. The reconstruction of the encrypted data to a 'readable' version using the encryption key is known as decoding.

In 1917 the engineer Gilbert Sandford Vernam formulated a mechanized encryption method, in which the information is encrypted letter by letter as it was transmitted. Using this method, the key determines the code's algorithm of. Without the key, it is not possible to retrieve the data from the encrypted file. This method is different from the traditional encryption method, in which the encryption is performed ahead of time and only then is the encrypted text transmitted. This encryption method is known as the Vernam Cipher, after its inventor.

Today there are two basic types of encryption keys, which use two different types of algorithms: symmetric encryption and asymmetric encryption. In symmetric encryption there is only one key for the decoding of the encrypted file, namely the 'symmetric' key. In asymmetric encryption, there are two different keys. One is used to encrypt the data, while the other is used to decrypt it. The keys are called 'private key' and 'public key', respectively.

Symmetric Encryption vs. Asymmetric Encryption

From the dawn of the invention of the encryption algorithm, the question has risen regarding whether asymmetric or symmetric encryption is the preferred encryption method.

Before us we have a question to which the response is not absolute, since in the world of technology it is not possible to compare two different systems of algorithms. Whitfield Diffie from Stanford University, California (1976) addressed this issue in his article "New Directions in Encryption"[159]:

> I object to the presentation of a public key encryption as a new form of encryption instead of as a method for the transfer of an encryption key. Some quickly indicated that RSA is very slow in comparison to DES and an encryption key is required, several times larger. Although it was clear from the start that the use of a public key is limited to the transfer of the key for conventional encryption, it seems that not everybody understand immediately the nature of the idea. Hence, the idea arose to build a hybrid system that integrates these two systems, and in this context the idea was considered an invention in its own right.

Put simply, symmetric encryption and asymmetric encryption are two fundamentally different encryption methods and they can solve different problems. Symmetric encryption is intended primarily to encrypt large information files. Encryption using the symmetric method is faster than asymmetric encryption, and its capacity to withstand technological attacks has been proven beyond all shadow of a doubt.

In asymmetric encryption it is possible to perform actions that are impossible when using symmetric encryption. Asymmetric encryption is intended primarily for the transfer of small data files and/or for dealing

---

[159] http://groups.csail.mit.edu/cis/crypto/classes/6.857/papers/diffie-hellman.pdf

with real time data being passed over cellular networks and the Internet. The method is especially effective for the management of encrypted information, for instance, as a part of the digital signature process.

Symmetric Encryption Key

A symmetric key or, as it is known professionally, a symmetric cipher, is an algorithm that uses the same key both for encryption and for decoding. In simple terms, a number of duplicated keys are provided for the same 'door' with each of the authorized signatories being able to them. A symmetric key is a direct method, as opposed to asymmetric encryption, in which the decryption key is different from the encryption key, and in which the decryption method and sits security are based on the difficulty in calculating the decrypted key, which is derived from the encryption key.

Technologically, in the symmetric encryption process there is no requirement that the decryption key be completely identical to the encryption key, but it will be possible to calculate the decryption key from the initial key data.

Symmetric encryption has existed from the dawn of cryptography. Traditional ciphers – such as the Caesar cipher and the Vigènere Cipher – are defined as symmetric ciphers, in which encryption and decryption are performed using the same key.

I would note that there also exists a symmetric encryption key in which the decryption key is different from the encryption key. It is still known as a symmetric cipher, however, since all that is required to decode the file is familiarity with the encryption key; in other words, when the encryption key is known the process of duplication or production of an alternative encryption key is a simple action.

This is an encryption process known professionally as DES – Data Encryption Standard. It is a standard for the encryption of data that was developed in the 1970s by IBM in cooperation with the United

States National Security Agency. This is symmetric and active encryption, or in other words, the encryption algorithm is performed repeatedly a number of times pre-defined times and saved in a sub-division called block ciphers[160]each of 64 bits[161] long. This is a 64 bits secret key. In essence, the key can be a secret code or a password.

The standard was replaced in 2001 by a new standard called the Advanced Encryption Standard. I would point out that although it was replaced in 2001, this method of encryption is still used, primarily in the field of global banking.

Advantages of Symmetric Encryption

Symmetric technological methods are quick and especially when accessing the computer hardware. Certain symmetric algorithms can encrypt hundreds of megabytes of information within seconds.

In general, symmetric encryption is characterized by the multiplicity of algorithms, which can provide a wide variety of effective encryption solutions. For instance random number generators, mechanisms for identifying and validating text, sound, picture, and additional technological characteristics. They can examine and validate the integrity of the transmitted data, and so on. I would further note that symmetric algorithms have a rich history, most have been well studied over the years, primarily following the development of computerization technology.

At the mathematical level symmetric encryption methods were also developed. The most common method is known as a 'one time pad' and is based on the Vernam Cipher. This is a mathematical proof in which the key used for encryption was chosen randomly, and therefore the encryption cannot be cracked.

I would note that I am aware that in the opinion of some of my

---

[160] http://csrc.nist.gov/publications/nistpubs/800-38a/sp800-38a.pdf
[161] On this matter see the chapter of terms and definitions.

professional colleagues this method presents more than a few problems. However, n to the best of my knowledge, until this point in time this method's algorithm has yet to be cracked, and thus I have great trust in it.

Asymmetric Encryption Key

Asymmetric encryption is also called public key encryption and/or public key in that the encryption key, which is public, is different from the decryption key, which is private. In other words, every user prepares a pair of keys – the first is the public key, which is in essence a public encryption key that is accessible to the private encryption key, which is then preserved secretly and used to decode the encrypted file. This is a unique key, namely, every public key has one matching private key and only one. The person who receives an encrypted file can only decrypt it using the matching private decryption key at his disposal.

The safety of the asymmetric encryption key method relies on the difficulty in calculating the private key from the public key, and hence, the name, asymmetric encryption, to differentiate from the symmetric encryption method, in which the decryption key is identical to the encryption key. In the symmetric encryption method even if the encryption and decryption keys are not identical, it is possible to easily deduce this from the encryption key.

The asymmetric encryption method can be illustrated with an analogy of a combination lock. A person sends his friend an unlocked box with an open combination lock. In order to open and close the box no previous knowledge about the secret combination code, which was defined by the sender, is necessary. The recipient can put anything they want into the box and then lock it. After it has locked, the box is sent back to the sender and since the same person is the only person who knows the secret combination, he – and only he – can open the box and reveal its contents.

On this matter, I would note that the person placing items in the box is not permitted to and cannot open the box after it is closed, since he does not have the key; namely, he did not create the secret key to lock the box. In actuality, a person who has access to the sender's public key can authenticate the digital signature that was signed using the sender's private key. In this way, it is possible to prove that the sender is the source of the document and that there was no technological manipulation of the document, namely, it is not changed by any unauthorized agents.

I would emphasize that the encryption of a public key provides validation and/or unique and indisputable identification as to the originality of the documents, including actions taken when processing the signature and encryption during data transfer from the encrypting computer to the main server. The manner of encryption obligates confidentiality of the two sides with relation to the key. This fact forces the sides to 'find' and use a safe method to convey the key between them. In a technological world of multiple participants, the management and maintenance of encryption keys has become a main problem in the field of information security due to the fact that all communicating parties must share a secret code. Therefore, and because of the limitations of information security, symmetric encryption necessitates the frequent change of keys, and those who are very strict tend to change the key for every communication between the sides.

To illustrate, I will describe a situation in which one of the sides hacked into the computer and as a result is able to open an encrypted file. In a case in which every communication between the sides involves a new and unique key, then the fear that the key will fall into hostile hands is eliminated, since the key discovered in the computer is either no longer in use and/or is no longer suitable for unlocking the encryption.

In addition, to negate fears of an outside factor being able to crack the encryption, the symmetric key algorithm obligates use of a very long encryption key. As the combination of letters and their number is greater, the chance of hacking it becomes impossible.

Advantages of the Public Key

The advantage of the public key rests on the fact that it is necessary to save only one key, namely, the private key. Conversely, a process for the authentication of the public key is required, since without it the private key will not work.

In general, I would note that in light of the complexity of the encryption, the management and the maintenance of public keys is simpler than the management and the maintenance of symmetric keys. Therefore, the asymmetric encryption key has a longer life span. In addition, in light of the fact that this method is used to encrypt small amounts of data and in real time, the public key enables implementation of digital signature mechanisms without competitors.

In the past, the encryption method using a public key was slow in comparison to the symmetric encryption method, since the key is very long, including thousands of digits and binary combinations. At the end of the 1980s, for the first time a public key system was developed, called ECC (Elliptic Curve Cryptography). This is an asymmetric encryption algorithm, with which the Diffie Helman protocol is realized using a unique geometric structure known as an elliptic curve.

Without entering into the root of the algorithm, I would note that although it is a complex method, it became known because of its relatively short encryption key, which led to computer performances no worse in speed than those of symmetric encryption. Therefore, today the method is used by most commercial information security systems.

As mentioned previously, a public key is used to transmit short messages, in continuous communication, in light of the period of time either defined ahead of time and/or for one time. Generally, this method is used for the purpose of a digital signature and/or transfer of data, such as credit card payments through the SSL (Secure Sockets Layer)[162] protocol, which is a communication via the internet that enables secure and encrypted communication between two

---

[162] On the topic of SSL, see the chapter of terms and definitions.

communicating applications.

I would note that, despite the aforementioned statements, none of the methods have been proved to be 100% secure mathematically. Most of the methods rely on reverse lamination, namely, a limited number of unresolved mathematical problems. I would further note that in contrast to the symmetric key, the public key has a relatively short history. This fact detrimentally influences the data that confirms the method's security. In my opinion, it is only a matter of time until there is a mathematical breakthrough, which will eventually lead to the absolute resolution of the last of the unresolved problems, and hence the elimination of the possibility of hacking in general.

To some extent, the two encryption methods, symmetric encryption and asymmetric encryption, complement one another, in their advantages and disadvantages. Today, modern information security systems use both methods, according to the nature, volume, and complexity of the transmitted information.

CHAPTER 7: DIGITAL EVIDENCE OBTAINED FROM CLOSED CIRCUIT TELEVISION (CCTV)

This chapter will address the legal aspects of closed circuit television systems (CCTV) and the issue of coordination between CCTV system owners and law enforcement authorities and the judicial authority. The topics at hand include issues regarding the maintenance and preservation of systems, including preservation of the data; management of the data and protection of privacy; and closed circuit television systems for the purpose of civil quality control and business preservation and for the purpose of the war against crime and terrorism.

Legislation on the issue of the right to privacy and the use of closed circuit television systems is required so as to reduce the phenomenon of abuse of such systems. On these matters considerable caution is required to ensure that the legal implications surrounding the use of closed circuit television systems are fully understood and were taken into consideration when the systems were planned, installed, and deployed. This chapter will address this topic.

Companies, organizations, and businesses that install a CCTV system of this type are committed to learn and to internalize the legal implications even before the first installation is completed. It is recommended that a legal-technological authority be consulted in all issues pertaining to all required technological and legal arrangements that must be met from the initial decision to install closed circuit television systems to their deployment. This is especially relevant and important in issues relating to the preservation and use of the data collected from the cameras.

The owners of the closed circuit television systems bear the responsibility to ascertain that the systems are installed according to local law and to examine all municipal bylaws. It is their duty to be and to remain up to date with procedures and regulations for the use of such systems, to be fully aware of the rulings of the Privacy Protection Law and the Wiretapping Law, and the punishments for negligent use and data preservation which resulted in harm and/or damage being caused to victims.

In actuality, the principles are simple to implement and are intended, first and foremost, for the protection of citizen's reasonable and logical expectation of privacy when they are in public places. The owners of closed circuit television systems must adopt all reasonable steps to protect the information gathered and stored by these systems. In addition, no information collected by the systems should be distributed to any agency other than to legal authorities.

Filming in a public place will only be carried out for a justified goal, which connects to the organization's activity and has the goal of preserving the location, order, management and control of the organization. Monitoring will be to the required extent, while painstakingly maintaining the privacy of visitors to the site. In other words, it is necessary to make sure that supervision in a public place will be proportional and for a justified goal. It is necessary to adopt strict steps to secure the information collected using closed circuit television systems in a public place in order to prevent abuse or inappropriate disclosure of the documented materials.

In the examination of the legal issues associated with closed circuit television systems, it is necessary to understand the evidence that can be extracted using this technology and to learn and understand the complexity of the legal issues and procedures, which are an unavoidable by-product of the deployment and use of the system. The main issues are as follows:

- Issues of privacy, including personal information and pictures. I have been exposed on many occasions to situations in which for some reason or another, a club owner provides information documented by security cameras to private investigators, in other words, persons who are not authorized by the legal system or law enforcement agencies, as a part of the investigation process. I will refer to this matter later.

- Issues of freedom of information, including legislation and judicial issues. The right of the public to know where the cameras are installed can be likened the road signs that tell drivers that speed cameras are installed at a specific location.

- Issues of information security and protection, including the use of the collected material by authorized agencies or parties. These topics include issues of support, data preservation, and the period of time data will be preserved, as well as a clear definition of procedures dealing with the access to information and the implementation of mechanisms of the inspection of the system usage of the.

The importance of these issues is that their goal is to ensure the ability of the Police and/or the different law enforcement factors, as part of the investigative process, to obtain data that was recorded using closed circuit television systems in public areas through a Court order that permits special access to the required information.

To illustrate the importance of the issues, I to the murder of the Maoz couple in Israel[163], regarding the failure of the Police's handling of the security camera that was installed in the deceased's home. Following this failure, evidence that could have verified beyond any doubt what happened on the night of the murder (the films) was destroyed t.

---

[163] Severe Criminal Case 54877-09-11 State of Israel v. Daniel Meoz.

Perception and Documentation: Films Recorded Using CCTV Security Cameras

This chapter will address the handling of digital evidence in general and digital evidence recorded by closed circuit television cameras (CCTV) in particular. I will begin with an explanation of the process involved in the collection and preservation of video footage obtained from closed circuit television cameras. The removal of video footage from the computer-based closed circuit television system is different from the removal of conventional digital evidence from the computer or from any other technological component that we have addressed previously.

At the first stage, digital evidence experts must all those with access to the system, including the owner of the closed circuit television, in order to ensure that have no access to the system or any of the materials gathered by it. It is then necessary to document the specific type of system used, including the number of cameras installed in the building, the areas covered by the cameras and the 'dead' zones, areas which are outside of the range of the cameras and for which no video information is available.

Today, most closed circuit television systems preserve the footage on a computer hard drive or on a central server. The server can record and preserve a large volume of data, and therefore it can manage a large number of cameras and create a shared imaging of all the data collected.

The digital evidence experts must seize the central server used to store the files. It is necessary to take the server to a digital forensics laboratory and copy the CCTV's server's hard drive including all of its stored video footage.

If this is impossible for technical or security reasons or for any other reason acceptable to representatives of law enforcement authorities, even before the start of the video copying process, digital evidence experts need to clarify whether the system documented the relevant video sequence and how was the recording made. In other words, are these cameras that record only when motion is detected or do they record continuously? In addition, it is necessary to examine the period of elapsed time between one picture and the next in order to track the changes and the sequence of photography. Finally, it is necessary to examine the time framework of the specific 'video scene' and to compare the time recorded in the system to the correct time and to note whether there is a difference between them.

As mentioned, it is necessary to document the product name and model of the closed circuit television system. It is possible that this information will be necessary to enable the re-showing of the films. In addition, to prove that a specific a sequence is part of the chain of evidence and its admissibility as evidence in the legal procedure, it is necessary to preserve all recordings from all cameras, including footage taken with the other cameras. It is possible that the defense team will make use of this as evidence in their attempts to present and proof scenarios that preceded and/or caused the event itself.

For this reason, and as I have already noted, digital evidence experts must document all the cameras connected to the closed circuit television system and clarify whether they record continuously or operate when motion sensors identify movement.

After all the video footage has been collected, it is necessary to examine the quality of the files seized and to confirm that these are the correct films and that no harm or damage was caused to the evidence during the process of removing it from the system. In addition, it is necessary to view the file using a video playback program, in order to ascertain and confirm that the final format works as expected.

It is necessary to document the collection and documentation process of the digital evidence in writing and also by recording and photographing the process, so that a third party, another digital examiner, can repeat the same actions and obtain the same results using the same technological tools. Because of the nature of electronic components and potential digital evidence, the guidelines for the preservation of CCTV systems are similar to those for the preservation of computers.

The Duty of Owners of Closed Circuit Television Systems on the Matter of Privacy

When installing a closed circuit television systems, it is necessary to take into consideration legal constraints regarding the management of personal information and the preservation of privacy. In essence, the goal of defense of privacy of information is to provide a legally obligating framework for the collection of information regarding the individual, its storage, and procedures for its use and disclosure.

In Israel, issues for the protection of privacy are anchored fundamentally in the Basic Law: Human Dignity and Liberty, section 7 (A), which determines that "All persons have the right to privacy". Over the years, in Israel, secondary legislation was developed, known as the 'Privacy Protection Law, 1981'. In 2005, in the opening statements on a seminar held by the Justice Committee of the *Knesset* (Israeli Parliament) regarding the protection of privacy in the information era, the attorney, Haim Klugman, then the head of the Public Council for the Protection of Privacy in Israeli Legislation, said[164]:

> The legislators of the law have two main goals.
>
> The first: To determine a norm of behavior that will respect the person's right to draw a line between his 'self' and 'society' so that his dignity is not harmed, he is not humiliated publicly, and he is not despised and his self-image is not harmed.
>
> The second: To provide the legislative instruments required for enforcement and protection of the person who was harmed by an invasion of their privacy without their consent. Without enforcement the appealing norms have no purpose.
>
> These goals were recognized in Israel in 1992 as a fundamental value with the legislation of the Basic

[164] http://www.justice.gov.il/MOJHeb/HaganatPratiut

Law: Human Dignity and Liberty, which determines in section 7(A) that every person is entitled to privacy.

In my opinion, the Privacy Protection Law in Israel failed in achieving the two previously mentioned goals. The first goal was not achieved due to the existence of forces with strong influence on the legislature, while the second goal was not achieved because of the fact that the State failed to allocate a budget to make this possible. In my opinion, it cannot be said that the existing order is satisfactory.

It is important to emphasize that the recognition of the norm that supports the person's privacy regarding his personal life is intended to determine an achievable quality of life. If the citizen's life, secrets, issues between them and others, state of health, lifestyles, abilities, image, and every activity is the province of all, then this is not an appropriate or acceptable quality of life. If the citizen is subject to detection or is followed, then he must live his life under constant electronic supervision with computers and cameras (see the example of the United Kingdom with its abundance of CCTV systems), fingerprint databases, DNA, retina scans, electronic identity cards, automatic identification devices on toll roads, and so on. It is reasonable to assume that such a situation could lead to a situation in which the individual has no control whatsoever over their privacy.

It is to prevent this situation that the legislature has stepped in. If we succeed developing and enforcing laws that act as a brake on the pervasive invasion of privacy while taking into account the legitimate needs and the constraints of the modern era, but that also set clear boundaries that must not be crossed with the citizen's consent, then we can provide ourselves an acceptable quality of life.

Indeed the attorney Haim Klugman was correct when he stated that: the closed circuit television system is an aggressive way of tracking the private person, while essentially harming his privacy. Since the closed circuit television system, by its very nature, captures information about the individual, the meaning is clear on the matter of maintaining the citizen's privacy. From a different perspective, security and law enforcement agencies are entitled to use these abilities and databases, subordinate to a legal warrant as required.

The duty of the owners of the closed circuit television systems is to obey the principles of privacy and to implement the appropriate procedures in the planning and installation of the system. It is necessary to prepare a list that documents all possible effects on privacy issues resulting from the implementation of the closed circuit television system. This list needs to address the spectrum questions that pertain to the principles of privacy in general and to the principles of information privacy, as stated in the Privacy Protection Law.

The owners and operators of closed circuit television systems must implement an 'actions' guide that will reflect conditions relating to the protection of privacy. The guide will include issues that address the determination of system goals, permitted uses, and technological specifications that will reduce the harm to privacy. In addition, they must define the role-holders permitted to use and access the systems in general and the server storing the information in particular.

The duty of those authorized to access/use the system is to confirmation and provide proof that they have no criminal record and must also meet trustworthiness checks. In addition, it is test each camera separately to evaluate its field of view and thus negate the possibility to an invasion of privacy. It is also necessary to examine the system configuration and how backups are implemented, controlled and saved.

It is necessary to take into consideration the possibility that the documented material will be required for the purpose of a police investigation, and hence it is mandatory to enable law enforcement agencies and officers with a legal order, access to the CCTV system. It is important to implement strict security procedures regarding those people permitted to release system footage into the hands of a third party who is not part of a law enforcement agency and/or does not have a legal warrant. In addition, it is required to define the way in which the video footage is saved and the way in which it is destroyed/erased after the set period of preservation. It is necessary to implement mechanisms for handling complaints and provide solutions to issues that may derive from the system's activity such as tracking, evaluation, and criticism and response.

The Legal Situation in the United States

American law in civil damages law addresses primarily the issue of the security of public areas, but also private ones. Lawsuits in the field of damages are primarily linked with the concealed use of CCTV systems and issues of private civil liability and governmental immunity[165].

Within the framework of the change to the country's laws, United States courts obligated business owners to adopt extra caution, for the safety of those who come into their businesses and/or in public spaces. The law determines that the business owner who owns an open, public area is subject to liability and bears responsibility for all damage to property and/or physical harm that is caused to visitors by chance, as a result of negligence or intentionally by a third party.

The business owner has civil liability if he does not adopt the cautionary measures required to identify actions of this type that occur and/or might occur and if he does not adequately warn visitors to avoid the harm and damage this may cause and/or does not protect them from such harm[166].

The law is derived from the principles of negligence and not from the obligation of strict liability, then responsibility is in the ability to predict the damage that may occur. It is, therefore, the responsibility of the business owner to anticipate the crimes and/or damages that may be caused by a third party to those who come into the business. The goal of the law is to deter and prevent negligence on the part of the business owner, even when the harm to the visitor is caused following a criminal misdemeanor by a third party. In a case when the business owner acted appropriately, namely, predicted ahead of time the likelihood of the existence of the offence and cautioned against it, they will bear no liability[167].

The concept of 'reasonable caution' changes according to the

[165] McIntosh v. Schops, 180 P. 593 (Ore. 1919)
[166] Restatement 2d, Torts, Sec. 344 (1965)
[167] See Restatement, 2d, Torts, Sec. 302, and Comment e.

circumstances. Generally it is possible to use parallel events and similar businesses so as to show and prove that the business owner was aware of the dangers and that he acted appropriately so as to protect his guest/customer/visitor and/or to alert against the danger.

Many diverse questions arise in this topic. The first is whether previous activity was supposed to attract the attention of the business owner and to motivate him to adopt reasonable means of caution, namely, to be concerned regarding the safety of visitors.

I would further note that in a natural and reasonable manner, the law provides a balance, taking into consideration the severity of harm caused to visitors and the burden placed on the business owner to reduce possible risk. In places where reasonable means were adopted to reduce the risk, the liability of the business owner is reduced or is eliminated completely. The business owner must adopt obligatory steps for the reduction of criminal activity that threatens visitors[168].

Until recently, Courts in the United States expressed their objection to the assignment of liability to business owners for harm resulting from criminal activity by a third party caused to those who came through their doors. Recently the trend has changed, and the Courts have extended the laws of negligence, including liability caused from criminal acts, so that today they apply also to areas such as supermarkets, restaurants, cafés, schools, summer camps, and additional public places where citizens gather for different reasons as part of their daily routine.

On this matter I would note that although criminal action is in essence a real action, the business owner's awareness exposes him to liability in a case in which it is possible to expect, ahead of time and in a reasonable manner, the criminal act. It is important to emphasize that these are places over which the business owner has complete control, namely, the duty to provide reasonable security in all areas under their control[169].

---

[168] Id, at 578.
[169] Nebel v. Avichal Enterprises, Inc., 704 F.Supp. 570 (D.N.J. 1989)

With regard to the use of the CCTV system and the implementation of the law, a failure to use a system of this type is without a doubt negligence on the part of the business owner. In civil damages law, the claimant is entitled to present evidence such as an industrial standard, as proof of negligence. Although the standard in itself does not establish negligence, it constitutes a parameter for the examination of the systems installed in the business under examined.

For instance, the owner of a motel situated in a high crime area in the State of New Jersey maintained that the defendant's workers (a company that provides CCTV systems) were careless in that they did not usable equipment including television cameras and closed circuit monitors. The Court opined that the claimant's obligation, in cases in which deficient security is argued, is to prove that the defendant's negligence is the main cause of harm.

It is further their duty to prove that the defendant was aware of those sections of the law and that the CCTV systems and/or other means of security were supposed to warn the criminals against the criminal activity that caused the harm[170]. The claimant presented expert evidence that proved a prior prediction that it was possible that a robbery would be committed and thus the installation of security systems, including the installation of closed circuit cameras, is an obligation. The jury ruled in favor of the claimant and recognized the damages.

Often the question arises as to whether the use of CCTV is an adequate substitute for security guards or security officers. In cases in which it is possible to install cameras, arguments against this question are few. In my opinion, technology can serve as an aid but not as a substitute.

An example is the case in which a client was attacked, robbed, and injured in the parking lot adjacent to the defending restaurant. The attacked victim filed a damage suit against the restaurant owner[171]. The

[170] Morris v. Krauszer's Food Stores, Inc., 693 A.2d 510 (N.J.App. 1997)
[171] 460S.E.2d 809, 812.

claimant argued that the defendant knew of at least four previous cases of violence that had taken place at the same location over the past two years, including a case in which one of the restaurant's checkout clerks was shot at.

In the lawsuit the victim argued that the defendant, who had hired security staff for the evening hours only and had left the area without security guards during later hours, installed a hidden CCTV system near the restaurant's cash register. She further argued that, at a later stage, the defendant (the restaurant owner) employed guards to supervise the parking lots and accompany the workers on their way to their cars, especially on Fridays and Saturdays, when the workers receive their salaries.

In light of the fact that the restaurant was situated in a high crime area, namely, in an area of higher risk than most of the defendant's recreational sites, and in light of the fact that the claimants were aware of the potential for criminal attacks, the Court ruled that the defendant did not provide reasonable security measures for his clients.

The CCTV systems may inspire a sense of security, but sadly this is not justified. Victims of robbery and assault may argue neglect in cases where there is proof that the CCTV system was not designed and/or maintained appropriately.

The issue facing us addresses the sense of security that the CCTV system instills, which for the most part has no basis in reality, and in the person behind the system. This is an argument according to which the security system using closed circuit cameras is not subject to supervision, or in other words, may mislead visitors. From the visitor's perspective, the very existence of the cameras creates a feeling that there is supervision and hence a sense of security. In this way, the cameras encourage a sense of false security among visitors, who may take risks that they would not have taken had they known that the security system was not subject to supervision.

See, for example, the Kutbi Trial[172], in which a regular client of an bar claimed that the defendant's workers acted negligently in all pertaining to the guests' security, in that they duplicated the keys to the business in an unsupervised manner and were careless in the maintenance of the CCTV system, since they failed to maintain a security watch on regular clients rooms thus creating a false sense of security among those clients. This argument was based on the fact that the employees did not reveal the fact that the footage taken using the security cameras was not supervised.

The Court determined that, since the defendant presented evidence that the security system operated normally and was under appropriate supervision on the night of the robbery in the claimant's room, the lawsuit was dismissed.

On the matter of the issue of security cameras and government immunity, there is a 'public liability doctrine', which limits responsibility on the matter of public areas, in that it removes from all the analysis the constitutional separation of powers and legal enforcement by the Police of the executive local authority.

In simple words, if a victim who files a lawsuit privately proves the defendant's negligence, then he is entitled to financial compensation based on the argument that the owner of the public area, for example, a public library, dedicated too few financial resources to the area's security. The obligation of public and government organizations is to be cautious and to behave in a reasonable manner with regard to this limited immunity. In cases where the visitors enjoy a legal connection with the owner, for instance, a public library or an academic campus, the duty of the owner on the matter of negligence is strict liability.

Federal Law in the United States

In the United States, the right to privacy is anchored in constitutional law and in all State laws[173]. One of the most well-known

---

[172] Kutbi v. Thunderlion Enterprises, Inc., 698 P.2d 1044 (Ore. 1985)

events in this field is the trial of Katz v. the United States[174], in which the fundamental assumption was that the government's wiretapping of the defendant's telephone conversations held from a public telephone booth was a fundamental violation of his privacy. On this matter the question arises as to whether the defendant, as any other reasonable person, has a subjective expectation of privacy, an expectation that society will identify as logical and reasonable.

In the question under discussion here, a subjective and objective examination constitutes a theoretical measure in legal cases involving closed circuit television[175] in particular and additional legal issues in general. Conversely, I would note that after the Katz trial all actions occurring outside of the domestic residence are accorded a reduced degree of expectation of privacy.

The Fourth Amendment to the Constitution of the United States does not support surveillance through closed circuit television in public places, such as sidewalks and parks, and this since the ordinary person does not have a logical and reasonable expectation that they will be subject to surveillance in public situations and in general. Conversely, I would argue that a reasonable person, in public, is aware of the fact that they are constantly exposed to some form of surveillance. A person who is speaking on a cellular phone in an elevator or in a café, for instance, cannot complain when others listen to his conversations.

The basic assumption is that there is a real expectation that the use of closed circuit television will be reasonable, namely, not invasive and that surveillance will not be implemented in which there is a reasonable expectation for privacy, even if this is in a public area. This is also true regarding the focusing of the camera on a specific person, close ups to enable lip reading in a conversation between two or more persons and so on.

[173] See U.S. v. Martinez, 498 F.2d 464 (6th Cir.1974), cert. denied, 419 U.S. 1056. See 18 U.S.C.A. §2510

[174] U.S. 347 (1967)

[175] See People v. Smith, 360 N.W.2d 841 (1984)[Defendant's reasonable expectation of privacy will be determined by totality of circumstances], Cited in Granholm, supra., at footnote 26.

Conversely, I would argue that the suspect will always aspire to increased privacy, as part of the effort to conceal his actions, to differentiate from the reasonable person, who has no reason to conceal what they have said to others in a conversation in the street. Therefore, on this matter reliance on democratic principles is misplaced, and it is necessary to allow video surveillance in public places including enlargement capabilities, such as telescopic lenses or devices for filming video clips..

It is true that CCTV cameras are invasive and fundamentally disruptive to privacy. To a certain extent systems of this type contradict the democratic outlook, which is based on the expectation of privacy in public as well as private places. It should be noted that the public with concerns about privacy in public places is also concerned about their health and wellbeing at the same locations, and hence there is a foundation for the preservation of the balances required between maintaining a person's privacy and maintaining public safety in general.

To reinforce my statements, and in a different analogy, I would mention Mr. Rudi Giuliani (the mayor of New York City from 1994 to 2001), who decided to remove crime from the streets of New York by placing larger numbers of police on the streets. CCTV cameras can be compared to the policemen who patrolled the streets of New York so as to eliminate crime in the city. As a result, in those locations where security cameras were installed, the percentage of crime was reduced. This can be seen as an indication that the benefits and value derived from maintaining public safety are greater and override issues of personal privacy providing a proper balance between the two is maintained.

Over the years, different and diverse arguments have been raised against the invasion of privacy. The most prominent of them is the argument put forward by Jennifer Granholm which stated that mass surveillance of the individual's behavior contradicts the American constitution, since it lacks a basic preliminary condition, that of a reasonable suspicion of the commission of an offense – to differentiate from cases in which, for example, drug tests, alcohol tests[176], etc. are performed – or justification of mass search, such as the search performed on citizens in airports and in government buildings.

Granholm argued that cases that permit mass search in airports and government buildings are based on the existence of real and proven danger of violence at those locations, dangers that do not exist in general surveillance scenarios[177].

In addition, she maintained that the crime related threat shown by statistical data does not justify the use of technology for increased supervision and surveillance. This argument is based on the fact that closed circuit television systems are not installed in areas with high crime rates where the safety of poorer citizens is threatened but rather in locations such as shopping centers and prestigious recreational areas, and where the intention is primarily to protect the economic wellbeing of the business owners and those frequenting their businesses.

It is my opinion that Granholm is mistaken in her approach, since if the security cameras were to be removed from shopping centers and prestigious recreational areas, then crime would spread to these places as well. Hence the basis of her argument is erroneous. With regard to the matter of balance, I would direct the reader to the decision of the Supreme Court in the case of Griswold v. the State of Connecticut[178], which rejected the right to privacy in public places in favor of the public interest to prevent crime.

This is a complex issue, and each case must be discussed on its individual merits. Often, federal courts have found a certain degree of acceptability regarding the existence of checkpoints and/or buildings. In those cases the Courts deal with the invasive nature of the closed circuit

176 Regarding the constitutionality of government checkpoints set up to detect drunk drivers, see Michigan Dept. of State Police. Sitz, businesses (1990)

177 Citing Downing v. Kunzig, 454 F.2d 1230 (6th Cir. 1972); U.S. v. Lopez, 328 F.Supp. 1077 (E.D.N.Y .U.S. v. Bell, 335 F.Supp. 797 (S.D.N.Y.), aff'd 464 F.2d 667 (2d Cir. 1971), cert. denied, 409 U.S .and Federal Regulations at 14 C.F.R. 121.538, and 14 C.F.R. 107.123 (1987) Requiring AirCarriers to use screening devices designed to deter passengers from carrying explosives or weapons aboard an aircraft, or to allow unauthorized vehicles access to air operations areas.

178 U.S. 479 (1965) 381.

television systems, especially in places where there is a legitimate expectation of privacy, in other words, places where the need for supervision must be justified.

To conclude this issue, I would note that it is definitely possible to balance the justified desire to maintain the person's reasonable expectation of privacy and the use of technology against those committing crimes. There is no reason to focus a camera on the lips of a pedestrian, just as there is no reason to enable the commission of a crime. Early and correct planning of installation and use of closed circuit television systems enables the two variables to coexist and thus reduces the depth of the question faced by the Courts.

State Law

In the various states of the United States, most of the concepts that address privacy issues were shaped by the states under constitutional conditions and legal declarations. In addition, some states such as Oregon, Pennsylvania, Hawaii, Montana, Illinois, California, Alaska, Florida, New Hampshire, and Michigan, established clear constitutional defense measures to maintain privacy, including supervision using media of different types.

Conversely, a number of states have permitted use of closed circuit television systems and this has received support from the public in these states. This is the preference of the public interest in the war against crime, which outweighs concerns for the privacy of the individual.

In the reverse interpretation, an interesting story involves the case of Ricks v. Maryland[179]. In this case, Baltimore Police operated a closed circuit television system secretly and without a court order as required, as a part of an extensive drugs investigation in areas that were supposedly used by the defendants, namely, a house for growing and

---

179 520 A.2d 1136 (Md. App. 1987); aff'd, 537 A.2d 612 (Md. 1988) 520

processing drugs.

Eventually, following the defendants' arrest, the Appeals Court approved the surveillance. The Court noted the defendants' admission to the fact that the closed circuit television system was not installed according to a 1968 law for monitoring crime and keeping the streets safe, following which the Telephone Wiretapping Law was passed in Maryland[180]. The video system is not included explicitly in the State of Maryland's law, and therefore the Court permitted the use of a concealed system for surveillance of suspicious criminal activity.

On the issue of the Fourth Amendment to the United States Constitution, the Court argued that the burden of proof for the use of CCTV systems by law enforcement officers and agencies lays with the defendants, and that they must prove a legitimate expectation for privacy in a place where the boundary was encroached[181]. The Court believed that the defendant must show and prove that there is a subjective expectation of privacy and that this expectation is such that society is willing to acknowledge it as logical.

In other states, laws were enacted that forbade the Police to use closed circuit television cameras in public places such as streets and forbade the use of zoom lenses and/or other invasive surveillance means. In the state of Montana, for instance, the Police must prove that there is a reasonable suspicion of delinquent activity that justifies invasive surveillance. Take, for example, the Court Ruling State of Montana v. Mr. Brown[182].

Canada defined the conditions for the concept of 'invasive aspects' in the use of closed circuit television. The Supreme Court rejected the probabilistic aspect, which permits monitoring in situations in which the individual can logically expect privacy, while examining the variables and implementing judgment regarding the question as to whether the reasonable person would have assumed that security cameras which

181 537A.2d at 619, citing Katz v. United States, supra., and Rakas v. Illinois, 439 U.S. 128 (1978) 537
182 State v. Brown, 755 P.2d 1364 (Mont. 1988)

violate his privacy may have been installed in a specific location. The Court defined the logical expectation for privacy under circumstances in which a normal person expects privacy. In these locations, the state does not need to obtain a court permit for surveillance. In Israel and in the United Kingdom the situation is similar.

This determination of the Canadian Court indicates that constitutional defenses against search and seizure are not acceptable and do not give the state the right to use scientific and technological developments which enable invasion of privacy more easily and extensively. According to the Court and in light of the developments in surveillance technology, probabilistic examination sets a standard without meaning on the matter of privacy.

Employer's Use of Closed Circuit Television in the Workplace

In the United States, as in Israel, Britain, and in many other countries in the world, a thought provoking discussion is being conducted regarding employees expectations of privacy, alongside the employer's concern regarding the worker's inappropriate behavior.

In the case of Brazinski v. AMOCO Petroleum Additives Company, eight workers in a chemistry laboratory filed a suit against the installation of television cameras by the employer in the ceiling of the room where employees changed from their street clothing into work clothing[183].

The defendant explained that the installation of the cameras resulted from an inappropriate act of a sexual nature by one of the company's workers. In addition, the company asserted that the lawsuit is based on a collective agreement between the company and the complainants union, and therefore it is necessary to file the lawsuit under section 301 of the Work Relations Management Law (Taft-

183 F.3d 1176 (7th Cir. 1993) 6

Hartley Act, 29 U.S.C. § 185).

For these reasons, the lawsuit was removed from the court's list and transferred to the District Federal Court. In the end, a ruling was made in the company's favor, since the claimant did not file a lawsuit within the framework of the collective agreement. In statements summarizing the ruling, the Court pointed to the state's civil damage laws, which may support the lawsuit, and which state that the employer is required to prove that they did all they could do prevent harm to the worker's privacy and if such a harm were caused by the closed circuit cameras, then the harm itself constitutes grounds for a lawsuit on the part of the victim.

In addition, the Court noted that the person who randomly found themselves at the site and who was photographed or filmed, for example, when they were undressed (whether partially or totally) cannot file a lawsuit[184]. In addition, the Court cautioned that the employer must prove that he acted adequately and appropriately to reduce any harm to the employees to the extent possible and, when such action can be proven to have been taken, the grounds for the action should be dismissed. Conversely, the claimant must prove that they were seen in a live broadcast and/or was seen in the recorded footage.

Further on this issue, I would also note that because of the inherent technical difficulties, it is enough that the worker be able prove that they had been in a location where surveillance was being performed and that, in the event that the equipment was indeed used, it would be possible to show them speaking or to hear their voice. In general, it is necessary to note that the use of closed circuit television in work areas open to the public at large, even without the worker's clear knowledge regarding the existence of the CCTV system, is considered a less invasive action than is the installation of cameras that film the desks, folders, drawers, and/or any other private space where the worker is found.

The installation of closed circuit television cameras is part of the

184 F.3d 1176, 1183 6

effort to eliminate theft or damage that may be caused to the organization by workers or by people outside in, for example, publically accessible locations. The predominant approach of the Courts entails the creation of a system of balances between the employer's right to preserve their property (whether physical or intellectual) and the protection of the worker's right for privacy. Therefore, the employer is prohibited to record using closed circuit cameras any activities that fundamentally entails an 'un-based fear' of a specific occurrence. Moreover, even in those cases where the filming is justified as a legally acceptable precautionary means to prevent violence or crime, the employer must adopt care and also maintain the worker's right to privacy.

In addition, it is necessary to implement policies and procedures for training workers, in those locations where a closed circuit television system is installed as the sole means of security or in order to increase security. The business owner must be take care and act according to designated policies in order to ensure that employees rights to privacy are respected and maintained in all issues pertaining to the installation and use of technology[185].

To conclude, I would note that it is necessary to careful consideration should be given to the expectations of privacy in the workplace and in public areas, in order that the use of closed circuit television systems will constitute a deterrent, as well as a law enforcement resource for the protection of the public against all types of crime. In general, the widespread assumption is that as long as there is no misuse of technology, it is necessary to support the installation of surveillance cameras in public places, and that the use of closed circuit television systems by the Police, without legal authorization or permission, must be limited to public streets where the Court believes that citizens do not have a reasonable expectation for privacy.

The issue raises serious questions. Where can privacy be expected – and where not? Does the person committing a crime have the right to expect privacy while he is committing his crime? Is it possible to see the

---

[185] Cohen v. Southland Corporation, 203 Cal. Rptr. 572 (Cal. App. 1984)

camera as a law enforcement official who is tracking the person suspected of committing a crime and is the policeman who is tracking the public violating the offender's expectation of privacy? These questions and many others surface as a result of the use of these technological systems in particular and of control and surveillance systems in general.

It is my opinion that the emphasis is not on the protection of the victim of a crime and neither is it on the privacy of the person committing the crime. This approach will pave the way to the installation of as many security cameras as possible. I would further note that it is necessary to use technology so that it will support the elimination of crime, while meticulously maintaining the reliability of the data alongside the implementation of processes that ensure that there will be no abuse of the data collected using security cameras.

The Legal Situation in Israel

In Israel the dominant feeling is that visual evidence surpasses all other forms of evidence: "One picture is better than a thousand words". Video footage that presents the crime and/or the offense is the strongest evidence that indicates where the alleged offense did or did not take place.

Since reality does not reinforce this statement and video footage taken using closed circuit security cameras must meet the stringent standards I have discussed earlier in the book, I will discuss the conditions under which the reliability of the footage will be ensured as an additional reference to issues pertaining to laws of evidence.

As mentioned previously, the aim of deciding the admissibility of video footage retrieved from closed circuit television systems is to bring before the Court, in as much verifiable detail as possible, the facts and events that occurred in relation to the case under consideration. In other words, every reliable means that can bring the Court to a closer and better awareness and understanding of the facts is an admissible evidential means. Often the Courts in Israel have addressed recorded video footage as a 'mechanical' witness, when stating: "The recording medium is a mechanical witness, which brings before the Court the content of what was recorded".

This statement can be seen as correct when it refers to evidence brought before and presented to the court by an individual and when that individual testifies as to the truthfulness of the events based on their personal knowledge. This is not the case with regards to recorded video footage relating to a controversy/dispute the parties involved, and insofar as the reliability of the recording was not examined; namely, as long as the recording was not examined and the possibility that the video footage and transcription of any conversation presented to the court was not, in any way, manipulated through the use of technological means.

On the matter of closed circuit security cameras, to the best of my understanding the footage retrieved from closed circuit security cameras should not be seen as a 'mechanical witness', as long as the reliability was not examined and as long as the way in which the electronic evidence was dealt with and processed in general was not examined. In other words, since the film is a 'mechanical witness' that presents what the camera saw, and the act took place outside of the Court walls, it is obligatory to examine the trustworthiness of the recording, the manner by which the evidence was preserved, the trustworthiness of documenting software, and other contributing elements that I addressed at the beginning of this chapter and in the topic of "Processes of Collection and Preservation of Films and Pictures from Closed Circuit Television Cameras (CCTV)".

Even before the era of closed circuit television cameras, the admissibility of a recording was examined by the Courts in Israel, in a series of rules drawn from American law such as in the case Anonymous v. the Attorney General of the Government[186] and in the case Mohammed Snir and others v. the State of Israel[187]. The Supreme Court determined, on the matter of voice recordings, that it is necessary to discuss the technical means that were used to examine the admissibility of digital evidence and to examine whether things are as they seem to be and as first voiced and whether there is no distortion of the act, mistakenly or maliciously.

> In order that the Court be able to decide as to the admissibility and/or acceptance of the recorded video footage or audio recording, it is necessary to first prove or to show the existence of a number of preliminary conditions, namely: (1) that the device or other means used for the recording operates appropriately and can record things that were said, (2) that the person who performed and later dealt the recording was fully able to perform his task as appropriate, (3) that the filming or recording are reliable and correct, (4) that no changes, additions or subtractions were made in the film, (5) that those appearing in the video footage and/or audio recording are identified and (6) that the contents of the recorded conversation and the associated testimony was made out of the speaker's free will, without coercion and without temptation.

This is the real verification of the admissibility of evidence

[186] 28/59 Anonymous v. Attorney General to the Government.
[187] Criminal Appeal 869/81 Mohammed Snir and others v. The State of Israel.

produced from a voice recording. I would note that there is an almost absolute correlation between this field and evidence produced from closed circuit television systems. The missing component in this matter is that of information security, alongside advanced processes made possible because of technological advances which I addressed at the beginning of this chapter.

The fourth rule listed by the courts addresses the dependability of those persons charged with recording procedures. On this matter it is necessary to prove that there has been no technological manipulation of the recording, namely, nothing was removed or eliminated and/or nothing was added that was not in the original.

I would note that it cannot be learned from this rule that it is necessary to disqualify the recording in a situation in which there is a break in the continuity of the recording or when a passage is missing either at the beginning or at the end of the recording. Over the years, the technological 'arms race' has emptied of meaning the statement that video footage cut in the middle is of doubtful trustworthiness. If it is not proved beyond all shadow of a doubt that the film is trustworthy, including the presentation of proof and acceptable arguments on the matter of the reason for the break in the film's continuity, then the evidence as a whole must be disqualified.

Further on this matter, I would direct my readers to the subchapter "Processes of Collection and Preservation of Films and Pictures from Closed Circuit Television Cameras (CCTV)". This section indicates how to collect, preserve, and document films from a closed circuit camera system.

Regarding the sixth rule, the Court says[188]:

> Essentially closely related to the fourth question
> and the sixth rule deals with a similar situation, that
> the possibility that the recording was handled in

---

[188] Criminal Appeal 869/81 *** Mohammed Snir, Mohammed Turk v. The State of Israel Court Ruling 38 (4) 169.

such as way so as to raise suspicions that one or
more of the parties to the recorded conversation
was guided to say certain things, was forced to say
them or alternatively, was prevented by force from
speaking: an act of violence as already mentioned
can, for example, be performed, if an attempt is
made to create an artificially distorted picture, which
arises from the lack of a response of one of the
speakers, where such a response could reasonably
be expected , then the circumstances was not as
argued by the anonymous defendant.

On this matter, there is indeed an essential difference between
voice recording, in which the parties are only heard rather than seen,
and video footage from closed circuit camera systems. Despite the
obvious difference, technology exists that allows for the analysis of a
voice recording to determine if any of the parties in the recording were
speaking under duress or freely. This can be seen as proof that no
pressure was applied to any of the parties to the conversation (or the
opposite of course).

Further on this matter, I would also note that the law teaches us
that the burden of proof regarding the admissibility of evidence applies
to the person submitting the evidence if the court is to be able to make
a decision regarding the admissibility of digital evidence. It is necessary
to prove a number of preliminary conditions. The main conditions are
as follows:

- That it was proved beyond all reasonable doubt that the
  technological system operated appropriately and as expected
  and that the events documented indeed occurred.

- That the person who dealt with technological systems in general
  and the digital evidence in particular has knowledge, as required,
  for the handling of this type of digital evidence.

- That it was proved beyond all reasonable doubt that the documentation is original and that there was no technological manipulation that resulted in the distortion, addition, and/or removal of document sections.

- That the digital and/or documented evidence was obtained with the agreement of the speaker and/or in the course of a normal conversation and that the speaker was not under duress, being coerced, encouraged or under the influence of any substances that could cause the person to make the recorded statements submitted as evidence.

In addition, the person submitting the evidence must prove that the evidence is original, that it was tampered with in order to remove things and/or adding content that was not in the original. Further on this matter, I would also note that if it is not possible to interpret and/or understand parts of the documentation and/or parts of the documentation were erased whether mistakenly or intentionally, it is necessary to disqualify the evidence in its entirety, because it will be impossible to know whether things were taken out of context and/or whether the evidence was manipulated technologically .

We must not make the mistake of allowing a gut feeling that visual or verbal evidence is the best to overly influence our attitude towards digital evidence. Digital evidence whether film, picture, or sound recording and/or video footage from closed circuit television systems are subject to distortion by those utilizing technologies which enable the user to manipulate the evidential material in a wide variety of ways and with the end result that a false picture of the actual events may be presented as factual evidence. Furthermore, such is the level of distortion that it is often impossible to determine if such a manipulation has taken place even when there is reasonable suspicion that it did, indeed, take place.

It is our duty to ascertain ahead of time that this is original evidence, and as long as this has not been proven, the doubt as to the reliability of the evidence must be expressed. The Court must be convinced that what was seen indeed happened before a decision was made regarding the documented matter and/or before the evidence was submitted, and hence there is a duty of caution and exactness when dealing with the admissibility of evidence obtained from camera systems.

If at the end of the examination, doubt still exists regarding the reliability and credibility of the evidence, then it is possible to use physical methods, including, for example, questioning those involved in the event thus creating a sequence of events relating to the from its start to its finish and cross reference the evidence shown bin video footage with the physical evidence collected from the respondents. In this way, we 'validate the rule of 'best digital evidence', namely, we ensure that, given the circumstances of the event, this was the case.

I would further note that under the rule of 'best digital evidence', the Court must examine the appropriate weight under existing circumstances and that it may be necessary to reduce the significance awarded as required.

In December 2011 a circular was submitted to the *Knesset* Committee of Science and Technology that focused on 'Surveillance Cameras for the Purposes of Security in the Pubic Space". About a year before, attorney Hagit Lernau (the Deputy Public Defender) and attorney Yishai Sharon from the Public Defender's approached the office of the Attorney General, , Yehuda Weinstein, in a letter entitled 'Networking of Urban and Public space using Surveillance Cameras". The following is an excerpt from their letter[189]:

> The use of cameras awakens serious legal considerations, which focus on the constitutional harm caused to the privacy of thousands of citizens. What are the reasons that justify this harm to privacy? What is the authority of the local authorities to network urban public spaces with cameras? What is the division of responsibility

---

[189] http://index.justice.gov.il/Units/SanegoriaZiborit/News/Pages/camera.aspx

between the Police and the local authorities on the operation of the cameras and the use of the filmed material? There is a need for a legal arrangement covering the issue as a whole, while setting clear and uniform standards regarding the place and number of cameras, the manner of documentation, information security, saving and erasing of the information, means of signage and informing the public, the identity of the agencies observing the information and training them properly, mechanisms for the transfer of information to another body, imposition of sanctions for abuse, and so on.

Indeed these are serious issues, which the issues we are examining here raise questions regarding the method of documentation, information security procedures, how information is saved, as well as a range of issues with regard to the examination process in order to ensure that the information will not become accessible to unauthorized person or agencies. Additional question arise as to possibilities of data being erased (in error or deliberately), the persons and/or agencies permitted to see the information, how information is transferred to another factor, and so on.

In general, I would note that even in Israel the predominant assumption is that as long as there is no abuse of technology, it is necessary to support the installation of surveillance cameras in public areas and that the use of the Police and/or the local authorities of closed circuit television systems without permission must be limited to public streets where the Court believes that the citizens do not have an expectation of privacy.

As mentioned previously, I believe that the emphasis is placed on protecting the public from harm and/or a crime and that the right to privacy does not protect the person committing the crime or causing harm. This approach will pave the way to the installation of as many security cameras as possible. Every intelligent person understands that the normal citizen is not concerned about their privacy while they are walking in the streets, shopping malls, and public parks. Anxiety is the province of the criminal or the person planning a crime which will force them to deal with the presence of technology that aims at protecting the innocent bystander.

In November 2010 the Ministry of Law's Authority of Law and Technology published a position paper on the topic of "Surveillance Cameras –Applicable Law and the Manner of Use". Following are some of the points raised by the position paper[190]:

> Already in the beginning, we would emphasize two places that require caution in the operation of surveillance cameras. As will be detailed later, there are special problems in the placement of surveillance cameras in public areas due to the difficulty in obtaining the agreement of the people who will, potentially, be filmed two of the invasion of their privacy that is inherent in the operation of the video security systems. In many cases, the initial question arises as to who or what agency is entitled to film in the public space and, since filming obligates consent, whether the consent to film in public places is given freely and is genuine –this if citizens do not have freedom of choice and do not have the practical possibility to avoid entry into the area under surveillance and being filmed. This difficulty obligates special care and greater control of the use of cameras in public areas. It is necessary to emphasize that not only open areas that are found in public ownership (such as roads, parks, and city squares) are considered 'public' for this purpose, but also areas where the ownership is private but the public has free access to them, for instance, shopping areas ...

[190] http://www.justice.gov.il/NR/rdonlyres/AFA7C4A5-8481-4FC1-A939-B844F0170111/23249/cctv.pdf

On this matter, it is my opinion is that the Authority for Law and Technology erred in its assessment that the normal citizen has free choice whether to enter into a public space or not. A person who has not committed any wrong is not afraid to be exposed to the camera. The question at hand is not the individual's desire or choice regarding whether to be exposed or not. Rather, the relevant question is who is exposed to the documented materials and how to ensure that the information will not fall into unauthorized hands.

Section 7 of the same position paper addresses the issue of minors and states:

> Special attention should be also dedicated to the use of surveillance cameras in places where children tend to assemble, such as educational institutions or community centers. Given the lack of explicit consent as defined by the law regarding the use of surveillance cameras, it is doubtful that it is possible to be satisfied by passively informing the children being filmed through cautionary signs, as the foundation for the system's proper use: in principle, children are not able to take legal action such as, for example, agreement (and if only implicitly) to an infringement of their privacy. Therefore, it is necessary to use caution when installing cameras in areas where children assemble and at locations regularly frequented by children (and possible their parents) such as schools, playgrounds etc. parents of the children who will or may be filmed by the surveillance system must be asked, individually, for their explicit agreement as a condition for use of surveillance cameras and it is necessary to moderate, as much as possible, the use of cameras and to ascertain their placement and the use made of information collected through them.

Special attention should be dedicated to the use of closed circuit television systems in places where children assemble, such as educational institutions and community centers, and so on. With regard to the matter of the protection of minors, the relevant questions we mentioned previously remain: who sees the films, what steps are taken to safeguard the information, and what is the process used to destroy/erase the filmed material when this becomes necessary? Assuming that an appropriate answer is given on the issue of information security, this is a technology that is supposed to, in itself, protect minors and not violate their privacy.

Later on in the position paper, in the chapter "Making the Decision to Place Surveillance Cameras", section 19 says:

> Use of surveillance cameras in the public space, especially by public authorities, must therefore meet conditions of constitutional limitation: explicit consent in law, appropriate purpose, and meeting tests of proportionality. To establish the appropriate and proportional purpose, the decision to use a surveillance camera must be made in an intelligent and conscious manner, after the examination of the needs and alternatives of use of the camera. The placement of a surveillance camera is not a decision that can be made casually merely because its installation is possible, for example, due to a budget being available for its purchase and installation f or because of a local event that creates pressure to install the system.

Limitation rulings discusses issues of explicit agreement in law, the appropriate purpose, and the test of proportionality. I will examine, in-depth, the question of appropriate purpose. In my opinion, the normal person, like the legislature and the law enforcement authorities, wants security and safety, the wellbeing of their children, and the certainty that they can stay in a public space without fear. Placing a camera as a deterrent against law offenders will increase the citizen's sense of security and will enable tremendous economic savings in the law

322

enforcement and in the implementation of justice. This is the contribution of closed circuit systems to public financial savings and to the cumulative wellbeing of all the citizens of the state.

On the matter of proportionality, an area that is defined as private and/or in which a person has an expectation of privacy should be seen as an area in which closed circuit cameras should not be placed. To emphasis the topic, such places include changing rooms in stores, restrooms, and any other space where the normative person has a reasonable expectation of privacy and does not expect to be exposed to the public. However, this does not mean that public restrooms should not have a camera placed at the entrance and exit.

In general, I would recommend that all Western countries bring this question before the public and hold a referendum so as to obtain the support of the public. This will ensure the public's wellbeing as well as result in a significant reduction of crime in public areas.

A document of the State of Israel's Law and Technology Authority entitled "Surveillance Cameras – The Applicable Law and the Manner of Use"[191], addresses most of the issues related to closed circuit cameras, including the issue of information security, whether the preserved documentation created from the use of surveillance camera is a database, the preliminary conditions of harm to privacy, and so on.

So far I have addressed the issues and general conditions pertaining to the issues of the database, including issues in the field of information security and management of parties permitted access to and use of the system and its recorded materials.

I will now address issues relating to the potential harm caused by an evasion of privacy.

Sections 16 and 17 of the memorandum state:

~~A basic principle~~ of the Privacy Protection Law is

191 http://www.justice.gov.il/NR/rdonlyres/AFA7C4A5-8481-4FC1-A939-B844F0170111/23249/cctv.pdf

that a person's privacy shall not harmed without their agreement (section 1 of the law). Regarding State authorities, the Courts[192] have already ruled that it is not enough to have the victim's consent that harm to the right of privacy, as harm to other rights laid down in the Basic Law: Human Dignity and Liberty, is permitted only "by a law befitting the values of the State of Israel, enacted for a proper purpose, and to an extent no greater than is required" or according to law, as mentioned, by the force of explicit authorization.

It was seemingly possible to argue that the constitutional demand does not need to apply to the private agency that is not 'a government authority' that seeks to install a surveillance camera in the public domain or in a public space. However, because of the nature and areas of influence, in most cases it is impossible to obtain agreement from all those individuals whose privacy is harmed or could be harmed because of the camera, certainly not explicit agreement. At best, it will be possible to ascribe to them implied consent for invasion of privacy (see details following). With this in mind, tit is possible to argue that even placing cameras in the public domain by a private agency, should be examined from a constitutional perspective.

On this matter and ironically, I would ask whether a police officer or all normative individuals of the community who witnessed the commission of a crime and reported what they say to the police, as required by law, did, in essence, infringe on the criminal's right to privacy? Additionally, I would ask if there are any differences between the eye witness accounts of an offence and the events recorded by a ~~surveillance camera. The expe~~ctation of privacy is a subjective term,

---

192 Supreme Court 8070/98 The Association for Citizen Rights v. The Ministry of the Interior and Others.

namely, there is no equality between the individual's expectation and that of the general population. Hence, the following question is asked: should the norm create uniformity in the public domain?

Indeed, the Law and Technology Authority quoted statements of the Court regarding the protection of privacy as a part of the Basic Laws of the State of Israel and argued on the application of the topic with regard to private bodies. In my opinion, the center of the issue is the public's awareness of the existence of the surveillance cameras. In a simple analogy, there is a correlation between the installation of the closed circuit camera, which passersby are aware of, and speed trap camera installed at the side of the road.

Another example is public awareness in Britain of cameras installed at almost every street corner in London. Given that the average person is aware of the existence of the cameras, which constitute an inseparable part of daily life, they will see in it an advantage since the purpose is to avoid harm to themselves and their family.

Section 19 of the memorandum addresses the issue of the agency and/or person responsible for the operation of the surveillance system. This is a serious question, in the framework of which it is necessary to examine, in-depth, an number of questions: whether it is appropriate to leave the responsibility for this matter in the hands of the local authorities or whether it is necessary to instruct the Police to handle this issue, and how to address security cameras in public areas of a private location such as shopping malls, colleges, pub and bars, or any other place that is open to the public.

In my opinion, the important question is not who is responsible for operating the cameras but where and how the recorded material is stored. We live in a world where technology is so advanced that there no longer exists a physical relationship between the position of the camera and the position of the recording device and/or the agency viewing and examining the material. Put simply, in order to maintain the right to privacy of the public as a whole, it is possible to separate the physical location of the surveillance system's cameras and the location where the information is collected/stored and viewed by the authorized persons and/or agencies. In a simple analogy familiar to all, this is similar to the situation at control and monitoring facilities which remotely monitor and control devices away from the facility itself.

On the matter of security cameras in spaces open to the public in private areas (as described earlier), it is possible to implement the same method. In my opinion, it is necessary to obligate by law the owners of private areas to install closed circuit security cameras, and the material documented and collected must be transferred to a central control unit. Thus, we ensure that the documented material is indeed original and we can bring to the Court absolute evidence that indicates what actually occurred.

This issue, of course, raises a whole range of questions that pertain to the invasion of privacy of those who did not commit any offense and who are still interested in maintaining their privacy. An example of this case is a person who betrays their partner, an action that is not considered a legal violation in the Western world. The Law of Human Dignity and Liberty, alongside the laws protecting privacy in general, balance between the different rights proportionally.

In my opinion, definitions relating to the issue of collection and handling of information and the right to view what is recorded, are related to the issue of proportionality and required balance. Let us take the case of a police officer who is an eye witness to an event. The question is asked: What will they do with this information? In the case in which they witness a man cheating on his wife, since this is not a violation, they are not obligated to say or report anything.. To differentiate from the police officer, the security camera documents what is done without the human ability to differentiate between good and bad, acceptable or unacceptable or what is legal or illegal.

I would further note that to the best of my understanding the delegation of authority for the local authorities will lead to an increased use and distribution of all seeing surveillance camera and will enable many more sources of information leaks . Hence, it is my opinion that is necessary to keep what is recorded in one central location, stored using meticulous procedures for information security that include a comprehensive set of permissions and procedures for backing up the information, the destruction of material that does not depict a crime and/or suspicion of a crime.

With regard to the purchase and installation costs of this type of closed circuit TV systems, I would point out that these systems constitute a defense system that can oversee a wide physical area as well as areas of importance such as national security issues. These factors, when taken into account, reduce the costs significantly. Moreover, management of a civil or criminal trial, in every country in the Western world, entails considerable economic costs large portion of which relates to the efforts of the parties involved in the case to being before the courts convincing evidence.

Closed circuit security cameras, in the proposed configuration, can, beyond any shadow of a doubt, provide what is required. Put simply, the use of these systems results in a considerable increase of the wellbeing of society as a whole, and therefore, in terms of cost-effectiveness and benefits, when we examine the benefits to society, the balance is tilted sharply in favor of the benefits provided by closed circuit television systems.

The Law and Technology Authority addressed the issue of data bases. Section 10 of the memorandum lets us learn that the Authority's conclusion that materials recorded by closed circuit surveillance systems constitute a database for all purposes. The Authority stated that:

> ...In our opinion, there is no doubt that the recorded films of the surveillance cameras will be categorized as a 'data base' that addresses the identified information or information that can be identified regarding an individual, according to the meaning of section 7 of the Privacy Protection Law, 1981:

> Camera systems that implement technologies such as identification of car license plates ... which

already today provide automatic identification on a high level of precision.

Systems that alongside input from surveillance cameras also draw from additional databases, in a way that allows for the cross-checking of information from both sources and processing that enables a high level of precision in the identification of the filmed objects; for instance, film from a surveillance camera situated at a factory, which is cross checked with a database of pictures identified as the factory workers.

Every camera system that uses automatic face identification on a minimal average level of accuracy; as a rule of thumb, we would note that in our opinion a system that provides identification at an average level of precision of at least 20% - is certainly considered information that can be identified 'about the person' that enters the 'data base' according to section 7 of the law.

To clarify this I will begin with a short explanation and definition of what a data base is. A data base is a collection of data in a certain field or in a variety of fields, which are collected and saved in one place, from which it is possible to retrieve data to produce information necessary to the user. From a technical perspective, the database is divided into two main components: hard drives where the information is actually stored and a data collection management program, without which it is not possible to perform data searches and retrieve the desired information.

I accept the definition of Israel's Ministry of Justice, Law and Technology Authority, for the concept of information, as stated in section 7 of the Privacy Protection Law 1981[193]: "Information – data on the person's personality, personal status, intimate affairs, and state

[193] http://www.nevo.co.il/law_html/law01/087_001.htm#Seif5

of health, economic status, professional training, opinions, and belief".

In addition, I would point out Amendment Number 12 of the Privacy Protection Law[194]: "And on the matter of sections 23 (13) (4) and 23 (15) – information of any type". Hence, my conclusion is that according to the legislature's intention, this is a data base: from the filmed documentation it is possible to learn about the individual's daily routine, including their economic and family situation, their professional training, and their state of health.

Conversely, I would note that these data are found at the state's disposal even without documentation collected through the use of closed circuit surveillance systems. Therefore, I would argue that the nature of the issue is the definitions, procedures, and manner in which the data base is held and maintained rather than any potential or actual harm to the privacy of the person in the street or public place. On balance and since the information, in general, is already found in the State's hands, then, it is my understanding and conclusion that there is nothing to prevent the installation of closed circuit TV systems in every public space.

My statement is based, as mentioned previously, on the understanding that the normative person does not expect privacy when they conduct their daily routine in public places, alongside the fact that 'surveillance' of individuals can, in actuality, be performed in different ways.

For example, credit card companies can analyze their clients' patterns of behavior according to credit card data and create different advertising packages for each individual based on the conclusions drawn from an analysis of buying behavior and patterns. This is also true of cellular companies, banks, HMOs, and all other organizations which provide the public individual services on a regular basis and can use the data collected regarding each individual to conduct a statistical analysis that indicates everyday behavior patterns.

[194] http://www.justice.gov.il/NR/rdonlyres/A301D378-F0B7-4BE5-B67F-E0288923A273/31447/627.pdf

Therefore, the relevant question, in my opinion, is not whether to install cameras in public places but rather, what is the correct way of operating them? Moreover, what information security procedures and what procedures for the preservation and later erasure/destruction of information should be put in place and enforced, including definition of strict conditions regarding those authorized to access and view the recorded materials?

To conclude, I would note that, in my opinion, the advantages of installing closed circuit TV systems in public place far outweigh the disadvantages. We only need to consider the security and safety of our children, the reduction in act of vandalism and assault in the public domain, about the decrease crime, the increase of the Police's ability to investigate different crimes and to do so more easily and with greater success – a fact that will in itself lessen the costs of Police work, the judicial system and the Courts and thus save the public's coffers (and indirectly the public itself) considerable sums of money.

General Explanation, Definitions and Appendices

Computer Structure, Layers

In general I would note that computers consist of four layers of operation.

The first is the basic foundation for the system, , the hardware that physically connects and bridges between all other components and layers..

The second is the basic operating system. This is the BIOS (Basic Input-Output System). This system is installed on the hardware and is the basic software burned on the hardware for the purpose of booting the computer and implementation of software programs.

The third layer is the operating system. There are a number of types of operating systems, including Linux and Microsoft Windows. These operating systems, and many others, are linked to the hardware through the BIOS. The operating system is a set of integrated software program that create a bridge between the user and the hardware via the input-output system. This is the first program that the user sees when he turns the computer on, and it enables the user to act on the three different levels, namely, the user interface, the drivers, and the application interface (API).

The fourth layer is that of user installed software programs, such as business management programs, email programs, customer management programs (CRM), word processors, such as Office, and others.

A **server** is, in all respects, a computer with software programs installed in its third and fourth layer to handle different types of events and specifically events that the end user is not aware of. Apart from the differences in the third and fourth layers, the server's hardware components are built so that it can handle a larger number of events (compared to a standard computer) at any given moment and at a higher speed. Another type of server, which many people have certainly heard of, is the virtual server (VM). The difference between a physical server and a virtual server is that the physical server is, as mentioned, a computer that includes all four of the previously mentioned layers. With a virtual server (VM) on the other hand, the two top layers of the physical server are replaced by a specific file type, in other words, the hardware component is temporarily eliminated. The file can be run on different hardware, while defining hardware resources in favor of the file. Since, in this model, the virtual server is hosted by an Internet service provider (ISP), such as Bezek Benleumi (in Israel) or BT (in the

United Kingdom), control is only possible in the two upper layers and there is no access to the server hardware. This is in contrast to the physical server, in which control of all system layers is possible.

Terms and Definitions

- **API – Application Programming Interface**. In professional jargon, the library of code, orders, functions, etc. The main functions provided in the application programming interface are memory management, data storage and retrieval, links to other applications, and so on. Generally programmers use the application programming interface in most software components.

- **PGP** - **Pretty Good Privacy**. An algorithm that enables encryption of messages in a simple and easy manner, the product of a software development venture of the entrepreneur Phil Zimmerman in 1991.

- **Mirror Image**. The mirror image is accepted professional jargon for the copying of the hard drive (or hard disk) that results in a copy that is faithful to the original. In the physical world, looking at a mirror obtains a reverse image. This fact creates a feeling of confusion in the legal world. On this matter I would note that when a technical expert refers to a 'mirror image', he refers to a copy that is faithful to the original of the original disk.

- **Making a legally acceptable copy of a copy that is faithful to the original**. The copying of a hard drive that is faithful to the original is known in professional jargon as a bit by bit copy. This creates, at the end of the process, a precise copy of the original drive. As a part of the copying process, the duplication machine examines the working order of the drive performing the copies and the drive that is copied and, at the end of the process, produces output that indicates the integrity of the copy or shows a logical or mechanical flaw that occured during the copy process. This same output also contains a digital signature (HASH) that indicates that the copy is totally identical to the original and that no change and/or distortion has been made in the hard drive from which the copy was made.

To clarify the issue, I emphasize that if there is any difference between the copying drive and the copied drive, the digital signature will not be identical. This can indicate that there has been a change in the copied drive and that it is not identical to the original and that it is not possible to determine the nature and the scope of the change. In simple terms, if the digital signature is not identical, then is the copy is classified as unoriginal digital evidence and that the copy has been changed from the original which, in turn, cast doubt as to its reliability and its admissibility.

General Explanation and Significance as a Part of the Investigation Process

The hard drive can be compared to a public library. At the entrance there is a librarian, who has an index of all the books kept at the library. Without the index, it will be impossible to identify and locate a specific book amongst the total collection. If the position of a book is not documented in the index, or it documented location is incorrect, then locating it will be impossible and, indeed, its very existence may not be known.

When a copy that is faithful to the original disk is made, a bit by bit copy, even erased files are cloned and can be recovered through the use of special procedures and techniques. When the digital signature of the copied hard drive is identical to that of the original hard drive, this is an indication that the copy includes all the data on the original frive and is, indeed, a morror image. . Lacking an identical digital signature, it will be impossible to determine if content of the original drive is missing or different on the mirrot image. I would note that lacking copies that are faithful to the original, it is impossible to examine and verify the evidence presented as part of the legal process and it is impossible to focus on its nature and its evidential importance.

- **Hot Copy**. This is a copy that is faithful to the original hard drive or hard drives undertaken without turning off the computer or the server and without booting the operating system. A 'hot copy' is made in a situation in which it is not possible to turn off the computer or the server, for instance, in companies and organizations where there are hundreds of workers and core actions which are dependant on the continued operation of the server. In other words, turning off the server could harm the. It is important to be aware that data which changed during the hot copy process will not be included in the copy.

- **Hard Drive or Hard Disk**. This is a non-volatile memory device that is used to store large volumes of data in a digital format. The hard drive appears in two main configurations: internally, as a component installed in the computer or the cellular phone and externally, as an independent unit that connects to the electronic component through different types of cable .

- **CPU – Central Processing Unit**. The hardware component that acts as a central data processing unit. The modern CPU is composed of a number of units that can perform a number of different actions in parallel; in other words, each of the units operates separately. The leading companies in the global market for the production of processors are the American international corporation Intel, which holds nearly 80% of the market share of global processor production, and AMD (Advanced Micro Devices), which is based on Sunnyvale, California.

- **Bad Sector**. A unit or area in the hard drive or in the flash memory that it is impossible to use as a result of damage caused to it and/or because the operating system is unable to access it.

- **RAM - Random Access Memory**. This is volatile memory that exists only as long as the computer or the electronic device is in an active state. It enables the computer processor to directly access every memory bit rapidly and efficiently and to write and erase data on the non-volatile memory.

- **ISP - Internet Service Provider**. This is the link that connects the user to the outside world of the Internet. The ISP provides the user with access to the Internet through specific identification (a user name and password).

- **MB - Motherboard**. The basic computer component that links between all the computer's components that are active in the system. Some manufacturers produce motherboards that already include additional hardware components, such as network cards, graphic processing units, memory cards, and so on.

- **Cookie**. A small file that contains a chain of letters and digits, used generally to verify the user's data and to follow up and store information about the surfer on a website. The chain is created by the website, which transfers the file through the web browser and saves it in the memory of the user's computer. The chain creates a relationship with the website every time that the surfer connects to the website through the browser.

- **Log**. A file that documents the system's activation condition that the mechanism that enables this process is implemented. On this matter I would note that every log file documents a type of action or system and if we want to document different types of system activity, a log file must be saved for every required system. The log file saves itself for a limited period (generally four months) and is then erased or 'overwrites itself' and replaces the saved data for new data. The log file can be compared to a security guard at the entrance to a building who can testify As to the state of affairs when an event took place and following.

- **Log data**. Files that are created by programs and applications and/or operating systems that document activity such as tracking and capture of on-line key strikes or files that can be used so as to reconstruct events, such as "history", "meeting", "event", or "last files".

- **BIOS - Basic Input-Output System.** A mechanism that incorporates hardware with software burned into it and which is generally used to boot the computer, to implement software in the upper system layers, which support input and output. The central roles of the input-output system include: identification of hardware devices, determination of basic hardware definitions, activation and deactivation of different devices as needed, determination of the order in which storage devices are accessed, initial examination of hardware integrity, and so on.

- **RAID – Redundant Array of Independent Disks**. A method by which a number of hard drives are combined into one logical unit, which is managed by an information controller. The combination of the drives enables access to a number of data location parallel and thus improves computer efficiency and its speed. When a malfunction occurs that causes a loss of data, the array mechanism enables the reconstruction of the data that was lost as a result of the malfunction.

  There are different methods, at the hardware level and the software level, for the management of an array of drives, each of which has its advantages and disadvantages. The higher computer layers, namely, the operating systems and applications that operate on the server, address the drive array as one hard drive.

- **The Net - Internet**. A global network of computers that links individual computers and local networks from around the world (what has become known as the 'global village'). In order to connect to the Internet, a computer, cellular phone, or tablet is needed, as well as a connection to an Internet Service Provider (ISP).

- **ISP - Internet Service Provider.** The technological infrastructure through which information moves on the Internet. This can be the cellular network, telephone infrastructure, and cable infrastructure. The ISP provides the technology and mechanisms required to link surfers to Internet content.

- **Hosting Services.** A commercial organization that owns computers with advanced technological abilities, including large volume disks and memory capacities using a direct method of communication. The host allows companies and individuals to place content on the Internet or to store content on the supplier's computers. This service provided for a fee or free of charge (subject to the structure of business contract with the organization or the individual). Hosting services have recently become very popular, since the implementation of company organizational structure and the move to **cloud** computing and data storage.

- **Cloud Technology.** A relatively new work environment in which commercial companies, organizations, and even private individual's store their information on remote servers. The transition to cloud technology is part of the lessons learnt from the terrorist attack on the Twin Towers in Manhattan, in which a large part of the business and private information stored physically on servers in the Twin Towers, without remote backup, was completely lost, without any possibility of restoration.

- **Content providers.** The organizations that provide information on the Internet, such as CNN, Fox News, Sky News, Yahoo, Amazon, and so on. In recent years we have been exposed to a new type of content, in the guise of social networks and blogs in which the individual can provide information freely, while maintaining complete anonymity.

- **IP Address IPv4.** A series of four groups of numbers that indicate the country, the Internet provider, the region, and the precise position from which or through which the device is connected to the Internet. Since every Internet provider is allotted its unique range of addresses, it can identify the ISPa specific surfer if necessary.

- **IP Address IPv6.** An improved version of the Internet browsing protocol. The primary innovation in version 6 is a significant increase of the number of available IP addresses.

- **Virtual Private Network VPN.** A method for the transfer of private information in a secure manner, through a public infrastructure, namely, through the Internet.

- **Firewall.** A system for the monitoring and blocking of undesired traffic on a communication network and/or the Internet. This is an important step in the security of the organization's information, alongside additional protection systems, such as anti-virus software.

- **Proxy Server.** A server that acts as a representative or emissary. Its main role include providing rapid access to external resources on the Internet. In the world of Internet crime, anonymous proxy servers are also used to mask the IP address from which the surfer connects to the Internet.

- **Metadata.** The source of information that provides file information and specifically the history of the picture, the file, or the datum found on the Internet. The use of metadata makes it possible to locate the identity of different data stored in different places, for instance, databases, files, and so on.

- **Control Panel.** The operating system's graphical management interface that enables the computer user to change definitions that are the basis of the third and fourth computer layers, using predefined templates.

- **User Internet Protocol for Sending and Receiving Email (SMTP, POP3).** Email is sent through SMTP (Simple Mail Transfer Protocol) number 25, which an email program uses to transfer the message to the email service, which will then send the message to the recipient. The recipient uses POP3 (Post Office Protocol) protocol number 110, which enables the delivery of the email message.

- **OST**. Structure of data storage for the main email server system (exchange server from Microsoft).

- **Exchange Server**. The email server program used extensively by organizations and companies. The main functions of the server are the provision of the email infrastructure, calendars, contact lists, and tasks. In addition, it supports access to information through mobile phones via the Internet.

- **PST**. A file for saving Microsoft Outlook. The difference between an OST file and a PST file is that PST is used only on personal computers while OST has higher survivability and is used to store much more data from Exchange servers.

- **Logging Events**. The log file documents system events.

- **Cross-Over Cable**. A cable that transfers data from the broadcasting computer to the receiving computer. The cross over cable is different from a regular network cable, which can also be used to transfer data to other computers, which in turn can retransfer the data onwards.

- **Anti-Forensics**. A general name for digital anti-forensics systems. The purpose of anti-forensic techniques and applications is to blur the basic data that indicates that some type of transfer was indeed performed, including the hiding of the performer's identity,

- **Blacklist**. A list that collects names of users, email messages, or the IP addresses of serial offenders, so as to limit or refuse them access to a service or a resource via the Internet. The Internet and cellular providers are generally those responsible for the collection and documentation these lists, as are information security companies and/or producers of defense systems and anti-virus systems. The lists are updated on a regular basis and thus lists of offenders are also updated.

- **eMule and KaZaA**. File sharing websites, which enable all those connected to the internet to download and install a program on their personal computer. This acts as a network of "friends" that allows for the transfer of files between other computers on the same network. This enable's all content stored on a connected computer, pictures, movies, music etc., to be shared with all other connected users.

- **Fishing or Phishing**. The attempt to steal information by deception on the Internet. The information may include financial data and the user name used for accessing social networks such as Facebook or for accessing email accounts. Phishing is accomplished by pretending to be a legitimate agent with which the victim is in continuous contact, such as a cellular supplier, bank, global shipping company, or credit card company. The imposter sends the victim an email message, in which the user is asked to press on a link. After pressing the link, the user reaches a fake website, which is very similar to the website that the user knows, for example, the bank's homepage, and there the user is asked to fill out the details that the imposter is attempting to steal.

- **VoIP (Voice over Internet Protocol)**. A general name for technology that enables the transfer of voice over the Internet, namely through an IP address.

Mobile Phone Terms and Definitions

- **IMEI (International Mobile Equipment Identity).** A unique number for the international identification of mobile equipment allotted to every mobile phone during the manufacturing process. The number enables cellular suppliers to identify the device and to manage its connection to the cellular network.

- **SIM Card (Subscriber Identity Module).** User module printed on an electrical circuit.

- **Secure Digital High Capacity (SDHC).** The 'big brother' of the SD memory card, found in mobile devices such as cellular phones, digital cameras, and handheld computers. SHDC cards are similar in shape to SD cards but are different in their technology and storage capacity. Older generation cellular phones, digital cameras, and handheld computers cannot utilize the maximum volume that the new SDHC cards technology makes possible.

- **Multimedia Messaging Service MMS.** A technology for the transfer of messages content rich , including pictures and movie clips, through the mobile network.

Internet and the Cyberspace Terms and Definitions

- **Cyberspace.** The cybernetic space that links people and organizations, regardless of geographical location or distance. This is a virtual environment that is unconnected to the physical world. The gate to the cyberspace is, as mentioned, the Internet.

- **E-business.** The totality of business applications that are influenced by communication technology and cyberspace.

- **Browser.** A program that enables browsing on the Internet. The most commonly used programs are Microsoft Explorer and Google Chrome. However, there are many other browser programs.

- **Web Service (WS)**. Internet services technology used primarily for the purpose of data transfer of between system interfaces and websites. These interfaces are based on technologies with a common denominator that operate in conjunction with information security authorizations for software platforms via the Internet, such as XML and HTTP. The aim of the technology is to integrate software and information components in real-time for the parties involved.

- **Object**. An object is software code installed on the computer, on a website, or in software, which constitutes a value, including an identifying reference, with technological significance. As mentioned, an object can be a variable, a function, or a data structure. With the appearance of object-oriented technological systems, the expression 'object' assumed additional meaning regarding the specific instance of a class, which constitutes, as mentioned, part of a software program or a website.

- **Intranet**. An intra-organizational network based on Internet technology and which facilitates the increased efficiency of the work operations and a more efficient exploitation of available work hours.

- **Virtual Community**. A group of people whose geographic location has no significance and who have shared areas of interest, occupation, profession, ideas, opinions, and/or attitudes, who make use of the Internet, in cyberspace, so as to share and/or to exchange information, and act.

- **Sub domain**. As already explained, the domain name signifies an entity that has registered to use a specific identifying tag for its internet activities. Examples include Microsoft.com, and NYU.edu (New York University). Note: the 3 digit suffix is an indication of the domains area of interest – com = commerce, edu = education, ac = academic and so on. A sub domain is a domain associated with upper level domain and, in the event that the upper level domain is not active, then the sub domain will also be inactive and unusable. The sub domain enables organizations, institutions, and Internet website owners to extend the name of the domain at their disposal to different divisions and tasks. For instance, in academic institutions it is customary to allocate a sub domain for every faculty. For example, the domain name of New York University is www.nyu.edu, while the sub domain name for the university's school of law is www.law.nyu.edu.

- **CRM - Customer Relationship Management.** A software program for the management of a company's customer database. This is a method that increases the efficiency of company activity, including client documentation and service improvement.

- **ERP - Enterprise Resource Planning.** A system that incorporates all the functions required for management of a business/company into one computerized system that can provide an answer to the needs of the organization as a whole.

- **FTP – File Transfer Protocol.** An Internet data communication protocol o that enables the transfer of different types of files via the Internet.

- **HTML – Hypertext Markup Language.** A markup language (not a programming language) that enables the editing of contents and is used primarily to create Internet websites.

- **DHTML – Dynamic HTML.** An advanced model of HTML that enables the introduction of dynamism and interactivity with the user, such as movement of objects, opening of toolbars in different ways, and so on.

- **HTTP - Hypertext Transfer Protocol.** The Internet protocol that enables the transfer of hypertext files from the server to the client. Hypertext pages are decrypted on the client's computer using the browser program.

- **URL - Universal Resource Locator.** A generic name that expresses the address of the website and/or the exact address where files are stored.

- **ActiveX.** Small software routines that extend browser capabilities and which provide the user with a wide range of possibilities Such as watching video clips, playing on-line games etc.

- **Applet.** A small software program that performs one specific action. These programs are integrated into HTML pages and add dynamics and pyrotechnics to the page.

- **E-Commerce.** Electronic commerce, is commerce carried out via the computer and/or a system of computers that connects through the Internet to cyberspace.

- **E-Procurement.** Electronic procurement. All virtual property, such as Internet websites, software, applications, or virtual services, meets the definition as electronic property.

- **Hits.** The financial value of a website is measured by the number of visits. Hits are the number of the clicks or the number of visits to a website.

- **Homepage.** This is the main "contents" of a website and/or of software.

- **IRC – Internet Relay Chat.** Communication protocol that enables the creation of virtual conversation groups. This protocol can manage the traffic of thousands of different communications channels in real time.

- **EDI - Electronic Data Interchange**. A communication protocol that enables different computers, in different companies, to transfer and process data between them without the involvement of a human mediator. This can be used for instance, to transfer funds and information between banks, charges from large companies to credit companies, and so on.

- **B2B – Business to Business**. An expression of commerce between businesses.

- **B2C – Business to Consumer**. An expression of commerce between a business and the end consumer.

- **C2C – Consumer to Consumer**. An expression of commerce between individuals. The most well known example is ebay.com.

- **P3P – Platform for Privacy Preferences.** A technology that enables browsers in the cyberspace to define their degree of privacy and the amount of personal information they are willing to disclose.

- **SSL - Secure Socket Layer.** Technology for the encryption of data in transfer through cyberspace This is usually sensitive data that could result in harm to the receiver and/or sender if revealed to unauthorized agents. Data is usually transferred from one party to the other to information servers and/or Internet store, Data remains encrypted as long as it is in movement through cyberspace.

- **Java, JavaScript, .net, C#, PHP, and others**. Website development languages, with which the Internet websites and their components are developed and built. The development language is chosen by the programmer, in most cases due to economic considerations, functionality and according to the work environment that they know best.

- **Auctions**. The business model for auctions and tenders is one of the main business innovations of electronic commerce (e-commerce).

- **SEO – Search Engine Optimization**. A collection of methods used to improve a web site's position (ranking) in search engine results..

  Black Hat Coding Methods. The goal of black hat coding is to 'bomb' search engines to such an extent so as to create a false representation of a specific website thus causing search engines to assign it a much higher ranking. Search engines combat this form of "attack" as the provision of high ranking to irrelevant results to a search request harm the surfer's experience and the credibility of the search engine. I would note that websites using these and other improper techniques to improve their ranking may be penalized by search engines. In those cases where improper promotion is detected, the search engine will stop reporting the offending website and in extreme cases the website owners will be forced to transfer the website to another domain and even to store it with another supplier (search engines identify the IP address of the website).

- **Ad Words**. Google's paid advertising system. Search results appear in the first three places at the beginning of the page and with a gray or cream light-colored background. In addition, the search results appear in the left or right column (depending on the computer language). On its website, Google states that advertisers will only pay for visits to their site which are initiated by a click on a Google ad and that registration for Google Ad Words is free. (https://www.google.com/adwords/)

- **Bit coin**. A virtual, tradable currency. The Bit coin is not backed by any regulatory organization such as a bank or a government. The crypt currency is saved using a designated software program installed on a local computer or a distant server (cloud). The software program enables the currency to be saved and traded. As mentioned previously, this is not an official sate of bank backed currency. Nevertheless, companies and private individuals around the world, and in Israel as well, are willing to accept payment in bit coin as if it is a valid currency in all respects. I would emphasize that this is a virtual currency (compared to a stock traded on an Internet website). I would further note that in the United States, Canada, and Europe the public has been cautioned against the use of the Bit coin. Furthermore, the idea of a virtual currency has expanded to include a number of other "currencies" such as Light coin, Doge coin, and Isra coin.

- **IIS – Internet Information Server**. A group of Microsoft Corporation technological internet tools implemented by the Microsoft Windows operating systems. They can handle HTTP, FTP, SMTP and other applications. In addition, the tools include software for building and management of websites, search engines and also support the writing of established applications.

- **DNS – Domain Name System**. An Internet service that translates the domain name into an IP addresses. In essence, the main goal of this service is to 'humanize' that the language used by the computer (machine language). The DNS service creates a correlation between the IP address and the website name (domain). The data is saved on DNS servers and shared between them throughout the world. Thus all surfers, regardless of their geographic location, will be able to access all available websites.

- **Subdirectory Folder**. A secondary directory is a directory of files that is found within another directory. A similar term can be used to describe a folder within another folder in the user interface. Thus, for example, www.cnn.com/EUROPE - in other words, the word EUROPE is a subdirectory folder associated with the main domain name.

- **Redirect**. The redirection of the domain name to another page or website. I would note that there are many uses of this type of redirections. Some are prohibited according to Google search engine guidelines , for example, code 301 that misleads the search engine by causing it to 'think' that this is another website and thus to improve its ranking .

- **Advertising Links**. Or in its popular name "pay for clicks advertising". This is an ad link, such as those displayed in a Google search result. It is a cyberspace marketing tool with which the user can market the website and/or product or service by themselves. The type of promotion enables reaching more people at the correct time, to focus advertising on a predefined geographic region, to only pay for the visitors to the website and to manage the advertiser's budget. From the surfer's viewpoint, advertising is shown on three results shown at the top of the Google search page results and on the bottom of the page, on a cream or light gray background. In addition, advertising appears in a column on the left or right side of the page (depending on the browser's defined language).

Appendices

- Israel Internet Association. The association works to promote the Internet and its use in Israel.

- Evidence Ordinance [New Version], 1971.

- Evidence Ordinance (Number 15), Source and Copy as Evidence, 2006.

- Israeli Association for Information Technology.

- The Courts in the United States, b2008.

- Civil Case 11831-03-10, Confidential (publication of identity is forbidden) v. Philip Kushmaro.

- The United States v. Councilman 2004.

- The Courts in the United States, c2008.

- Civil Appeal 6205/98 Unger and others v. Ofer and others.

- American Express 2005.

- State of Israel v. Meoz, Major Criminal Case 54877-09-11.

- Proposal for a Law Amending the Evidence Ordinance (Number 15), Source and Copy as Evidence (2006).

- Report of Bank Supervision Activity – Bank of Israel, for the year 2004, chapter 3.

- Criminal Appeal 5121/98 Private (Reserves) Raphael Yissachrov v. Chief Military Prosecutor.

- Criminal Case 40061/06 (Tel Aviv District) State of Israel v. Ruth and Michael Efrati.

- Section 1521 California Evidence Code.

- Special Elections Case 16/01 Shas Union of Sepharadi Jews v. Knesset Member Ofir Pines Court Ruling 55 (3) 159.

- Section 152 (3, 4) of the Criminal Procedure Law [Combined Version] 1982.

- Civil Appeal 601/68 Bider v. Levy Court Ruling 23 (part 1) 597.

- Police Law, 1997 (England).

- Law of Police Evidence and Criminal Evidence, 1984.

- Supreme Court 5016/96 Horev v. Minister of Transport Court Ruling 51 (4) 1 (hereinafter: the Horev Ruling), p. 43.

- Supreme Court 4541/94 Miller v. Minister of Defense Court Ruling 49 (4) 94 (hereinafter: the Miller Ruling), p. 138.

- 1514/01 Gur Aryeh v. the Second Authority of Television and Radio Court Ruling 45 (4) 267, pp. 284-285.

- Different Civil Requests (Jerusalem Magistrates Court) 4995/05 Anonymous v. Bezek Benleumi Ltd. 2006 (1) 11480.

- Different Civil Requests (Kerayot) Mor v. Bezek Benleumi Ltd. 2006 (3) 16405.

- Mor Incident, Section 4 of the Court Ruling of the Honorable Judge Rivlin. Section 51 of the Court Ruling of the Honorable Judge Rubinstein.

- Birnhek, Self-arrangement, chapter 3, number 2, and Dr. Keren Barzilay-Nahon, "Who Controls the Virtual Communities", *Panim*, 30, 7-76.

- Opening Summons (Tel Aviv) 541/07 Sabo v. *Yediot* on the Internet, District Precedent 2007 (4) 5805.

- Baba Kama Chapter 8, Mishneh Torah, Rambam, Laws on Injuring and Damage, Chapter 3.

- Honorable Judge Dalia Marek-Horntzik, Tel Aviv-Jaffo Magistrate Court, A 064981/04, Section 80.

- Different Civil Request (Haifa) 12387/07 Rami Mor v. Barak 013 Internet Services Ltd.

- Y. Zamir, Freedom of Speech on the Internet, *Law and Government*, 2013, 353.

- N. Elkin-Koren, Self-Arrangement of Creator Rights in the Information Era, *Law*, 2012, 319, 322.

- Civil Appeal 440/75 Zendbank v. Danziger Court Ruling 30 (2) 260.

- Civil Case (Tel Aviv Yaffo) 29488/04 Computer Skey v. Prime Medical Company.

- Aharon Barak, Judicial Legislation, *Law* 13 (1983) 25 p. 50.

- Paper of Position, Israel Internet Association. June 2011.

- Different Civil Requests, 4995/05 Anonymous v. Bezek Benleumi Ltd. (Published on Nevo, February 28, 2006). For discussion of this approach, see Birnhek, Exposure of Surfers, pp. 74-75.

- Appeals Authority 850/06 1632/07 Mor. v. Yediot Internet Ynet, Forum Systems (published in Nevo, April 22, 2007).

- Opening Summons (Tel Aviv) 1244/07 Mizmor Productions Ltd. v. Maariv Publications Intelligence Ltd. (NRG Internet website).

- Yuval Karniel, "Anonymity and Defamation on the Internet – Between Freedom of Expression and Lawlessness".

- Supreme Court 683/82 Aldin v. Israel Police and Others, Court Ruling 37 (3) 472, 474. The interest of a person who relied on property rights may be harmed as a result of confiscation.

- Directives of the preliminary section and general section of the Penal Law, 1977.

- In Israeli Law it is required to prove the mental and factual basis so as to link the accused with the offense, for instance Criminal Appeal 538/89 Warshevsky and Others v. State of Israel, Court Ruling 44 (2) 870.

- Aviv Ayalon, Lawyer, and Amiad Raviv, Cybernetic Aspects of the New Law against Terror in the United States.

- Professor Wyman Gabi and Yariv Zefati Terror on the Internet, Online Journal of Haifa University, March 1, 2008.

- Supreme Court 320/80 Kosama and Others v. Ministry of Defense and Others, Court Ruling 35 (3) 113 132.

- Supreme Court 168/91 Morcos v. Ministry of Defense Court Ruling 45 (1) 467, 470.

- Yuval Karniel and Haim Vismonsky, "Freedom of Expression, Pornography, and Community on the Internet".

- Ministry of Finance – Department of the Capital, Insurance, and Savings Market, Circular for Agents and Consultants, October 2, 2012.

British Institute of International and Comparative Law, http://www.biicl.org/.

Casey, 2011: Kenneally, 2001a: Rothstein et al, 2007: Volonino, 2003.

Rule 702. Testimony by Expert Witnesses.

http://www.knesset.gov.il/laws/special/heb/yesod3.pdf.

G8 Proposed Principles for Forensic Evidence.

U.S. Department of Justice Office of Justice Programs National Institute of Justice, Forensic Examination of Digital Evidence: A Guide for Law Enforcement.

International Standard ISO/IEC27037, First Edition 2012-10-15, Information Technology — Security Techniques — Guidelines for Identification, Collection, Acquisition and Preservation of Digital Evidence.

Federal Rules of Evidence.

http://7safe.com/electronic_evidence/ACPO_guidelines_computer_e vidence_v4_web.pdf.

http://www.nij.gov/pubs-sum/199408.htm.

http://www.oas.org/juridico/spanish/cyb_best_pract.pdf.

www.legislation.gov.uk/ukpga/1990/18/contents.

http://www.inss.org.il.cdn.reblaze.com/upload/(FILE)1306930376.pdf

http://www.legislation.gov.uk/ukpga/1997/50/contents.

USC § 2511 - Interception and Disclosure of Wire, Oral or Electronic Communications Prohibited.

http://elyon1.court.gov.il/files/08/880/049/o06/08049880.o06.htm.

http://www.legislation.gov.uk/ukpga/1984/60/pdfs/ukpga_19840060_en.pdf.

http://csrc.nist.gov/publications/nistir/nistir-7250.pdf.

http://www.iwar.org.uk/comsec/resources/nist/pda-forensics-sp800-72.pdf.

https://viaforensics.com/resources/white-papers/iphone-forensics/.

https://viaforensics.com/android-forensics/.

http://www.7safe.com/electronic_evidence/ACPO_guidelines_computer_evidence.pdf.

http://csrc.nist.gov/publications/nistir/nistir-7250.pdf.

http://www.isoc.org.il/hasdara/hasdara_code.html .

http://www.moital.gov.il/NR/rdonlyres/689B0383-5FA7-4AC8-B964-11D974DD1AD2/0/isakov.pdf.

http://www.legislation.gov.uk/ukpga/2000/23/section/1.

http://www.legislation.gov.uk/uksi/2000/2699/contents/made.

http://www.ico.org.uk/upload/documents/library/data_protection/practical_application/ico_emppraccode.pdf.

http://eurlex.europa.eu/LexUriServ/LexUriServ.do?uri=CELEX:31997L0066:EN:HTML.

http://www.nevo.co.il/law_html/law01/077_001.htm#Seif9.

http://www.knesset.gov.il/mmm/data/pdf/m02219.pdf.

http://csrc.nist.gov/publications/nistpubs/800-101/SP800-101.pdf.

American Express v Vinhnee 2005.

U.S. v. Boucher, D.Vt. 2007-09.

Jones, 2009: Kenneally, 2001b: Kerr, 2005a.

HMRC - Poynter Recommendations – ICO Audit Executive Summary Version 1.0.

Practice Direction 31B – Disclosure of Electronic Documents.

Ieong, 2006: Kenneally & Brown, 2005.

International Standard ISO/IEC27037.

Sixth Amendment to the United States Constitution.

Supreme Court of the United States. Daubert v. Merrell Dow Pharmaceuticals.

http://www.microsoft.com/security/resources/botnet-whatis.aspx.

http://www.justice.gov.uk/courts/procedure-rules/civil/rules/part31#IDARPTBB.

http://www.bailii.org/uk/cases/UKHL/1973/6.html.

http://www.psakdin.co.il/fileprint.asp?filename=/plili/public/art_ccid.htm.

http://www.fcc.gov/encyclopedia/communications-assistance-law-enforcement-act.

http://www.iana.org/.

http://transition.fcc.gov/

EnCase   http://www.guidancesoftware.com/.

AccessData FTK http://www.accessdata.com/products/ftk/.

X-Ways http://www.x-ways.net/forensics/.

ProDiscover http://www.prodiscover.com/ProDiscoverDFT.htm.

SMART http://www.asrdata.com/tools.

Sleuthkit http://www.sleuthkit.org/.

Andersen (2006), "International Air Centers, LLC, v. Jacob Citrin", 05-1522, Argued October 24, 2006,

Bitsum (2006), "PECompact: For Maximum Compression and Speed", http://www.bitsum.com/pec2.asp.

Carrier (2006) The Sleuth Kit [online] http://www.sleuthkit.org/.

http://www.legislation.gov.uk/ukpga/1990/18/contents.

Dear (2005), "An Exploration of Future Anti-Forensic Techniques" [online] http://www.assuremind.com/antiForensics.pdf.

El-Khalil, R. (2004), "Hydan: Information Hiding in Program Binaries" http://www.crazyboy.com/hydan/.

http://www.knesset.gov.il/mmm/data/pdf/m02219.pdf.

Foster and Liu (2005), "Catch me, if you can", Black Hat Briefings 2005.

http://www.utexas.edu/law/journals/tlr/sources/Issue%205/Richards/fn83.Ehrlich.pdf

Garfinkel and Malan (2005), "One Big File is Not Enough: A Critical Evaluation of the Dominant Free-Space.

http://ieeexplore.ieee.org/xpl/mostRecentIssue.jsp?punumber=5412864.

Sanitization Technique", The 6th Workshop on Privacy Enhancing Technologies, Robinson College, Cambridge, United Kingdom, June 28

- June 30.

Geiger (2005), "Evaluating Commercial Counter-Forensic Tools," DFRWS 2005.

http://www.dfrws.org/2005/proceedings/geiger_couterforensics.pdf

http://7safe.com/electronic_evidence/ACPO_guidelines_computer_e vidence_v4_web.pdf

Goldschlag, Reed and Syverson (1999), "Onion Routing", Communications of the ACM, 42(2), pp. 39—41.

Grugq (2002), "Defeating forensic analysis on UNIX", Phrack Magazine, 11)6-6, 28 July http://www.totse.com/en/hack/hack_attack/167627.html

Grugq (2003), "To the Art of Defiling", Black Hat Asia 2003 Presentation. http://opensores.thebunker.net/pub/mirrors/blackhat/presentations/ bh-asia-03/bh-asia-03-grugq/bh-asia-grugq.pdf

Grugq (2003a), "The Design and Implementation of ul_exec" Security Focus http://securityfocus.com/archive/1/348638/2003-12-29/2004-01-04/0.

Grugq (2005), "The Art of Defiling," Black Hat 2005,http://www.blackhat.com/presentations/bh-usa-bh-us-05-grugq.pdf

http://grouper.ieee.org/groups/1149/1/.

http://www.knesset.gov.il/Laws/Data/law/2153/2153.pdf.

http://ieeexplore.ieee.org/xpl/mostRecentIssue.jsp?punumber=54128 64.

http://en.wikipedia.org/wiki/Telecommunications_data_retention.

https://www.google.co.il/#bav=on.2,or.r_cp.&fp=4314e9f7a27de014
&q=US+law+about+ISP+Record+keeping.

http://www.eeoc.gov/employers/recordkeeping.cfm.

http://www.out-law.com/en/topics/tmt--sourcing/data-
protection/data-retention-laws-what-they-mean-for-communication-
service-providers/.

http://www.cybertelecom.org/security/records.htm.

http://www.cybertelecom.org/security/records.htm.

http://www.law.cornell.edu/uscode/text/18/2257.

http://torrentfreak.com/how-long-does-your-isp-store-ip-address-logs-
120629/.

http://www.hamoked.org.il/items/1670.htm.

http://www.isa.gov.il/Download/IsaFile_1216.pdf.

http://elyon1.court.gov.il/files/98/050/062/g15/98062050.g15.HTM.

http://www.knesset.gov.il/protocols/data/html/huka/2006-06-26-
01.html.

Boddington, R., Hobbs, V. J., & Mann, G. "Validating Digital Evidence
for Legal Argument," The 6th Australian Digital Forensics Conference,
2008.

Qishi Wu, Yi Gu, Xiaohui Cui, Praneeth Moka, Yunyue Lin. "A Graph
Similarity-Based Approach to Security Event Analysis Using
Correlation Techniques", GLOBECOM 2010.

http://www.utexas.edu/law/journals/tlr/sources/Issue%205/Richards
/fn83.Ehrlich.pdf

http://groups.csail.mit.edu/cis/crypto/classes/6.857/papers/diffie-
hellman.pdf.

Icove, D. Computer Crime. O'Reilly, 1996.

Rothfeder, J. Privacy For Sale: How Computerization has made everyone's private life an open secret. Rothfeder, 1992.

Hoffman, L. Building in Big Brother: The Cryptographic Policy Debate. Springer-Verlag, 1995.

Bloombecker, J.Introduction to Computer Crime. National Center for Computer Crime Data, 1988.

Cavazos, E. and Morin, G. Cyberspace and the Law: Your Rights and Duties in the On-Line World. MIT Press, 1994.

Cunningham, W. et al Private Security Trends 1970-2000. The Hallcrest Report II. Hallcrest, 1990.

Johnson, D. Computer Ethics. Prentice-Hall, 1994 (2nd edition).

Forester, T. and Morrison, P.Computer Ethics. MIT Press, 1994 (2nd edition).

The Honeynet Project's Forensic Challenge

Basic Steps in Forensic Analysis of Unix Systems, David Dittrich (Pasos BAsicos en AnAlisis Forense de Sistemas GNU/Linux, Unix, modified, updated and translated to Spanish by Ervin S. Odishoo).

Course notes for Black Hat '00 Unix forensics class, Dominique Brezinski and David Dittrich

Dan Farmer & Wietse Venema's class on computer forensic analysis

[forensics.tar.gz contains the slides in 6-up portrait PostScript format for printing on just 25 double-sided pages

Forensic Computer Analysis: An Introduction -- Reconstructing past events, By Dan Farmer and Wietse Venema, Dr. Dobb's Journal, September 2000

What Are MACtimes?: Powerful tools for digital databases, By Dan Farmer, Dr. Dobb's Journal, October 2000

Strangers In the Night: Finding the purpose of an unknown program, by Wietse Venema, Dr. Dobb's Journal, November 2000

Computer Forensics Column, Errata

The Law Enforcement and Forensic Examiners Introduction to Linux, a Beginner's Guide, Barry J. Grundy, NASA Office of the Inspector General

Brian Carrier's Sleuthkit (formerly TASK, formerly TCT-Utils(

Notes on updating Red Hat Linux 7.1 to support >2GB images with TCT, TCTUTILS & Autopsy (see also Large File Support in Linux(

Forensic Analysis of a Compaq RAID-1 Array and Using dd with EnCase v3, by Keith J. Jones

Forensic Analysis Using FreeBSD - Part 1 by Keith J. Jones

International Organisation on Computer Evidence

European Network of Forensic Science Institutes -- Forensic information technology Working group

International Association of Computer Investigative Specialists (IACIS)

Law and Legal Process

Judicial Gatekeeping in Texas, by Thomas F. Allen, Jr. and Robert Rogers, Harvard Law School '99 (Daubert)

September 2000 Market Survey -- Computer Forensics, by James Holley, SC Magazine (ranks Linux dd a Best Buy! ;)

Cybercops Need Better Tools -- Law enforcement agencies are falling behind hackers, says exec of CIA tech incubator, by Matthew Schwartz, Computerworld, July 31, 2000

Crime Seen (Cover story on digital forensics), by Bill Betts, Information Security Magazine, March, 2000

Disk Shows Love Bug-Like Virus, by Dirk Beveridge, AP, May 16 2000

Computer Forensics: Investigators Focus on Foiling Cybercriminals, by Illena Armstrong, SC Magazine (cover story), April 2000

CD Universe evidence compromised -- Failure to protect computer data renders it suspect in court, by Mike Brunker and Bob Sullivan, MSNBC, June 7, 2000

Crime & Clues -- The Art and Science of Criminal Investigation

FBI Forensic Science Communications

Reverse engineering

Reverse Engineering Malware, by Lenny Zeltser, May 2001

The Honeynet Project's Reverse [engineering] Challenge

SecuriTeam.com TESO Burneye Unwrapper

Advanced in ELF Runtime Binary Encryption - Shiva, by Neil Mehta, Blackhat USA 2003 (PDF)

Unpackers/decrypters/unprotectors(Generic/universalunpackers/depr otectors/dumpers)

Packer and Unpackers

EXEStealth executable protection

Generic ExeStealth Unpacker v1.0.

FIREVue FireWire 400 / IDE Bridge Boards

DK-9 Removable Hard-Drive Enclosure USB 2.0 + Firewire 1394 with Ultra Quiet Cooling Fan

F.R.E.D.D.I.E.

The Image MASSter Solo 2 Forensic system

Project Develops Model for Analyzing Security Incident Costs in Academic Computing Environments

A Study on Incident Costs and Frequencies, by Virginia Rezmierski <ver@umich.edu>, Adriana Carroll <adriana_carroll@hotmail.com>, and Jamie Hine

Security Attribute Evaluation Method: A Cost Benefit Approach, by Shawn Butler, Carnegie Mellon University, International Conference on Software Engineering 2002 (ICSE 2002) Proceedings

Multi-Attribute Risk Assessment, by Shawn Butler, Carnegie Mellon University, Proceedings from Symposium on Requirements Engineering for Information Security (SREIS 2002)

Attack Trees: Modeling security threats, by Bruce Schneier, Dr. Dobb's Journal, December 1999

Attack Modelling for Information Security and Survivability, Andrew P. Moore, Robert J. Ellison, Richard C. Linger, Technical Note CMU/SEI-2001-TN-001, March 2001

A Quick Tour of Attack Tree Based Risk Analysis Using Secur/Tree, whitepaper by Amenaza.com, May 2002

Electronic Data Discovery Primer, by Albert Barsocchini, Law Technology News, August 28, 2002

Solving the Perfect Computer Crime, by Jay Lyman, www.NewsFactor.com, February 27, 2002

NT Incident Response Investigations and Analysis, by Harlan Carvey, Information Security Bulletin, June 2001

"A harder day in court for fingerprint, writing experts: US judge limits testimony of forensic analysts, in a ruling that might alter how evidence is presented at trial," by Seth Stern, Christian Science Monitor, January 16, 2002

Cybersleuthing solves the case (and related stories) by Deborah Radcliff, Computerworld, January 14, 2002

Digital sleuthing uncovers hacking costs, by Robert Lemos, Special to CNET News.com, March 22, 2001

Icove, D. Computer Crime. O'Reilly, 1996.

Rothfeder, J. Privacy For Sale: How Computerization has made everyone's private life an open secret. Rothfeder, 1992.

Hoffman, L. Building in Big Brother: The Cryptographic Policy Debate. Springer-Verlag, 1995.

Bloombecker, J.Introduction to Computer Crime. National Center for Computer Crime Data, 1988.

Cavazos, E. and Morin, G. Cyberspace and the Law: Your Rights and Duties in the On-Line World. MIT Press, 1994.

Cunningham, W. et al Private Security Trends 1970-2000. The Hallcrest Report II. Hallcrest, 1990.

Johnson, D. Computer Ethics. Prentice-Hall, 1994 (2nd edition).

Forester, T. and Morrison, P.Computer Ethics. MIT Press, 1994 (2nd edition).

Frye v. United States 293 F. 1013 (D.C. Cir. 1923)

Time is of the Essense: Electronic documents will only stand up in court if the who, what, and when they represent are unassailable, by Charles R. Merrill, CIO.com, March 15, 2000

How to Time-Stamp a Digital Document (PostScript), by Stuart Haber and W. Scott Stornetta, Journal of Cryptology, Vol. 3, No. 2, pp. 99-111 (1991)

Improving the Efficiency and Reliability of Digital Time-Stamping (PostScript), by Dave Bayer, Stuart Haber, and W. Scott Stornetta, in Sequences II: Methods in Communication, Security, and Computer Science, eds. R. Capocelli, A. DeSantis, and U. Vaccaro, pp. 329-334, (Springer-Verlag, 1993)

Secure Names for Bit-Strings (PostScript), by Stuart Haber and W. Scott Stornetta, in Proceedings of the 4th ACM Conference on Computer and Communication Security, (ACM, 1997).

Evidence Examinations -- Computer Examinations, Handbook of Forensic Services, U.S. Department of Justice, FBI

Digital Evidence: Standards and Principles, Forensic Science Communications, US DoJ, April 2000, Volume 2, Number 2

Recovering and Examining Computer Forensic Evidence, Forensic Science Communications, US DoJ, October 2000, Volume 2, Number 4

RFC 3227: Guidelines for Evidence Collection and Archiving, by Dominique Brezinski and Tom Killalea

An Introduction to the Field Guide for Investigating Computer Crime, by Timothy E. Wright (Security Focus Incident Handling focus)

The Field Guide for Investigating Computer Crime: Overview of a Methodology for the Application of Computer Forensics, by Timothy E. Wright (Security Focus Incident Handling focus)

The Field Guide for Investigating Computer Crime: Search and Seizure Basics, by Timothy Wright (Security Focus Incident Handling focus)

Recovering from an Intrusion, by /dev/null.

http://www.judiciary.gov.uk/wp-content/uploads/JCO/Documents/Reports/super-injunction-report-20052011.pdf

Hansard (HC) (13 Oct 2009, Col. 163ff); Hansard (HC) (21 Oct 2009, Col. 272WHff) (Hansard (13 October 2009) and (21 October 2009)) (http://www.publications.parliament.uk/pa/cm200809/cmhansrd/cm091021/halltext/91021h0008.htm)

Hansard (HC) (13 Oct 2009, Col. 163) (The Speaker (13 October 2009)) (http://www.publications.parliament.uk/pa/cm200809/cmhansrd/cm091013/debtext/91013-0004.htm)

Hansard (HC) (13 Oct 2009, Col. 164) (David Davis MP (13 October 2009)) (http://www.publications.parliament.uk/pa/cm200809/cmhansrd/cm091013/debtext/91013-0004.htm)

Hansard ((HC) 19 Oct 2009, Col. 1234W) (Paul Farrelly MP (19 October 2009))

(http://www.publications.parliament.uk/pa/cm200809/cmhansrd/cm091019/text/91019w0006.htm#0910197000895)

Hansard ((HC) 21 Oct 2009, Col. 289WH) (David Heath MP (2009)) (http://www.publications.parliament.uk/pa/cm200809/cmhansrd/cm091021/halltext/91021h0007.htm)

Hansard ((HC) 21 Oct 2009, Col. 279WH) (Paul Farrelly MP (21 October 2009)) (http://www.publications.parliament.uk/pa/cm200809/cmhansrd/cm091021/halltext/91021h0006.htm)

Hansard (HC) (21 Oct 2009, Col. 294WH) (Bridget Prentice MP (21 October 2009)) (http://www.publications.parliament.uk/pa/cm200809/cmhansrd/cm091021/halltext/91021h0008.htm)

Hansard (HC) (28 Oct 2009, Col. 422W) (Jack Straw MP LC (28

October 2009))
(http://www.publications.parliament.uk/pa/cm200809/cmhansrd/cm
091028/text/91028w0016.htm#09102844002613)

Second Report from the Committee of Privileges 1978 (HC 222) (1978
– 1979).

Joint Committee on Parliamentary Privilege, Report, (HC 214-I (1998 –
1999), HL 43-I/HC 241-I (1998 – 1999)) (1999 Joint Committee
report) (http://www.parliament.the-stationery
office.co.uk/pa/jt199899/jtselect/jtpriv/43/4302.htm#evidence).

House of Commons, Culture, Media and Studies Committee, Report
on Press standards, privacy and libel, Vol. 1 (9 February 2010) (HC
362-I) (CMS Report Vol.
I)(http://www.publications.parliament.uk/pa/cm200910/cmselect/cm
cumeds/362/362i.pdf

House of Commons, Culture, Media and Studies Committee, Report
on Press standards, privacy and libel, Vol. 2 (9 February 2010) (HC
362-II) (CMS Report Vol. II)
(http://www.publications.parliament.uk/pa/cm200910/cmselect/cmc
umeds/362/362ii.pdf)

Ministry of Justice, Report of the Libel Working Party (23 March 2010)
(MoJ Libel Working Party)
(http://www.justice.gov.uk/publications/docs/libel-working-group-
report.pdf)

The Government's Response to the Culture, Media and Sport Select
Committee on Press Standards, Privacy and Libel (Cm 7851) (April
2010) (The Government's Response to the CMS Report)
(http://www.official
documents.gov.uk/document/cm78/7851/7851.pdf)

Ministry of Justice Business Plan 2011 – 2015 (November 2010) (MoJ
(2010)) (http://www.number10.gov.uk/wp-content/uploads/MOJ-
FINAL-Business-Plan.pdf)

McKay et al (eds), Erskine May on Parliamentary Practice (LexisNexis) (23rd edition) (2004) (Erskine May)

Trafigura, Eight key facts about the draft Minton report, (Trafigura (16 October 2009))
(http://www.trafigura.com/PDF/TrafiguraStatementOnMinton.pdf)

Judicial Communications Office, Committee to examine 'super-injunctions' (06 April 2010)
(http://www.judiciary.gov.uk/media/media-releases/2010/1510)

Lord Judge CJ (2009), Statement of the Lord Chief Justice on "Super-Injunctions", (October 20, 2009) (Lord Judge (2009))
(http://www.judiciary.gov.uk/media/media-releases/2009/statement-jco-super-injunctions-09) (Transcript of answer given at press conference.)

ABOUT THE AUTHOR

Dr. Ehud Roffeh, arbitrator and mediator, counselor for legal and technological issues, provider of professional opinions regarding technological and legal matters, startup valuation, websites, databases, domain names, issues involving computer crime – began his professional career within the computer domain as a soldier in one of the Israeli Defense Forces elite computer units..

Eight years after finishing his military service Dr. Roffeh was nominated as the development manager of a company which dealt with the development of computer security systems. Over the years he has accumulated great experience and gained a reputation for expertise and excellence. In the beginning of 2000 – during the days following the " Bug 2000" panic, he served as Assistant Director General of Business Development at Maof College and as a lecturer on topics concerning data protection, ERP systems, CRM systems and Internet.

In 2000, following the introduction of ADSL networks in Israel, Dr. Roffeh was asked by the college's administration to manage a unique and first time project – the establishment of the first radio station in Israel which broadcasted on the Internet. At the same time Dr. Roffeh continued lecturing, writing syllabuses and training new lecturers.

Two years later, with the successful completion of this project, Dr. Roffeh established a multinational company specializing in program development, computer system integration and for the development of Web CRM solutions. At first the company specialized in integrating systems within organizations, including analyzing needs, characterization and designing marketing strategies. However, over time the company has changed and today its main occupation is in the world of digital evidence and computer investigations.

Over the past two decades Dr. Ehud Roffeh has acquired unique expertise in the digital investigation domain and especially in all issues regarding computers and the Internet. He is a well-known and internationally accepted expert in advanced software systems analysis, data protection issues and information theft by employees, digital picture analysis and investigation, email messages, harassment within internet sites and intrusions into organizational computer systems and more.

Dr. Roffeh lectures at Beit Berl for B.A. degree studies and in the college's criminology class. The courses he teaches include digital evidence, computer laws, data protection, computer and Internet crime and various courses concerning business administration.

Over the years Dr. Roffeh has written and presented dozens of expert opinions to Courts of Law, for both civil and criminal procedures. The opinions he provided dealt, amongst other issues, with the Internet, social networks (Facebook, Twitter, YouTube etc.), sexual harassment, rape, murder cases and money laundering and on-line gambling, code theft and copyright issues. Moreover, he is frequently appointed by the courts as a mediator and as an arbitrator in the domain of law and technology.

Dr. Roffeh has been involved in, for many years, with research on the issue of digital signatures and his professional opinions have confirmed the use of digital signature systems amongst some of Israel's largest insurance companies' l.

Education

Ph.D. in Law (Doctor of Law), proficiency in computer and internet crime – IUBL University, California.

MBA – Bar Ilan University.

Graduated (LLB) in Law, the Academic College of Kiriyat Ono.

B.Sc. in Computer Science and Mathematics, Mercy College, NY.

Directors Course, Bar Ilan University.

Various courses in data protection, data restoration, computer investigations, internet programs, program engineering and digital evidence examination.

Software engineering and information technology (with merits), administration school, Tel-Aviv.

Made in the USA
Lexington, KY
02 April 2015